SEED FALLING ON GOOD SOIL

Seed Falling on Good Soil

Rooting Our Lives in the Parables of Jesus

Gordon W. King

CASCADE *Books* · Eugene, Oregon

SEED FALLING ON GOOD SOIL
Rooting our Lives in the Parables of Jesus

Cascade Books
An Imprint of Wipf and Stock Publishers
199 W. 8th Ave., Suite 3
Eugene, OR 97401

www.wipfandstock.com

Paperback ISBN 978-1-49827-936-9 (paperback)
Hardcover ISBN 978-1-49827-938-3 (hardcover)
Ebook ISBN 978-1-49827-937-6 (ebook)

Cataloging-in-Publication data:

Names: King, Gordon W.

Title: Seed falling on good soil : rooting our lives in the parables of Jesus / Gordon W. King.

Description: Eugene, OR : Cascade Books, 2016 | Includes bibliographical references.

Identifiers: ISBN 9781498279369 (paperback) | ISBN 9781498279383 (hardcover) | ISBN 9781498279376 (ebook)

Subjects: LCSH: Jesus Christ—Parables. | Christian life.

Classification: LCC BT375.3 K46 2016 (print) | LCC BT375.3 (ebook)

Manufactured in the U.S.A.

Dedicated to the Memory of
Jaime Goytia
Bolivia 1931–2014
Teologo del Camino

Table of Contents

Preface

IT WAS A NIGHT of great tastes and great conversation. It was a time of sharing a meal with old friends and a new friend from the Southern United States. He had just become involved in a number community development projects focused on some of the poorest areas in the South and his excitement was contagious. These ingredients mixed with dialogue, laughter, and tears blended to create one of those "leaning in" magical memorable evenings. We were fully engaged and full of passion as we shared our own journeys of discovering a faith lived at the margins and in the dislocated areas where the need for justice and compassion merged out of our loving encounter with God.

Our new friend shared his passion about the actions of justice and compassion of which he was a part.

Another friend talked about her own sense of call to the poor and to the particular areas of vocation in which she had focused her doctoral studies.

A pause and then a question directed to our friend from the United States, "When did you begin to have a social conscience?"

Before our friend could answer, a counterpoint question was posed, "When did you become a Christian?"

It was an intriguing question that evoked silence as we each reflected on its truth.

When in our history as the church did we remove the implications of following Jesus and replace them with individualistic pietisms that appear to give us permission to pick and choose the responsibilities we must live out? At what point did we begin to think that having a concern for justice, for the poor, the disempowered or the "other" was a special call rather than an essential aspect of the Christian life?

It is obvious from the teachings of Jesus that simply believing in him is not enough. So when did we begin to believe that one could trust Christ and not intend to obey him? We pray, "Your kingdom come, your will be done, on earth as it is in heaven," but fail to join in the activity that might make a present taste of that kingdom possible. Somewhere, sometime, we moved away from discipleship that was firmly rooted in the idea that believing in Jesus meant that we should also believe in the things that Jesus believed in and actually participate in doing them.

Alan Jones, the former dean of the Anglican Cathedral of San Francisco, says that the first question God will ask us when we get to heaven is, "Where are the others?" Given the individualistic nature of the North American Christianity, we might muse, "What has that got to do with me?"

Gordon King challenges any attempts to compartmentalize. He guides us through this exploration of the "parables" in such a way that we begin to see that doing the things of Jesus are actually the revolutionary center of faith in the first place. Our encounter with Jesus is but a beginning to an upside down life and subversive spirituality that puts the heart of God for those on the margins at the center.

It shouldn't surprise us. The Gospel has always been much more revolutionary than we have wanted to be. William Willimon said it well,

> The Gospel is not a set of ideas about which we are supposed to make up our minds. The gospel is intrusive news that evokes a new set of practices, a complex of habits, a way of living in the world, discipleship. The obedience we owe to Christ makes Christianity far more than an ethical code it is a way of life. It is a way of living as if the Kingdom of God has already come about.[1]

Gordon King in *Seed Falling on Good Soil* takes us to an amazing place where the familiar, parables we have heard all our lives, become utterly new. He helps us see that these parables were deeply embedded in a context. These socio-economic, spiritual and political realities of the time elicit deeply challenging and dissident messages that will alter our lives. They challenge the status quo and confront the powers, principalities and systems that have lost touch with the marginalized and the "other." We will begin to realize that they point to challenging and truthfully more dissident places than we might ever have imagined. And we will begin to realize that these are the places of our faith's possibilities.

1. Willimon and Hauerwaus, *Where Resident Aliens Live*, 44.

As you read this book, I implore you to keep in mind that the themes unpacked in this book are not merely fresh exegetical offerings: They are passions and responsibilities deeply embedded in the author. I have known Gord for a long time. From our shared work in a small inner city church in Vancouver, to his life in Bolivia, his work with World Vision and then our years of working together at CBM/The Sharing Way, Gord's love for the marginalized and disempowered resides deeply in his heart and is demonstrated in his daily walk with Jesus. This book calls us to a life of character and foundational virtues that are the heart of God and embodied in His servant Gord. As his friend, Gord has opened my eyes and heart to see, understand and engage aspects of faith in Jesus that I never had seen, understood nor acted on before. My faith has never been the same. My hope is that after reading this book your faith will be changed as well.

—Gary Nelson
President Tyndale University College & Seminary
Author, *Borderland Churches: A Congregation's Introduction to Missional Living*

Acknowledgments

I MAKE A HABIT of reading the acknowledgments of authors at the beginning of books. The brief comments remind us that there is a history of relationships and events in the background of every book. My acknowledgments, as those of other authors, are partial, incomplete, and inadequate.

I want to begin by thanking Gary Nelson, my friend and former boss. I served under Gary's inspirational leadership when he was General Secretary of Canadian Baptist Ministries (CBM). Gary encouraged me to follow my passion in exploring the parables of Jesus and using them to develop a theology of mission for community development. The friendship of Gary and Carla Nelson has been a wonderful gift over the years.

Dr. Dave Diewert and Karen Hollenbeck Wuest made invaluable contributions to the writing of *Seed Falling on Good Soil*. Dave directed my doctoral work on the parables at Carey Theological College. He has a keen sensitivity to biblical narratives and to the stories of people on the margins. Karen took on the task of editing the book through various stages. She excels in her craft using words that convey the deep emotions of suffering, solidarity, and faith. I valued her work and her prayers over the months we labored together.

I owe an immense debt to the women and men that I met through my work with World Vision and CBM. We learn more from people than from books. There were many long journeys on dusty roads to rural villages where we listened to the stories of people on the margins. I want to say a special thanks to three people. Rupen Das was my colleague at both World Vision and CBM. His friendship and insights have enriched my understanding of community development and God's kingdom. Rene Padilla introduced Integral Mission to CBM through his teaching and example. Simon Gasibirege, a Lay Franciscan in Rwanda, has used the sharing of life stories to facilitate the healing of wounds and the nurturing of reconciliation in communities. There were so many other people who contributed to this book by the manner in which they worked for human dignity and transformation. Readers will meet a few of them in the following chapters. I am indebted to both those mentioned and those who names are not found in the following chapters.

It has been a privilege to serve with CBM since 2002. I owe particular gratitude to those who cared for me during the unexpected medical crisis that ended my international work and the transition period into a new role. Thank you for your understanding, patience, and support. Terry Smith was appointed executive director of CBM during the final stages of preparation of the manuscript. He will bring commitment, creativity, and energy to the challenges faced by mission organizations in this period when the strength of the Christian Church lies in the Global South.

My partner Regine sustained me through the writing of the book while teaching at the University of Manitoba and struggling to meet her own deadlines. Regine introduced me to her family and her country (Rwanda). I continue to learn from her that grace and healing can be found in places of cruelty and violence. I am proud to be part of Regine's family and to share my life with her.

I thank my father and my three children. My father set an example of community service as a farmer and, later, as a member of the Canadian Parliament. Tara, Lucas, and Tasha were born in Canada, Costa Rica, and Bolivia respectively. I celebrate their lives, accomplishments, and love. Now I find myself praying that our grandchildren, Charlie, Millie, Alice, and Nick, will shape the world they inherit with justice, compassion and faith.

Finally, I have dedicated this book to Jaime Goytia, a dear friend from Bolivia who died during the time of writing. Jaime served as General Secretary of the Bolivian Bible Society and the Bible Society of the Americas. In retirement he was Rector of the Seminario Teologico Bautista in Cochabamba, Bolivia. No trip to Bolivia was complete without a raucous and joyful family meal in the Goytia home. During a troubled period of my life, Jaime visited me in Vancouver and assured me that my service to God's kingdom had not ended. Jaime's Bible, gifted to me by his family, is a treasured possession. *Gracias querido hermano.*

INTRODUCTION

Seed Falling on Good Soil
Rooting our Lives in the Parables of Jesus

> Stories are wondrous things. And they are dangerous...You have
> to be careful with the stories you tell. And you have to watch out
> for the stories you are told. —THOMAS KING[1]

> ...we become the people we are because of the stories we tell our-
> selves. —EMMANUEL KATONGOLE[2]

Living with Stories

WE LIVE AND DIE with stories. Some are personal. Others are passed down
to us by our families or the cultural environment around us. My life has
been nurtured by stories of the Bible for over sixty years. These "ancient"
stories have struggled to find their place among newer narratives circulat-
ing in the places where I have lived and worked. As someone who enjoys a
good story, I am attracted to John P. Meier's comment that we must learn
to do theology by story.[3] This recommendation is helpful for readers of the
gospels, as it invites us to create spaces where the story of Jesus and the
stories of the world around us can interact with the stories we write with
our lives.

1. King, *Truth About Stories*, 9–10.

2. Katongole, *Mirror to the Church*, 52.

3. John P. Meier is a New Testament scholar who teaches at the University of Notre
Dame. The quotation is take from *A Marginal Jew* 2:922.

This book is about stories Jesus told as recorded in the Gospel of Luke. I have tried to understand them in their original social and political context. The book also features stories of people who live in what has been called "the underside of the world." Each of the following chapters begins with what I call a story from the margins. Years ago, Archbishop Oscar Romero observed that the stories of the poor can cut through our illusions and reveal to us what the world is really like.[4] I hope that the stories from the margins function in this way. Most of the book is about the parables and their meaning within the current world order. The final chapter will be more personal in nature. It will address the theme of the story that you are writing with your life. I hope that the parables chapters will prepare you to examine your sense of vocation and calling.

It seems appropriate to tell you one of my own stories here in the beginning pages of the book. I was able to travel to El Salvador during the civil conflict that divided the country from 1980 to 1992. Toward the end of that period I visited development projects in an area controlled by the FMLN resistance forces.[5] A community development worker, who I will call Esteban to protect his identity, drove me by night from the capital city into the beautiful hills of Chalatenango. We stopped for breakfast with FMLN combatants at San Jose de las Flores. We shared food beside a church that had a large mural of Oscar Romero. We moved on to the community of Arcatao near the border with Honduras. Like most communities of Chalatenango, the people of Arcatao were loyal to the FMLN. Families supported the revolutionary army with food, lodging, and the sacrifice of their sons and daughters who volunteered as soldiers. The threat of government retaliation hovered over the entire area. At any time, government troops might descend in helicopters to destroy crops, kill farm animals, plant land mines, and round up people who subsequently disappeared.

Along the way from San Salvador to Arcatao, Esteban shared his story. He was born in Spain, served with revolutionary forces in Angola and Nicaragua, and eventually settled in El Salvador. He now worked with communities in areas of the country held by the FMLN. They were deprived of schools, health care, and other government services. Roads were often blocked to stop the transit of produce in and out of these zones. I asked about the risks of his work. Esteban told me that a few months earlier he

---

4. "The poor are the ones who tell us what the world is and what service the church must offer to the world." Romero, *Violence of Love*, 2005.

5. Farabundo Marti para la Liberacion Nacional.

had been in Arcatao when the Atlacatal Battalion descended unexpectedly by helicopter. This unit of the government army was feared for its brutal violence and repression. Having been warned that the soldiers had orders to find him, Esteban hid in a peasant's home. He was discovered and taken to the central square for public execution.

The battalion commander inspected Esteban's documents and discovered that he held a Spanish passport and was, therefore, a citizen of a European Economic Community country. Not wanting to create an international incident, he ordered Esteban to leave El Salvador and threatened him with death if he ever returned to Arcatao. Within a month, Esteban had resumed development work in the community, serving people whom the national government considered to be enemies of the state.

The story of Esteban has lived with me for almost twenty-five years. At one level, his story invites me to ponder the mysterious nature of the people who are brought into our lives to tear down walls of ideology and culture in order to mold us into God's servants. Esteban was a committed Marxist. I was the son of a Canadian politician who admired Ronald Reagan, played a role in NATO, and worked for the downfall of the Soviet Union. We were unlikely traveling companions. At a second level, Esteban's story troubles me with probing questions about the nature of my commitment to the values of peace, compassion, justice, and faith. Are there causes for which I am willing to place my life on the line? Does my heart really understand that faithful service will inevitably lead us to places of loneliness, conflict, and danger? I live with these questions each time I remember the story of Esteban. His example calls me to live my vocation with the same courage.

I believe that we all have stories that leave us inspired or unsettled. They are gifts from God, intended to guide us into a deeper understanding of ourselves and our faith.

Background to the Book

I have served with a number of national and international organizations over the past thirty-five years. My colleagues have included women and men who worked among the poor in countries such as El Salvador, Nicaragua, Bolivia, Rwanda, Kenya, Angola, Malawi, Indonesia, the Philippines, India, the Middle East and Canada. Their stories and experiences have shaped my understanding of the world and have challenged me to live faithfully, truthfully, and meaningfully. My friends Gary and Carla Nelson introduced me to the concept of "borderlands." Like the term "margins," the word borderlands signifies social locations where people live outside those places where other people enjoy relative security, order, and some level of prosperity. Visual images may be more helpful than technical definitions. In the borderlands, people have insecure employment, medical attention is difficult to obtain, schools are crowded and poorly equipped, houses need urgent repairs, violence is prevalent, and despair has settled in like a fog that conceals the sun. Zygmunt Bauman has written about "the underclass," whose members are viewed as a social problem and deprived of meaningful roles in their communities. He uses the term "horrifying wilderness" to describe the locations in which they live silenced, excluded, and humiliated.[6] We need to grasp that expressions like "margins," "borderlands" and "horrifying wilderness" represent both geographical zones that can be identified on a map as well as the painful experiences of people who exist on the "outside," with few prospects for moving into a life of dignity, stability, and security.

Over the past years, visits to Rwanda and friendships with people of that country have further shaped my theology and understanding of the world. Most of Rwanda is a borderland with stories marked by themes of genocide, poverty, AIDS, and abandonment by the international community. I met my wife Regine in Rwanda. She was a genocide survivor who invited me to enter into her stories and those of her family. These narratives revealed the entrenched evils of ethnic divisions along with miracles of human transformation and grace. Regine has dedicated her life to healing trauma, brokenness, and social divisions through her teaching at the University of Manitoba and her participation in grassroots community work.

I have been privileged to engage in academic studies of the New Testament at Acadia Divinity College, Princeton Theological Seminary, the University of Sheffield, and Carey Theological College. I have taught Scripture courses at the Seminario Teologico Bautista in Bolivia and more recently to students in Africa, India, and Canada. As someone who has lived at the intersection of New Testament studies and community development work, I have been stirred to bring stories from the margins to my reading of the gospels. Four years ago, my life took an unexpected turn when my health collapsed in India. I am still learning to live with the restrictions and relapses associated with Still's Disease. One of the gifts of a chronic illness is the way it creates space to reflect on the stories of the past and to consider

6. Bauman, *Collateral Damage*, 153.

the time that remains. I am being forced to write the lines of a new chapter of my life story. Although the call to serve the poor remains constant, the plot has taken a course that I did not choose. I hope this book makes some small contribution to others who are seeking to write the themes of justice and compassion into the stories of their lives.

I wrote this book for two kinds of readers. The first group is composed of those men and women who have said "yes" to the call to serve and live out their faith in difficult places. I sometimes think of them as community workers, environmental educators, and pastoral leaders who work in the borderlands. The second category of readers are people who are disappointed and disillusioned by organized religion and congregational life. They long for something deeper, more engaging, and more transforming. I hope that the content of the following chapters will provide spiritual nourishment for both groups.

Stories as Agents of Change

My sleep is often interrupted in the night due to my illness. Sometimes I listen to a radio, using an earphone in order not to bother Regine. One such night, I was riveted by a BBC interview with Dr. Mukesh Kapila,[7] who described an afternoon in March 2004 when he sat behind a desk in Khartoum writing a report for his superiors at the United Nations in New York. Kapila was the UN's senior representative in Sudan. He held little hope that the lines he was writing about Darfur would have any greater impact than his previous reports.

A tall woman in torn, dirty clothes unexpectedly appeared outside his office, having somehow made it past the security guards and administrative staff. She introduced herself as Aisha and chose to sit on the floor rather than to use a chair. She explained that she had come from Darfur to Khartoum in order to tell him her story. Aisha had been with her family in her town's market when Arab militia attacked on horseback and in vehicles. They rounded up the women and girls and raped them systematically "like a production line in a factory." She passed out after being abused by several men. When Aisha gained consciousness, houses were burning and the men of the town had disappeared (and never returned). Somehow she journeyed 1,000 kilometers (620 miles) to Khartoum to meet with Mukesh Kapila.

7. See Kapila and Lewis, *Against a Tide of Evil*, 2013.

Kapila had received third-party reports about Darfur over the past months. Now he was confronted with the personal story of a survivor. His subsequent actions would cost him his UN career and lead to years of death threats. He booked a flight to Nairobi and called a press conference without the permission of his superiors. He exposed the violence sponsored by the Government of Sudan and the inaction of the UN to protect vulnerable populations in Darfur. He had been ambushed by Aisha's story and felt compelled to make a series of dangerous personal commitments.

The interview with Mukesh Kapila shows how stories can shape our lives. This theme is brilliantly analysed in Arthur Frank's book *Letting Stories Breathe*.[8] Frank proposes that narratives are dynamic, living entities that have the capacity to touch our emotions, challenge our perceptions, and work as agents of change in different social contexts. His theory of socio-narratology gave me valuable insights for approaching the parables of Jesus. Three concepts have been particularly important.

First, Arthur Frank suggests that each person creates an "inner library" of stories in their personal memory banks. These narratives come from diverse places—family histories, the prevailing culture, religious faith, folk tales, the media, movies, books and even malicious gossip. We use some stories again and again to reinforce a particular worldview or value system. We move other stories to the back shelves of the inner library, where they fall into disuse and are almost forgotten. Using Frank's analogy, we could say that the parables of Jesus are carefully crafted stories that have entered into the libraries of diverse audiences throughout the ages. Some of these narratives have been given prominent places, which is reflected in the way we use phrases such as "a good Samaritan," "a prodigal child" or "a mustard seed project."

Second, Frank introduces the concept of "narrative ambush," where stories unexpectedly assault listeners and overwhelm their defences. These stories can shake us to the core and force us to examine our values, motivations, ideologies, and apathy. Though we often build walls against the rational discourse of people on the other side of political and ethnic boundaries, a powerful story can unexpectedly leap over these protective fences and penetrate our hearts. Third, Frank describes certain stories as "dangerous companions" that have a way of living with us or showing up at inconvenient times. These stories can inspire us to undertake risky journeys of

8. Frank, *Letting Stories Breathe*. Dr. Frank was very gracious in allowing me to read the manuscript prior to its publication.

great virtue or vice. They push us towards nobility or destruction. Aisha's *3 stories* story was a dangerous companion for Mukesh Kapila.

These three descriptive concepts, "inner libraries," "narrative ambush" and "dangerous companions," have shaped my approach to the parables. The stories told by Jesus were not "cute rural tales." They were not the "wise reflections" of a philosopher recounted while resting in a pleasant meadow. They were also not sermon illustrations told to reinforce a religious message. *The parables were the message.* They were memorable. They ambushed people by speaking of the coming of God's rule in territory controlled by the Roman Empire. They were dangerous because they encouraged people to take creative actions in ways that gave expression to the gospel saying about taking up the cross and following Jesus.

I conclude the introduction by noting that it was dangerous for Jesus to talk about the kingdom of God in a land ruled by an emperor who commanded legions of troops. It would have been a safer option to speak about the family of God or the age of the Spirit. Most of the people who heard his stories lived on the margins, where they contended with hunger, poverty, social exclusion, and a growing sense of resistance to the kingdom of the Romans and their puppet Herod Antipas. His audiences also included a few people who were agents of the elite minority and thereby benefited from the culture of domination and privilege. Jesus used parables to address both groups by casting the vision of an alternative kingdom which offered personal and social transformation. The following chapter will attempt to portray the social setting of Galilee and Judea in which the message of Jesus was proclaimed in deeds of healing, words of teaching, and, of course, stories.

CHAPTER 1

Stories from Foreign Lands

Deep down, we're inclined to assume that everyone thinks about and perceives the world as we do. —DAVID LIVERMORE[1]

If you don't enjoy a place, maybe you don't know enough about it. Seek the truth. . . . Give a culture the benefit of your open mind. See things as different, but not better or worse. —RICK STEVES[2]

Stories From the Margins

Ginugula Prabhakhar, a thirty-year-old farmer, tended two acres of cotton in the Indian state of Andhra Pradesh. Early in 2010 his wife, Kamala, borrowed 20,000 rupees (about $500) from an agent of a microcredit finance institution. A few months later, a cyclone destroyed their entire crop. Without income from the cotton, Ginugula and Kamala were unable to pay instalments on their debt. They received threats from agents of the lending institution. Seeing no way out, Ginugula committed suicide by drinking the pesticides that had protected his cotton from insects. He could neither find protection from a cyclone nor debt collectors.[3]

A tourist to India reading this report in a newspaper would most likely have understood Ginugula's suicide as a family tragedy caused by a personal debt. It could happen anywhere! I read the story in a hotel, waiting for colleagues with whom I would spend several days visiting rural development

1. Livermore, *Cultural Intelligence*, 87.
2. Steves, *Portugal*, 28.
3. *Times of India*, 19 November 2010, 5.

projects. They had oriented me to the issues that lay in the background of the story of Ginugula and Kamala. Farming families with small landholdings were usually denied access to credit from regular banks. Their needs were generally small, their collateral negligible, and it was hardly worth the paperwork involved. Furthermore, there were always unexpected risks involved in farming. Unscrupulous for-profit companies had stepped into the gap and were loaning money to rural families for seeds, fertilizers, and other inputs. The interest rates charged sometimes exceeded fifty percent. The collection agents were known to harass and threaten clients who were tardy in making payments. As a result, farmer suicides had become a major social problem in India.

This background information was not in the newspaper story. It was unnecessary. Indian readers were familiar with the issue. People with local knowledge were able to interpret Ginugula's suicide as a desperate act of protest against the unjust system of credit and profiteering in rural India. The average tourist would have missed the deeper meaning of the story without the help of informants who understood the "unstated" part of the narrative.

Crossing Borders: Entering the Cultural World of the Parables

To offer another story of a lighter nature, Regine and I were blessed by the participation of a few international guests at our wedding in Rwanda. They were initially surprised that Regine was not present at the commencement of the ceremony. They were further confused when a cow was brought in to stand at the center of the room. They were absolutely bewildered when a man in traditional dress moved forward to inspect the cow carefully and then signaled his approval through an exuberant song and dance. The cow was then taken to Regine's mother, who formally accepted it before it was led away. Regine did not appear in the room until the cow had made its exit. Friends from North America and Australia had never seen a cow at a wedding. They needed someone with local knowledge to explain that my family was offering a valuable gift in recognition that Regine's family was losing a daughter. She could not participate in the ceremony until the symbolic transaction was completed.[4]

4. The story of our wedding has been recounted in John Steward's book *Genocide to Generosity*, 157–60.

The tragic story of Ginugula and the account of our wedding illustrate that stories can transport us to foreign lands with different patterns of family and community life. Only naïve and inexperienced tourists expect customs, behaviors, roles, and worldviews to be like those of their homelands. Wise and experienced travelers heed the advice of Rick Steves found at the beginning of this chapter. They observe carefully, ask good questions, and resist the temptation to jump to conclusions so that they can enter sensitively into the culture where they have been received as guests.

Bruce Malina is a pioneer in weaving together the relatively modern study of social sciences and anthropology with biblical interpretation.[5] He uses the analogy of reading the scriptures as a journey into the foreign lands of the Bible. He advises readers to be constantly aware of the distance between themselves and the people who are found in the ancient narratives. Malina advocates the use of cultural anthropology to interpret the biblical texts responsibly and appropriately so that readers grasp the patterns of daily life and social organization behind the accounts of scripture. The following statement expresses his concern:

> . . . the Bible is necessarily misunderstood if one's reading is not grounded in an appreciation of the social systems from which the documents arose...Even such concrete items as house, courtyard, cup, sheep, and goat carry meanings lost to and/or replaced by the contemporary reader. The interpretative situation is even more hopeless regarding abstract values such as peace, wealth, poverty, humility and love.[6]

When it comes to the parables, we require information that makes explicit to us what was implicitly understood by the original audiences. Kenneth Bailey writes about the "cultural problem" of the parables, noting that they were narratives drawn from the community life of people who shared a particular cultural setting at a specific time in history.[7] "Any commentator who moves through any parable inevitably makes a series of culturally influenced judgments; the question is not, 'Shall we interpret,

---

5. Malina's book *Social Gospel* is a helpful introduction.

6. Ibid., 5

7. Bailey served as the chairman of the Biblical Department at the Near Eastern School of Theology in Beirut, a location that gave him proximity to cultural practices and attitudes associated with the Middle East. Bailey, *Poet and Peasant*, 27.

making cultural judgments as we go along, or shall we not?' Rather it is, 'Whose culture shall we allow to inform the text for us?'"[8]

Bailey signals a clear danger. Readers often impose their own values and customs as they interpret the parables. As a result, the message of the parables may be lost, distorted, or even used to justify abhorrent behaviors.[9] Klyne Snodgrass, author of a major book on the parables of Jesus, describes how the stories of Jesus have been twisted, summarized, subverted, realigned, and "psychologised" by generations of pastors, scholars, and lay readers who did not understand their social context.[10]

I advocate that the work of archaeologists, linguists, and social scientists serves as a kind of tourist guide for modern readers by offering us information about first-century Galilee and Judea that has not been available to biblical scholars since the time of the early church.[11] Their research allows us to enter the social world of the parables and to appreciate the characters, plots, tensions, and emotions that lie within the stories. When this information is combined with a socially tutored imagination,[12] a reader has an informed position from which to consider the meaning of a parable in its original context and then to reflect on its message for our time and circumstances.

This approach to the parables is important for the development of faith. The Christian scriptures are not a compendium of timeless doctrines that we memorize for a written examination. Most of the Bible consists of narratives embedded within a larger story of God's relationship with the world that he created. The stories include the call of Abraham, the liberation of slaves, the reign of kings, the building of a temple, the anointing of prophets, and the commissioning of apostles. In every story, God acts in the lives of individuals and in the broader social world in which they participate. The gospel is the story of Jesus of Nazareth, born in Bethlehem, acclaimed as a prophet in Galilee, executed in Jerusalem, and raised from the grave by God's power. By the very nature of our faith as Christians, we should be people with a deep appreciation for the power of stories and the importance of their cultural setting.

8. Ibid., 36

9 Saint Augustine interpreted the command "Compel them to come in!" from the parable of the great banquet (Luke 14:23) as a justification for forceful conversion of people he considered as heretics.

10. Snodgrass, *Stories with Intent*, 6.

11. Moxnes, *Jesus in His Place*, 19–20.

12. Malina, *Social Gospel*, 7.

The parables of Jesus account for more than one-third of the teaching material recorded in the synoptic gospels.[13] Some are so memorable that their vocabulary and images have become part of our global culture. Unfortunately, the very familiarity of Jesus' parables has left the impression that we instinctively understand them. Accordingly, they are robbed of their power to inform, challenge, and give direction to our lives. In this book, I attempt to offer fresh readings of selected parables from the Gospel of Luke by eavesdropping on Jesus and his audiences as they gather in Galilee and Judea during the first century. As we participate in the delight, laughter, surprise, and astonishment of the crowds among which we mingle, the parables will speak to us about the world of Jesus, our own world, and our participation in God's work of transformation and healing.

Hidden Transcripts of Resistance

The work of James C. Scott has shaped my understanding of the parables of Jesus in first century Galilee and Judea. Scott is a professor of political science and anthropology at Yale. His book *Domination and the Arts of Resistance*[14] influenced a number of New Testament scholars, including Richard Horsley and William Herzog II.[15] Scott argues that repressive regimes propagate a *public transcript*, which justifies the power imbalances that favor an elite minority. The public transcript uses words, symbols, and actions to communicate the content of what the privileged minority want their subordinates to believe about the world and their duties. Subjected people are compelled to participate in the public transcript through symbolic actions of subservience along with taxation and obligatory labor. Those in power use violence in an arbitrary and capricious manner, with few restraints and apparent consequences. Dominated people generally live with fear and resentment while nurturing the hope of a future reversal. Scott's theory helps us to understand the incongruity of massive demonstrations in support of repressive dictators in certain countries, where ordinary people are forced to play their roles in the public transcript.

According to Scott, some individuals and groups within the oppressed majority develop *hidden transcripts* of resistance. These hidden transcripts are nurtured in locations beyond the surveillance of those in power. You

13. Snodgrass, *Stories with Intent*, 22.
14. Scott, *Domination*.
15. See for example Horsley, ed., *Hidden Transcripts;* and Herzog, *Parables.*

might think of the village of Arcatao in the story of Esteban Lopez. The village developed a culture of resistance that could withstand the occasional invasions of government troops dispatched by generals in San Salvador. Like the public transcript, a hidden transcript is not restricted to public speeches. Music, jokes, art, theatre, and symbolic actions such as inferior work, theft, and evasion of taxes are also examples of these hidden transcripts of resistance.

The creation of hidden transcripts requires time, secluded locations, and people who take on the dangerous task of communication. The communicators generally share the social conditions of the oppressed, but have a degree of mobility that enables them to move from place to place, thereby linking scattered communities of resistance.[16] Members of the movement rely on networks of families, friends, and sympathizers rather than a formal organization. They make use of social or religious occasions in which they can meet and express dissent. Tension and danger is heightened when a public transcript of domination and a hidden transcript of resistance rub up against each other. Spokespeople of the hidden transcript will often choose to use ambiguous forms of communication, employing terms and symbols that require inside knowledge in order to avoid a direct confrontation between unequal powers.

I am particularly intrigued by Scott's observation that stories are used within hidden transcripts of resistance to critique the dominant social narratives and offer a competing version of reality. These stories create space for dissident views and establish a foothold in hostile territory. It seems to me that the parables work in this way. Scott also observes that at some point, the charismatic leader of a hidden transcript will inevitably collide with the officials of a public transcript of domination in a politically charged and dangerous event. The ruling elite will usually act decisively and violently. Terms such as "lunatic," "fanatic," "trouble maker," or "criminal" will be used to justify the removal of the hidden transcript's leader from the stage. The stories of fallen leaders often live on as part of a renewed hidden transcript directed against the powerful minority who maintain the public transcript of domination.[17] We are reminded that Jesus was arrested and executed as a criminal or social bandit.[18] He was accused of threatening to destroy the temple, perverting the nation, encouraging tax evasion,

16. Scott, *Domination*, 123–24.

17. Ibid., 202–27.

18. Mark 14:48 (Luke 22:52; Matt 26:55); Mark 15:27 (Luke 23:33; Matt 27:38).

and calling himself a king.[19] The lies, distortion of justice, and brutal use of power against Jesus correspond to Scott's theory.

Unmasking the Powers: the Parables as Hidden Transcripts

Scott's theory of public and hidden transcripts provides a helpful way to enter into the stories that Jesus told. First-century Galilee and Judea were repressive states that formed part of a large empire. Herod Antipas and the Roman procurator exercised power accountable only to the emperor in Rome. Their rule depended on the use of force to produce revenues and maintain public order. The imprisonment and beheading of John the Baptist due to his criticism of the marriage of Antipas gives an idea of the repression below the surface of the *Pax Romana* (Roman peace). Troops of the Roman general Varus had burned towns, sold women and children into slavery, and publicly crucified 2,000 men in Galilee around the time of Jesus' birth.[20] As Richard A. Horsley observes, "There is no way we can understand such practices as crucifixion, mass slaughter and enslavement, massacres of whole towns and annihilation of whole peoples, other than as purposeful attempts to terrorize subjected peoples."[21] Military presence and symbols of the empire were part of the public transcript of domination.

Members of the Jewish elite maintained their own public transcript within the confines of Roman rule. Their transcript justified their privileged position and an interpretation of Torah that focused on purity rather than economic and social justice. Their transcript included the temple system of sacrifices and festivals that created wealth for the high priestly families and their associates. Archaeological discoveries have shown that the high priestly families lived in spacious mansions in the area of Jerusalem above the location of the temple.

In *Jesus and Empire*, Richard Horsley argues that diverse hidden transcripts of resistance were nurtured in villages and towns in Galilee and Judea. Opposition to Roman power and the Jewish elite drew on stories from the Hebrew tradition, such as the defeat of Pharaoh, the liberation of the Jewish slaves, the struggle against enemies for the land of Canaan, and prophetic condemnations of the monarchy, Jerusalem power brokers, and the

---

19. Mark 14:58; Matt 26:61; Luke 23:2.
20. Josephus, *Jewish Antiquities* 17.295 and *Jewish War* 2.71–76.
21. Horsley, *Jesus and Empire*, 27.

temple.[22] Peasant communities found hope in the promises that God would intervene to establish his rule over the forces of oppression that robbed them of their dignity and peace. They expressed resistance through forms of protest, such as the evasion of taxes, inferior work, and social banditry.

The movement Jesus led would have appeared to be simply another form of a hidden transcript with similarities to other dissenting groups clustered around prophets, messianic leaders, and prominent social bandits. However, there was a decisive difference. Jesus announced that the Kingdom had drawn near. God was already acting on behalf of the poor and oppressed. His followers formed cells scattered throughout rural towns and villages. They embraced his message and sought to implement his teaching. Jesus used parables as an important component of his message about the coming of God's rule. Stories communicated his message in ways that could be grasped by his followers while being opaque or hidden from his opponents.

Unlike John the Baptist, who remained stationary on the banks of the Jordan, Jesus took his message into the public arena in villages and towns throughout Galilee and Judea. It is important to observe the places that he visited and also those locations that he avoided. The Irish scholar Sean Freyne notes that there is no record of Jesus visiting or preaching in the major Galilean cities of Sepphoris and Tiberius, where Antipas had troops and supporters.[23] He entered Jerusalem during the final days of his mission in order to provoke a showdown that he knew he would lose. It is not sufficient to say that Jesus had a personal preference for open skies and lake shores rather than the streets of large cities. He chose not to enter Sepphoris, Tiberius, and Jerusalem because these were the centers of the power that opposed God's rule. The final week in Jerusalem was full of tension and danger as the hidden transcript of the kingdom challenged the public transcripts of Roman power and the Jewish elite through actions such as the triumphal entry, the cleansing of the temple, public debates, and the prediction of the temple's destruction. The open proclamation of his message in word and deed resulted in a staged trial and execution as a political agitator and blasphemer.

22. Ibid., 62.

23. Freyne, *Jewish Galilean*, 144.

Interpreting the Parables: Remembering, Re-imagining and Resisting

Jesus told parables because they surprised (ambushed) people and encouraged them to envision God's rule and their lives in new ways.[24] Through stories, Jesus challenged his listeners to use their imaginations to contemplate personal and social transformation. I find modern analogies in theologian Sally McFague's description of entering a "wild space"[25] of insight about alternative ways of living and journalist Christopher Hedges' reference to the "sublime madness" that inspired biblical prophets and social reformers to work for justice and human dignity.[26] The parables were simple, memorable stories suitable for an oral culture rather than the complex narratives of a modern novel or movie. They stayed with listeners and could easily be re-told by women in the marketplace, men in fields, and families lying in their sleeping rooms at night. The serial telling of parables facilitated the spread of the kingdom transcript throughout the rural villages of Galilee and Judea.

The parables became a unifying force for Jesus' followers, who were scattered throughout Galilee and Judea. The stories were also a persuasive means of attracting new followers to the movement. Jesus would have repeated the same parables in diverse settings in different ways in order to convey the key ideas and values of his movement. The parables created a group identity that distinguished Jesus' mission from the agendas of other dissident movements. It was inevitable that the stories of God's rule would move into public spaces occupied by the dominant political, economic, and religious transcripts of those who exercised power and controlled wealth. The message of God's reign was political, in that it addressed issues of sovereignty, loyalty, and obedience; it threatened the imperial system of the emperor in Rome and the economic system that benefited a small minority of wealthy families. By speaking in parables, the message was expressed in ways that were veiled and puzzling to those who stood outside of his movement.[27] They were left to ponder his words, reflect on their meaning, and ultimately make a decision about how to respond.

24. Marcus J. Borg describes parables as invitations to see in a new way and thus embrace a radical change in perception. Borg, *Jesus*, 334.

25. McFague, *Life Abundant*, 48.

26. Chris Hedges, *Wages of Rebellion*, 201–26. Hedges attributes the phrase to the theologian Reinhold Niebuhr.

27. Wright, *Jesus*, 181, 287.

In the next chapter, I will seek to challenge the popular image of first-century Palestine as an area of happy peasant families enjoying simple lives tending sheep, growing crops, and fishing on the Sea of Galilee by noting the realities of wealth and poverty during this time. But before turning to this discussion, I will offer the following excursus on the Kingdom of God in the gospels, which will frame observations about God's rule in subsequent chapters.

Excursus: The Kingdom of God

The word "kingdom" is found 121 times in the first three gospels. Most of these occurrences are qualified as either "the kingdom of God" or its equivalent "the kingdom of heaven." The latter term avoids the use of the divine name. In this excursus, I want to provide a brief explanation of this important biblical expression for readers whose lives are far removed from times of monarchs and their realms. More substantial studies are available in academic books and journals.[28]

The word "kingdom" implies a monarch who claims power over a territory. Democratic states with presidents and prime ministers are not kingdoms. Consequently even The United Kingdom, The Kingdom of Thailand, and the Kingdom of Belgium are considered democracies that retain some of the traditions and trappings of a monarchy. Many biblical scholars prefer the use of terms such as the "reign of God" or the "rule of God." They argue that "kingdom" creates the idea of defined borders that can be drawn on a map and defended with armies. In contrast, "reign" or "rule" conveys a sense of action and activities involved in governing and exercising sovereignty. The discussion of terms among specialists has been helpful. When Jesus entered Galilee he proclaimed that God was acting to establish his sovereign rule rather than readjusting boundaries on an ancient map.

I had the good fortune to study under David Hill at the University of Sheffield. He used to tell his students that the kingdom of God signified that God was present in majesty and mercy. Hill's definition captures the awe of God's presence in a specific place and the nature of his care for broken and wounded people. Over the years I expanded his definition with a purpose clause. The kingdom of God is a phrase that expresses God's presence in majesty and mercy to transform the lives of individuals and

---

28. A good starting point is the article on the kingdom of God written by Joel B. Green in Green, ed. *Dictionary*, 468–81. The article includes an extensive bibliography.

their communities. The presence of God is both a current reality and a future hope for which we pray. The kingdom is and is to come. I have been drawn to two modern attempts to create equivalent expressions for God's kingdom. John Dominic Crossan proposes "the Great Divine Cleanup of this world."[29] Clarence Jordan, who earned a PhD in New Testament Greek before he founded Koinonia Farms, uses the simple translation, "God's movement."[30] Crossan and Jordan are seeking ways to express that God's kingdom creates personal and social transformation. God's presence gives dignity to human life in the borderlands, builds communities of justice and compassion, and challenges the cultural practices of exclusion and privilege. The kingdom is God's work of healing in a wounded world.

---

29. Crossan, *God and Empire*, 116.
30. Jordan, *Cotton Patch Gospel*.

CHAPTER 2

Entering the World of the Poor

Whose knowledge counts? Whose values? Whose criteria and preferences? Whose appraisal, analysis and planning? Whose action? Whose monitoring and evaluation? Whose learning? Whose empowerment?

Whose reality counts?

Ours or theirs? —ROBERT CHAMBERS[1]

Stories from the Margins

ANA SALOMAO GREW UP in a refugee family after her parents were forced to flee Angola during the war of independence.[2] Carrying only a few possessions, they crossed the border to Zaire,[3] a country that did not want them. Ana grew up in poverty among displaced people. She returned to Angola to attend secondary school during the civil war that followed independence. Living with an aunt in the regional centre of Nzeto, she was keenly aware of the family's sacrifices that allowed her to study. After completing secondary school, Ana won an international scholarship that allowed her to study community development in Kenya. Five years later, Ana returned to Angola with a university degree in her suitcase. She knew she had been called to work in rural communities and urban slums among her people.

---

1. Chambers, *Reality*, 101. Robert Chambers is a British professor and development practitioner.

2. 1961–75.

3. Now known as the Democratic Republic of the Congo.

They welcomed her home because she was one of them and she understood their needs.

Some people called to vocations in the margins of the world will identify with Ana's story. They may have been raised in places of poverty, violence, and oppression. Perhaps they had parents who valued education and sacrificed for their children. They were able to leave their homelands to study and begin careers in locations of relative security and affluence. But there was a decisive moment in which they decided to return home and dedicate their gifts and acquired knowledge to their people. They re-entered their homelands with an innate understanding of the contexts in which they would serve.

Other people raised in places of comparative privilege may somehow sense that their vocations will require them to leave the familiar in order to take up residence in the borderlands. Their calls are authentic, but they enter these new areas without the local knowledge and social familiarity of the people among whom they will serve. They must face the difficult and costly process of slowly learning what it means to live with different cultural codes, ways of understanding the world, and social patterns that sometimes clash with their former lives. I understand these feelings. I have been an awkward outsider at different times in my vocation. Although the call to serve on the margins is deeply rooted in the soul, the integration will require humility, sensitivity, humor, determination, and a supportive community. The transition from locations of privilege to the borderlands is challenging at every level—intellectually, physically, emotionally, spiritually, and socially. This is true whether we cross the world or simply enter into a new social location within our community.

I was struggling to align my life with Bolivian culture and issues when I read a book by Gustavo Gutierrez on the spirituality of service among the poor. The following quotation has stuck with me for over thirty years.

> Beyond any possible doubt, the life of the poor is one of hunger and exploitation, inadequate health care and lack of suitable housing, difficulty in obtaining an education, inadequate wages and unemployment, struggles for their rights, and repression. But that is not all. Being poor is also a way of feeling, knowing, reasoning, making friends, loving, believing, suffering, celebrating, and praying. The poor constitute a world of their own. Commitment to the poor means entering, and some cases remaining in, that universe with a much clearer awareness; it means being one of its

inhabitants, looking upon it as a place of residence and not simply of work.[4]

These words are a helpful orientation toward life in the rural communities of Galilee and Judea, where the parables were told to crowds that came out to meet Jesus. As I stressed in the last chapter, we enter into the social context of these communities as strangers and visitors. We observe patterns of interaction and practices that may seem strange and difficult to comprehend. We might be tempted to make quick judgments by comparing what we see and hear in the texts to the familiar patterns and cultural assumptions of our own lives. At times it will be helpful to return to the quotation of Gutierrez in order to remind ourselves that being poor involves a distinct way of feeling, knowing, reasoning, building relationships, believing, and praying. The goal of this chapter is to help you to enter the unfamiliar world of first-century Palestine in order to comprehend the forces that maintained people in poverty and the faith that challenged the status quo.

Wealth and Poverty in First-Century Palestine

I begin this section with a statistical analysis of Palestinian society during the time of Jesus. While the following numbers are estimates, they are useful in helping us to grasp the social divisions in Galilee and Judea.[5] The *urban elite*—which included families associated with the upper echelons of the Roman Empire in Palestine, the Herod dynasty, and the Jerusalem temple along with lay aristocrats—accounted for a mere 1 or 2 percent of the total population. This group was characterized by honor, power, affluence, and the ownership of large estates. We need to remember that in agrarian societies, wealth was generated by land ownership and the control of agricultural production. Although the affluent minority possessed a disproportionate share of farmland, they lived in exclusive areas of urban centers alongside other wealthy households. A second group can be categorized under the term *retainers*. These people served the administrations of Herod Antipas and the Roman procurator, the high priestly families in Jerusalem, and the urban elite through the roles of managers, administrators, military officers, tax farmers, scribes, and bailiffs. The retainers comprised approximately 5

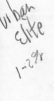

---

4. Gutierrez, *Our Own Wells*, 125.

5. Duling, *Proclamation and Parenesis*, 56; Rohrbaugh, "Ethnocentrism and Historical Questions about Jesus," in Stegemann, Malina, and Theissen, *Social Setting*, 35–36.

percent of the population. Most retainers lived with their families in the urban centers such as Sepphoris, Tiberias, and Jerusalem.

I use the awkward term "*sub-elite*" to designate a class of people that included merchants, artisans, and laborers with secure employment who lived in cities or towns.[6] They accounted for approximately 8 percent of the population. This group, like the retainers, lived modestly compared to the urban elite. However, they had confidence that their resources would be sufficient for future needs and allow them to maintain their honored status in the community.

Peasants were families with small landholdings, tenant farmers on rented property, casual laborers, fishers, and village artisans. They made up approximately 75 percent of the population. Their lives were economically vulnerable at the best of times. Palestinian peasants did not aspire to become wealthy or powerful, but simply wanted to feed their families.[7] This majority group lived with the fear of sliding into the bottom 10 percent of the population which I call the *vulnerable.* This last group included unemployed laborers, shepherds, beggars, widows, orphans, prostitutes, dung collectors, lepers, and other expendables. They can be compared with those who live in extreme poverty in our modern world.[8]

These statistics allow us to grasp that approximately 85 percent of the population struggled to survive. The social structure of Galilee and Judea was dysfunctional because inordinate power and privilege were given to a very small portion of the population.[9] An assessment by modern development workers would describe the majority population of Palestine as poor, chronically food insecure, malnourished, and disproportionately vulnerable to contagious diseases. An estimated 60 percent of children born in Palestine died by age six, and the average life expectancy was just over thirty.[10] Life was difficult for most people, and there was little reason to hope for positive change.

This information creates an appropriate place to refute the romantic notion that Jesus' mission was conducted in the pleasant and peaceful environment of hillsides and lakeshores under the bright sunshine of Galilee.

---

6. The more common term "non–urban elite" conveys the idea that these people enjoyed a portion of the benefits of elite status outside of the major cities.

7. Fiensy, "Ancient Economy," in Neufeld and DeMaris, *Social World*, 198.

8. Paul Collier refers to this group as "the bottom billion." Collier, *Bottom Billion*.

9. Hanson and Oakman, *Palestine*, 6.

10. Malina and Rohrbaugh, *Social-Science Commentary*, 383, 304–5.

We have sometimes imagined contented farmers and jolly fishing families that give up a few hours of work in order to hear the message of a religious teacher speaking about the deeper meanings of life. At one time I envisioned the setting of passages such as the Sermon on the Mount in this manner. I now judge that this portrait is about as accurate as the frequent and naïve observation of tourists that the poor in the global south seem so happy. It is more accurate to say that desperation, deprivation, and resentment characterized the lives of most people in Galilee and Judea.

The romantic portrait of rural Galilee completely overlooks the economic and social forces that were transforming daily life as the Roman Empire restructured the economy of Palestine. I will address this issue by making five points. The first is that under Roman rule, Palestine had transitioned from a barter economy to a "money" economy. The issuance of coins was a matter of economic control and political propaganda. Tributes and taxes paid to Rome and Herod required the use of coins. These coins carried the image of the emperor, along with symbols and slogans of Roman rule. In this way they were an important communication tool of the public transcript.[11] The temple tax imposed on Jewish males was paid with coins, along with the costs of sacrifices. Most debts were incurred in amounts of money.[12] Coins were used as a medium of exchange in markets controlled by elite families. The change from barter to money benefited the powerful at the expense of the poor.[13]

Second, the combination of tributes, taxes, tithes, and offerings to the Empire and the temple were an unbearable burden for rural families and communities.[14] In Galilee, agents of Antipas collected a land tax, a poll tax (based on the number of people in a household), along with further taxes and tributes in order to transfer wealth to Rome and enlarge the local ruler's personal treasury. The temple in Jerusalem claimed tithes, an annual contribution for each male, and the costs associated with sacrifices from Jewish people in Galilee and Judea. High priestly families and their administrators collaborated in the collection of taxes, tributes, and tolls for the Roman

11. Martin Goodman describes coins as the most pervasive medium for disseminating the image of the emperor and the claims of his empire. *Rome and Jerusalem*, 66.

12. The exception would be tenant farmers, who promised to pay the landlord in a percentage of produce of the crop. This figure was usually set at between 25 to 50 percent of the harvest.

13. Doug Oakman, "Money in the Moral Universe of the New Testament," in Stegemann, Malina, and Theissen, *Social Setting*, 343–44.

14. Herzog, *Prophet and Teacher*, 62.

Empire in Judea. The temple authorities even sent armed gangs to rural communities at harvest time to intimidate peasants and collect the tithes and taxes.[15] Herzog estimates that the combination of the Roman taxes and the Temple claimed 20 to 35 percent of a peasant's farm production.[16] In addition to these external demands, farmers needed to save approximately 20 percent of their grain harvest as seed to plant for the next crop cycle.

Third, the production on large estates was oriented toward cash crops rather than toward supplying food for the local population.[17] Even peasants had to balance food security requirements with the need to sell crops that would generate the coins required for taxes and other obligations. Money was gained through sales in the markets of towns or work as day labourers on large estates. Similarly, the fishing industry was controlled by elite interests with set prices, production quotas, and export agreements for pickled fish. The plight of fishing families was no less desperate than that of peasant farmers.[18]

Fourth, wealthy families used their economic power to expand their landholdings and further consolidate their positions of privilege. Money lending was a highly effective means of acquiring land. General poverty augmented by disasters (such as crop failures, accidents, and sickness) drove peasant families into debt. Interest rates were often high, and the consequences of defaulted loans often included the loss of family land. As a result, the ownership of agricultural land gradually became concentrated in the hands of the urban elite, including the high priestly families in Jerusalem.

Fifth, as cities grew, rural areas were compelled to provide food, labor, and basic goods for urban populations. The produce and services were purchased at terms controlled by the urban elites.[19] Peasant farmers lacked the power to negotiate fair and just prices for their crops and labor.

Sean Freyne notes several important aspects of the changing social and economic structure of Palestine under Roman rule:

> The new cities, even when the majority of their inhabitants were Jewish, were alien to and parasitical on the surrounding territory.

15. Josephus, *Ant.* 20.181, 206–7. This action was done at the expense of priests of lesser status outside of Jerusalem, who depended on the tithe for their livelihood.

16. Herzog, *Prophet and Teacher,* 62.

17. Hanson and Oakman, *Palestine,* 142, 178.

18. Hanson, "Galilean Fishing Economy," 99–111; Crossan, *God and Empire,* 121–23.

19. Ibid., 103.

An urban culture introduced new types into the population, scribal administrators, military personnel, and others in various retainer roles, acting on behalf of the ruling elite and the native aristocracy. It also made new demands for goods and services—thereby, however, increasing the burden of taxation on the peasantry. This pressure from the top inevitably led to an increase in the levels of poverty, and the slide from landowner to tenant farmer, to day labourers to beggars, all characters we hear of in Jesus' parables, was inexorable. As always, in such situations it is the poor who are the most vulnerable, exposed to the effects of disease and dispossession.[20]

At this point I want to return to the earlier quotation of Gutierrez. People in the borderlands develop their own ways of analyzing and understanding the social realities that keep them on the outside, looking into the lives of the privileged. Accordingly, it is legitimate to ask how the people living on the social and economic margins of first-century Palestine understood their situation. One important answer is that most of them shared a "limited good" theory of economics and social honor. This frame of reference can be contrasted with our prevailing theory of the unlimited capacity of the world to generate wealth and security.[21] A limited good worldview connects all participants in a particular social setting and assumes that the actions of one segment of the population directly affect everyone else. The following explanation of Malina and Rohrbaugh is helpful:

> . . . all goods existed in finite, limited supply and all goods were already distributed. This included not only material goods, but honor, friendship, love, power, security, and status as well—literally everything in life. Because the pie could not grow larger, a larger piece for anyone automatically meant a smaller piece for someone else . . . Profit–making and the acquisition of wealth were automatically assumed to be the result of extortion or fraud. . . . To be labelled "rich" was therefore a social and moral statement as much as an economic one. It meant having the power or capacity to take from someone weaker what was rightfully his.[22]

An awareness of the economic and social forces operating in Palestine, along with an appreciation of the limited good worldview, enables the modern reader to enter more deeply into the social world of the parables.

---

20. Freyne, *Jewish Galilean*, 134.

21. Environmentalists have challenged this "unlimited capacity" theory for decades.

22. Malina and Rohrbaugh, *Social-Science Commentary*, 324.

We are able to grasp that rural peasants and the urban poor lived with resentment towards the social elites that celebrated abundance in their villas and country estates.[23] Jesus was raised by a widow in a rural village within this broader social and economic context. He told stories to people on the margins about extravagant banquets, kings who demanded extortionate profits, estate owners who hoarded production in order to drive up local prices, slaves on estates, corrupt judges, and sick beggars who survived on pieces of bread tossed on the floor. The plots and characters resonated with the life experiences and emotional feelings of those who listened to his stories. They were his people. He understood and identified with their issues.

Land, Poverty and Oppression in the Hebrew Scriptures of Jesus

I return to the words of Gustavo Gutierrez for a final time. He wrote that being poor involves a distinct way of believing. This observation encourages us to inquire about how pious families drew on their traditions and scriptures to nourish their faith while living under the domination of the Roman Empire and their appointed rulers. In this section of the chapter I will address the themes of land ownership, debt, and the oppression of the poor from the perspective of the Hebrew Scriptures. I ask readers to recall that Jesus understood his call and mission within the larger story of God and his people as told in the sacred writings of Israel. Terms such as "the kingdom of God" and "the Son of Man" are signs of a deep connection with the ancient scrolls that Christians refer to as the Old Testament.

According to the Hebrew Scriptures, the land was God's gift to the descendants of the slaves he had rescued from Pharaoh's empire in Egypt. Family properties were an important component of the covenant relationship between God and his people.[24] Arable land was not a commodity for speculation and personal profit. Although Leviticus 25 permitted the temporary sale of land to repay debts, every fiftieth year the property was to revert to the family that had traditionally owned it (Lev 25:31). The intention of this provision was to preclude the emergence of a permanent social group of landless poor people.[25] However, monarchs and wealthy families

---

23. Goodman, *Rome and Jerusalem*, 425.

24. Davis, *Scripture, Culture, and Agriculture*, 102.

25. Ibid., 39.

abused their power to take over the properties of vulnerable families, as illustrated by the story of Naboth's vineyard in 1 Kings 21.

The Torah also contained a provision for the cancellation of debts in the final year of each seven-year cycle (Deut 15:111). This provision was meant to ensure that there would be no chronic or multi-generational poverty among the people of Israel (Deut 15:4). The Torah contained a stern warning about turning one's back on the vulnerable in the closing stages of the seven year cycle.

> If there is among you anyone in need, a member of your community in any of your towns within the land that the Lord your God is giving you, do not be hard-hearted or tight-fisted towards your needy neighbor. You should rather open your hand, willingly lending enough to meet the need, whatever it may be. Be careful that you do not entertain a mean thought, thinking, "The seventh year, the year of remission, is near," and therefore view your needy neighbor with hostility and give nothing; your neighbor might cry to the Lord against you, and you would incur guilt. (Deut 15:7–9)

The *prosbul* became an important exception clause to this part of the Torah. It was instituted by the Sanhedrin or ruling council during the time of Herod the Great.[26] The *prosbul* facilitated loans in which the borrower waived the right of sabbatical-year debt relief. This legal provision allowed wealthy people to make loans to desperate rural families that offered their traditional properties as security. The *prosbul* directly contradicted the intention of the Torah to protect the well-being of vulnerable families. At a superficial level, this legal clause was drafted by wealthy lenders and scribal experts as a way to enforce their ability to collect on loans without regard to the calendar. At a functional level, the purpose of *prosbul* was to facilitate the seizure of land for non-repayment. As William Arnal argues:

> . . . the main reason to lend money, whether in Jerusalem or Galilee, would have been the longing to acquire land, rather than interest in abstract financial return . . . it is only when the borrower fails to repay that any significant gain is made, whether in the form of exorbitant late-payment penalties or, more realistically, in the seizure of the lands or persons pledged against the loan . . . money lending would have been an extraordinary effective means for acquiring land.[27]

26. Goodman, *Jerusalem and Rome*, 421–23.
27. Arnal, *Village Scribes*, 139–40.

This background knowledge gives us insight into Jesus' condemnation of the scriptural experts and Pharisees for neglecting the Torah's demands of justice, mercy, and faithfulness (Matt 23:23; Luke 11:42).

The violation of sacred laws about land ownership and indebtedness fits into the larger theme of oppression in the Hebrew Scriptures. Here I owe a great debt to Thomas Hanks. I met Tom in 1979 when I was studying Spanish in Costa Rica. Tom was commencing his calling to teach theology in Latin America. His doctoral research had been on the relationship between poverty and oppression in the Bible. The result of his academic research was later published in the book *God So Loved the Third World: The Bible, the Reformation and Liberation Theologies*.[28]

Hanks observes that the Hebrew terms that signify poverty occur overwhelmingly in connection with the vocabulary and descriptions of oppression. A classic example of this link is found in the third chapter of Isaiah:

> The Lord rises to argue his case;
> he stands to judge the peoples.
> The Lord enters into judgment
> with the elders and princes of his people:
> It is you who have devoured the vineyard;
> the spoil of the poor is in your houses.
> What do you mean by crushing my people,
> by grinding the face of the poor? says the Lord God of hosts.
> (Isa 3:12–15)

In this passage, there is a clear link between the circumstances of the poor and the oppressive actions of leaders who crush and humiliate them. Hanks reaches the important conclusion that the oppression of the poor is the basic cause of poverty in biblical theology. Other factors, such as sloth or misfortune, are seldom mentioned.[29]

This consideration of the Hebrew Scriptures give us another entrance point into the faith of people who lived on the margins during the time of Jesus. I want to emphasize again that the Hebrew Scriptures shaped the formation of Jesus during the hidden years of preparation before he entered Galilee and proclaimed that the kingdom of God was at hand. Jesus did not explain the poverty around him as the unfortunate and temporary

28. Hanks, *Third World*.

29. Ibid., 33–35. Hanks goes on to criticize most English translations for concealing the radical socio–economic analysis of the Hebrew Scriptures.

consequence of the economic policies of the Roman emperor and senate. He believed that the poverty of Galilee and Judea was the direct result of social injustices and oppression that robbed people of their dignity and hope.

Luke the Evangelist: A Passion for the Poor

The final part of our journey into the world of the poor in first-century Palestine requires us to consider the unique contribution of Luke the evangelist. The third gospel has a special sensitivity toward those on the margins. This is evident in the way Luke uses the Jesus material to draw attention to the kingdom's inclusion of the poor, the blind, the lame, lepers, widows, prostitutes, Samaritans, and people dominated by demonic possession. I have often drawn on Luke's Gospel while teaching in Latin America, Asia, and Africa precisely because of his concern for vulnerable people. I am not suggesting that the evangelist forced his own theological framework on the Jesus tradition. Rather, I think he intentionally highlighted certain themes as he sought to follow Jesus and write the gospel account within the historical context in which he served. I pay particular attention to Luke the evangelist in this last part of the chapter because the parables treated in this book are drawn from the third gospel.

Luke's Theology of Reversal

The possession of wealth seldom raises ethical questions in North America. Investments, savings, and property are viewed positively because they provide security and privileges. Conspicuous wealth is even celebrated in electronic and print media as "living the good life." As we have seen in this chapter, the majority of people in first-century Palestine believed that the accumulation of wealth was neither morally neutral nor socially desirable.

It seems safe to surmise that the prayers of many Palestinian households implored God to intervene in order to restore justice and equity to their land. They longed for a reversal that would give honor and security to the poor while bringing judgement on the minority that held a disproportionate share of wealth and power.[30] John Q. York identified three types of literary expressions that feature this motif.[31] First, there are passages in

---

30. The theme of reversal is found in apocalyptic writings such as 1 Enoch. See E. Isaac, "1 Enoch," in Charlesworth, *Old Testament Pseudepigrapha, Volume 1*.

31. York, *Last Shall Be First*.

which the conditions of wealth and poverty or honor and shame are explicitly reversed. Here we might think of Mary's Magnificat (1:41–53) or the Lukan beatitudes (6:20–26).[32] Second, there are places where the reversal is implicit so that the reader discerns that God's action challenges the social order of the world. The conversation with the rich ruler (18:18–25) contains a hidden condemnation of the wealth of the elite and the means by which it was generated. This man will be saved and enter God's rule only through a dramatic act of reversal.[33] Finally, there are a number of short sayings that contrast the values of God's rule against those of the dominant culture. The statement that the first shall be last and the last shall be first is an example (13:30).[34]

The reversal theme portrays God transforming the world in order to restore the dignity of those who live at the margins and bring judgement upon those who participate in and benefit from a society plagued by economic disparity and suffering. Personal loyalty to Jesus' message and mission requires a parallel commitment to critique and reverse the public transcripts that maintain the oppressive world order.

The Nazareth Manifesto (4:16–30)

The Nazareth Manifesto presents Jesus as a prophet committed to God's action to give liberty and dignity to the poor. A similar incident in the Nazareth synagogue occurs in Mark and Matthew after a significant period of ministry (Mark 6:1–6a; Matt 13:53–58). Luke's version retains many of the same features, including the identification of Jesus as the child of a local family and the proverb that a prophet is not honored in his own region. However, the evangelist departs from the other gospels in placing it near the beginning of Jesus' mission, inserting a quotation from Isaiah 61, making reference to Elijah and Elisha, and describing the attempt to kill Jesus.

The setting is the regular Sabbath assembly in Nazareth. The village was close to Sepphoris, and it is possible that the leaders of the synagogue were wealthy men who divided their time between the city and their country estates. It is clear that Jesus' reputation has begun to spread throughout Galilee, since the leaders recognize him and hand him a scroll with the sacred scriptures. Jesus chooses to read from Isaiah 61.

32. See also 16:19–31; 18:9–14.
33. See also 7:36–50; 10:25–37; 12:13–21; 14:17–24; 15:11–32.
34. See also 9:24; 13:30; 14:11; 17:33; 18:14.

The Spirit of the Lord is upon me,

because he has anointed me

to bring good news to the poor.

He has sent me to proclaim release to the captives

and recovery of sight to the blind,

to let the oppressed go free,[35]

to proclaim the year of the Lord's favor.

After the scroll has been returned to its place, Jesus announces that this scripture has been fulfilled in the hearing of his audience.

The Isaiah passage was originally addressed to people who longed for God to respond to the injustices, inequities, and sinfulness of the post-exilic communities. The statement of Jesus makes two assertions. First, God has begun to establish his sovereign rule through his mission activities in Galilee. Second, the transformation will benefit those who live on the margins. The poor, the captives, the blind, and the oppressed are not four separate groups, but rather four descriptors of the vulnerable and broken people to whom God promised his saving action.[36] Taken together, they describe the majority of people who struggled to survive in first-century Palestine.

After an initial response of approval, the mood turns to homicidal anger when Jesus remarks that authentic prophets never measure up to hometown expectations. The reference to Elijah and Elisha remind the assembly that God's prophets had a pattern of working beyond the borders of the dominant culture. The reaction of the assembly foreshadows the opposition of the leaders, who will eventually orchestrate the violent death of Jesus in Jerusalem.

In summary, the Nazareth Manifesto in the third gospel stands as a programmatic statement at the commencement of Jesus' mission. The remainder of the gospel account will present narratives of marginalized people who are restored to full membership in the community through healings, exorcisms, repentance, forgiveness, and bold acts of faith. Table solidarity will be shared with people considered to be sinners by synagogue leaders. The symbolic gestures of welcome and inclusion challenge the public transcript of privilege and root the promise of reversal in specific social locations where the rule of God is proclaimed.

35. This particular phrase represents a deliberate and surprising intrusion from Isa 58:6. The Isaiah passage presents hunger as a consequence of the oppression of the poor.

36. Roth, *Blind, Lame, Poor*, 162.

Almsgiving: Redistribution and Radical Generosity

It is important to note at the outset that Jesus did not attempt to impose an economic system on the nation as a whole. Men and women were invited to make costly individual decisions to become his followers and embrace the values of God's kingdom. We should also recognize that Jesus extended membership in his movement to individuals and households of all social standings. In fact, the inclusion of wealthy disciples was necessary to facilitate the kind of voluntary vertical redistribution that would benefit the poor. Precisely because of the causal connection between oppression and poverty, it was expected that disciples in more secure circumstances would engage in substantial and practical acts of solidarity and the distribution of resources far beyond the usual standards of charity.

There were three broad levels of interaction in the social system of first-century Palestine. *Balanced reciprocity* was practiced among peers. Benefits and obligations were carefully calculated in order to maintain a level of equality regarding honour and social standing within one's group. *General reciprocity* occurred primarily within immediate family and kinship groups. Generosity was extended without expectations of immediate repayment and incurred obligations. *Negative reciprocity* was practiced among people outside of kinship and peer groups. One party would seek disproportionate benefit at the expense of the other. The losers suffered both material consequences and diminished honor because of their inability to protect their interests.[37] The economic structure of the Roman Empire was based on negative reciprocity. As we have seen, food products, taxes, tributes, and rents flowed from small rural producers to urban centers for the benefit of elite families, their retainers, and ultimately the emperor in Rome.[38]

The third gospel encourages the followers of Jesus to live by the principle of general reciprocity in their relationships with those on the margins. This means relating to them as family members to whom obligations of kinship are owed. Previously, we saw that the rich ruler's salvation depended on a radical break from his wealth and subsequent generosity with the poor (18:22). The tax collector, Zacchaeus, practiced what the rich ruler could not bring himself to do. As a result, Jesus states that salvation has come to this household (19:9–10). The parable of the rich fool, which will

---

37. Neyrey, "Ceremonies in Luke-Acts," in Neyrey, *Social World*, 372.

38. Oakman, "Countryside in Luke-Acts," in Neyrey, *Social World*, 156.

not be considered in this book, is a narrative about the selfish calculations of a man who lives in a community with hungry families but is unwilling to share the abundance of his harvest (12:16–20). Jesus introduces this story with a warning about the temptation to measure success in terms of possessions and personal security. He concludes by contrasting the accumulation of material treasures with deliberate decisions to live "rich toward God." The earlier teaching on generosity in 6:27–36 is striking because general reciprocity is extended toward people who could be classified as enemies (and therefore treated within the social norms of negative reciprocity).

I wish to draw attention to the two references to almsgiving in Luke's gospel (11:41; 12:33). Modern readers of the gospel may associate alms with trivial acts of charity. As Halvor Moxnes observes, "Almsgiving is seen as a strategy that is opposed to a real sharing of wealth, a way to keep the poor masses quiet and to avoid a redistribution of property. Thus, almsgiving becomes a condescending giving from the rich to the poor, in reality upholding the basic inequality of society."[39] This narrow and demeaning definition would have been challenged by Luke the evangelist. In a saying found only in his gospel, Jesus tells his followers: "Do not be afraid little flock, for it is your father's good pleasure to give you the kingdom. Sell your possessions, and give alms" (12:32–33). The action envisioned is substantially different from token expressions of kindness to beggars on street corners.

The second mention of almsgiving is found in an earlier saying that is also unique to the third gospel (11:41). The social context is a shared meal in the home of a Pharisee. The observation is made that Jesus did not follow the purity norms of washing before eating. Jesus' riposte is harsh. He accuses the Pharisees of a preoccupation with the cleanliness of tableware and a disregard for the inner motivations of wickedness and greed. He goes on to say that they follow minute aspects of tithing herbs, seek places of honor and recognition in the community, build tombs for dead prophets, and load unbearable burdens on people. Within his critique, Jesus proposes almsgiving from within as an alternative form of purification. This interior disposition toward the needs of people on the margins acknowledges God's demand for justice and love (11:41–42). Here we have a connection between the giving of alms and a radical generosity of the heart. There is a clear suggestion that such generosity can address the social consequences of greed and wickedness that Jesus mentioned at the beginning of the conversation.

39. Moxnes, *Economy*, 114.

The third evangelist encourages radical generosity as a means to establish some form of equity between the privileged and the marginalized. Voluntary vertical redistribution restores the dignity, security, and material goods that have been taken (in various ways) from the weak and oppressed who live in the borderlands.[40] Because almsgiving outwardly expresses the Torah's teaching about justice and covenant solidarity, the practice of radical generosity creates an inner purity in those who chose to live by the values of God's rule.

Conclusion

This chapter began with the story of Ana Salamao, a community worker who returned to her home country to live and work among her people. Ana did not require lectures, readings, and discussions on the violent history of Angola, the inequitable distribution of wealth, and the needs of the poor. Her life experiences informed her vocation to serve in the borderlands. The opening section of the chapter recognized that some women and men will sense a call to enter and serve in new places, requiring them to cross cultural and economic borders. They will need to suspend the ways used previously to understand the world in order to enter into the social context of those who live on the margins. The quality of their service will depend on their willingness and ability to embrace the suffering and joys, limitations and opportunities, fears and dreams, distinctive worldviews, and expressions of faith of people in the borderlands.

This same principle applies to our approach to the parables. We seek to understand them from the perspective of the poor to whom the good news of God's kingdom was proclaimed. The content of this chapter has taken readers into the marginalized communities of first-century Palestine. We have not spent time considering the glorious reconstruction of the temple in Jerusalem under Herod, the building of Caesarea in Galilee under Antipas, the quality of Roman roads, and the aqueducts that transported water from rural areas to urban centres. Though there were undoubtedly accomplishments and engineering marvels associated with the Empire, they were disproportionate to the suffering endured by the most vulnerable people. Our intent has been to understand the circumstances and faith of those who lived on the margins, longing and waiting for God to bring

40. Ibid., 120.

transformation to Palestine. The next chapter will introduce us to one of the most important parables of the Jesus tradition.

CHAPTER 3

Sower, Seed, and Soils

Faith and Productive Living in the Borderlands
(Luke 8:4–15)

I think that Jesus spoke of the seed because he was talking for us campesinos and not for the rich. . . . he used this example of the seed because he was talking our language. He was talking about seeds and birds that eat the grains . . . because that's our language and because the message is for us poor people. —Oliva[1]

The examples of Jesus are very clear for simple people. They say nothing to proud people, who despise this language of Jesus because it is simple. For some it's a revelation; for others it's an enigma. It's so simple that only the simple understand it. —Alejandro[2]

Stories from the Margins

IN LATE NOVEMBER 1956, Fidel Castro and eighty-one men set sail in a boat from Mexico, heading for Cuba. Ernesto "Che" Guevara was the only non-Cuban among the group. Their goal was to gain a foothold in Cuba

---

1. Cardenal, *Solentiname*, 2:38. Cardenal was a priest, poet, and community worker in Nicaragua. He served as Minister of Culture for eight years after the Sandinista revolution. The four volumes entitled *The Gospel in Solentiname* were based on readings of the gospel and conversations with campesinos who lived on the Solentiname Islands of Lake Nicaragua.

2. Ibid., 43.

and launch the revolution that would free the country from the brutality and corruption of the Batista regime. The men landed on a beach the night of 2 December. Government troops were waiting for them and decimated the small band.

A few days later, the remnants of the revolutionary group—with fewer than a dozen rifles between them—managed to meet on the beach where their comrades had fallen. Castro and Che were among the twelve combatants who had not been killed. The men embraced and recounted their harrowing experiences. Then Fidel Castro made an audacious statement to his followers: "We have already won the war."[3] His words on the Las Coloradas beach in December 1956 proved to be prophetic. Three years later, Batista fled the country, and Castro's troops entered Havana in triumph.

This story resonates with vision, courage, and defiant confidence. One might imagine, in contrast, the official report about the battle on the beach delivered by government soldiers to their commanders in Havana. It would have stated that the rebels had been routed and the regime's rule secured. Fidel Castro's message inspired his eleven followers to move into the Sierra Maestra mountains and begin to rally the peasant population. There would be further hardships and sacrifices. But the movement had been planted on Cuban soil.

I propose that this narrative of Castro and his followers on the beach helps us to enter imaginatively into the historical setting of the parable of the sower, the seed, and the soils. The Roman Empire was a formidable regime that maintained social order with armed soldiers, economic domination, and violence. The public transcript proclaimed peace and security, yet this message was buttressed with threats, displays of force, and public crucifixions. As noted earlier, Jesus did not frame his message around a safe theme, such as the family of God, practices of personal piety, or alternative forms of wisdom. He deliberately chose the provocative language of God's rule in Galilee, where the Roman emperor had troops and Herod Antipas dealt harshly with political opponents. The announcement that God was acting to establish his reign was a message of daring vision, bold confidence, and immense courage within a hostile environment.

[Handwritten margin note: Not sure Castro is best / Castro]

3. Sotolongo, *Che Guevara*, 70.

Background to the Parable

The parable is customarily divided into three sections, which I refer to as the first telling (8:4–8), the interlude (8:9–10), and the second telling (8:11–15). The same general format is found in the parallel passages in the gospels of Matthew and Mark. Some of the variants between the versions may be explained by the probability that Jesus used parables on multiple occasions, adapting them to different settings and divergent audiences.[4] There is discussion among New Testament specialists about the authenticity of the so-called explanation (which I prefer to call the second telling). My aim for this chapter precludes entering into these technical debates. My objective is to show how the parable as a literary unit worked as a narrative of resistance for the movement based around Jesus.

The immediate introduction to the sower parable (8:1–3) portrays Jesus moving incessantly throughout the towns and villages of Galilee with his disciples, preaching and proclaiming the good news of God's kingdom to the poor and oppressed.[5] Luke informs his readers that the followers of Jesus were a diverse group, including women, sustained by generosity and mutual sharing. I want to draw attention specifically to Joanna, the wife of Herod's chief steward.[6] Evidently, she abandoned her family in order to integrate into the company of itinerant disciples. This detail indicates that the message of God's rule had penetrated into the courts of power in the capital city of Sepphoris. We can be sure that Joanna's actions scandalized many people of high standing who had a tight code of family honor.

The mission activity of Jesus in the towns and villages of Galilee created initial expectations of liberation from the oppression of Roman rule. But with the passage of time, many people began to entertain doubts about the possibility of real social and political change apart from armed intervention.[7] Pilate continued as the governor of Judea at the pleasure of the emperor in Rome. Herod Antipas still crushed the peasant population of Galilee with taxes, troops, and torture chambers. In Jerusalem, the

4. Howard Marshall suggests that Luke had oral traditions that supplemented Mark's version of the sower. Howard Marshall, *Luke*, 318.

5. *Euangelizomenos* ("proclaiming good news") recalls 4:18, where Jesus reads Isa 61:1–2.

6. Both Mary and Joanna will be present at the empty tomb and will be the first to hear that God raised Jesus from the dead (24:10).

7. This would have been true among the readers of Luke's gospel, who would have wondered when the great reversal would shake the powers of the world.

corruption of the temple leaders remained unaltered. These signs could all have been interpreted as explicit evidence that God had not begun to rule.[8] The unceasing nature of oppression would have created doubts about Jesus' proclamation of God's kingdom and the strange command to love one's enemies.[9]

People who live in a borderland understand the fragile nature of hope. The longing and motivation for transformation (personal and social) can be crushed by a system that seems entrenched and unbendable before any winds of change. Today's optimism can turn quickly into tomorrow's despair leading to destructive acts of violence. Individuals who respond to a "call" to offer their lives in service learn never to take hope for granted in the margins. Sometimes it takes courage to nurture the dream of positive change in the broken world around us.

The Sower Parable: First Telling 8:4–8

> When a great crowd gathered and people from town after town came to him, he said in a parable: "A sower went out to sow his seed; and as he sowed, some fell on the path and was trampled on, and the birds of the air ate it up. Some fell on the rock; and as it grew up, it withered for lack of moisture. Some fell among thorns, and the thorns grew with it and choked it. Some fell into good soil, and when it grew, it produced a hundredfold." As he said this, he called out, "Let anyone with ears to hear listen!"

Jesus tells the sower parable to a great crowd of people (including disciples) who journeyed out from the towns of Galilee (8:4). In Luke's narrative, the Galilean crowds are a sympathetic audience to Jesus and his mission. They gather because they anticipate that the prophet will say something important about the kingdom of God and their communities. A literal translation of the first words of Jesus reads as follows: "The one sowing went out to sow his seed."[10] The listeners would picture a typical

---

8. Wright, *Jesus*, 223.

9. This is also the view of Alessando Pronzato, who states that Jesus unchained a wave of enthusiasm that within a short time turned into disillusionment. *Parabolas, Tomo 1*, 32.

10. Luke alone has "his seed." This construction further emphasizes the importance of seed for peasant farmers and seed as a symbol for the message of God's rule.

Palestinian peasant, a bag of seed hung over his shoulder, scattering seed over the land with flicks of his wrist.

Modern readers should be attentive to the simple nature of this image. It does not easily align with expectations of how God would overcome the power of evil in the world. In the historical period of Jesus, the Psalms of Solomon depicted a powerful king from the line of David through whom Israel's enemies would be defeated. The fourth chapter of the apocalyptic book of Ezra employed the symbol of a lion roaring from the forest. In contrast, Jesus depicts a peasant, his bag of seed, and, as the plot unfolds, his wasteful farming practices. I am drawn to Richard Longenecker's comment that the image of a peasant farmer who experiences crop failure would have jarred the messianic dreams of the majority of the audience.[11] It is important from the outset to recognize that the parable's main actor and plot separate Jesus and his message from other transcripts of resistance.

Palestinian peasants had much in common with most farming families in the global south in our own time. Family members work hard to cultivate small plots of land. The farms have been passed from generation to generation. Farmers combine different crops and small animals in order to meet their needs and to sell surplus production. Farmers with small landholdings know every square meter of their land, its different soils, slopes, exposure to the sun, capacity to retain moisture, and micro-climate variations. Crop production in Palestine was always risky and uncertain. In the period between harvests, farmers had to balance the hunger of the household with the need to save seed for the next round of planting. Seed stock was a valuable commodity which could not be wasted by unnecessary consumption or wasteful farming practices. The situation is captured in the comment of Ellen Davis, a biblical scholar who has given attention to farmers, land, and crops in biblical theology:

> The Israelite farmers know that they survived in that steep and semiarid land by the grace of God and their own wise practices . . . unlike their neighbors—the Philistines on the fertile plain of Sharon, the Egyptians and Babylonians ranged along the banks and canals of their great rivers—they had only the slightest margin for negligence, ignorance or error. . . . Seasonal aridity and periodic drought, a thin layer of topsoil, susceptibility to erosion—these mark the land of Canaan as a place under the immediate, particular care of God.[12]

11 Longenecker, "Luke's Parables of the Kingdom," in Longenecker, *Challenge*, 133.

12. Davis, *Scripture, Culture and Agriculture*, 26–27.

By aligning God's rule with the work of a peasant farmer, Jesus introduces elements of uncertainty, limitation, and struggle that might be under-appreciated by modern readers in urban locations.

The plot of the first telling unfolds with four vignettes of the farmer's work in seeding his field and the subsequent results. Three of these scenes portray failure related to unusual farming practices. First, the farmer tosses seed on a pathway, where it is trampled upon and eaten by the birds of the air.[13] Second, he scatters the seed on shallow soil that barely covers a hidden substratum of rock. This seed shows initial promise and then the plants wither for lack of moisture. Third, the farmer throws seed on soil that had not been adequately cleared of thorn bushes. As a result, thorns grow along with the seeds and gradually overcome the plants. The first three vignettes raise doubts about the farmer's ability to grow crops on marginal land.[14] Peasant farmers in the audience would consider the sower to be foolish, excessive, and wasteful.[15]

These same adjectives might have been hurled at Jesus by opponents in their criticism and sarcasm about his message and mission. They considered him to be careless and irresponsible in the way he spoke about God and entered into contact with tax collectors, "sinners," lepers, women, the demon possessed, and even Gentiles. As we saw in chapter 2, members of the synagogue in Nazareth attempted to kill him when he cited the example of Elijah and Elisha, who had broken social boundaries that separated the respectable in-group from perceived out-groups (4:24–30). As readers, we may use our imaginations to contemplate other voices in Galilee that were not recorded in Luke's gospel. People who hoped for a violent confrontation with Rome's legions would have considered Jesus to be naïve and unrealistic about the politics of power. Their hidden transcript would have looked to the emergence of a leader of armed men rather than meek disciples. The images of seed being trampled, eaten by birds, wilting in the heat, and competing for life with thorns depict a vulnerability and weakness that would

---

13. The Greek preposition *para* with the noun *hodos* (road, path) in the accusative case can mean "on the pathway" rather than alongside it. This option is preferable since it is difficult to comprehend how seeds would be trodden upon if thrown to the side of the path. See Arndt and Gingrich, *Lexicon*, 616.

14. This position is contested by some scholars, who maintain that the parable describes the typical practice of indiscriminately sowing land in which the loss of some seed was inevitable.

15. Nolland, *Luke 1–9:20*, 372.

hardly ignite the hearts of people who longed for change through a violent showdown.

In the final vignette, some seed lands in good soil, grows, and produces a crop one hundred times more than the amount that had been planted.[16] Peasants in Galilee would have celebrated a crop production ratio of 7.5 to 1 as an extraordinary blessing. The ratio in the parable was beyond imagination.[17] A hundred-fold harvest challenged the listeners to envision, at least for a moment, a world of abundance in which hunger was no longer a factor associated with suffering and death in their communities. In one narrative moment, a bountiful harvest removes any doubt about the farmer's knowledge and practices.

After concluding the parable, Luke writes that Jesus raised his voice and shouted repeatedly:[18] "Let anyone with ears to hear listen!" The command to hear resonates with the opening phrase of the *Shema*,[19] the daily prayer repeated by pious Jews, which began with the words: "Hear O Israel." In this prayer and in the parable, hearing means to embrace God's message deeply into the heart so that it shapes the way listeners conduct their lives and relate to others in their communities. The strange manner in which Jesus shouts repeatedly creates an urgent invitation to pay attention to this unusual story because it contains a message of great importance.

The Spanish scholar Alessandro Pronzato interprets the first telling of the parable as a portrayal of the mission of Jesus in Galilee.[20] The audience recognizes Jesus as the sower, through whom God is working to establish his rule. The common pastoral image of a farmer sowing a field implies that spectacular signs or blatant displays of military power are not part of God's plan of transformation. The first three scenes represent what opponents consider to be wasted time among unworthy people. Their critiques are severe and seem plausible. The final vignette encourages listeners to have confidence in the small beginnings and mixed results of Jesus' mission in

16. Mark's version had gradations: thirtyfold, sixtyfold and one hundredfold.

17. Malina and Rohrbaugh, Nolland, and Pronzato propose that a normal harvest was four to five times the amount of seed planted (Malina and Rohrbaugh, *Social-Science Commentary*, 10; Nolland, *Luke 1:1–9:20*, 376; Pronzato, *Parabolas Tomo 1*, 34). The only point of comparison is from the distant time of the patriarchs, when God blessed Isaac in Gerar with a hundredfold crop (Gen 26:12).

18. The corresponding section of Mark describes Jesus simply as speaking (Mark 4:9). The regular meaning of imperfect verbs is a repeated action.

19. Deut 6:4–9; 11:13–21; Num 15:37–41.

20. Pronzato, *Parabolas Tomo 1*, 34–35.

rural Galilee. They are exhorted to have faith that God will produce an outcome beyond all expectations. The conclusion celebrates God's ultimate triumph over the evils and injustices that reduce life to the daily struggle for survival.

The Interlude (8:9–10)

> Then his disciples asked him what this parable meant. He said, "To you it has been given to know the secrets of the kingdom of God; but to others I speak in parables, so that 'looking they may not perceive, and listening they may not understand.'"

The small section, which I refer to as the interlude, has puzzled readers since Jesus does not address the question posed by the disciples in the presence of the crowd.[21] The response divides the listeners into two broad groups. The followers or disciples of Jesus have received the gift of understanding the mysterious nature of God's rule. The "others" hear only puzzling stories that seem to be riddles with concealed messages. Jesus goes on to draw on the words of Isa 6:9, where the eighth-century prophet was warned that his message would be rejected by people who willfully chose to be blind and deaf to God's word.

I want to make two comments about the interlude. First, James C. Scott's theory of hidden transcripts provides insight into the nature of these two groups and the function of the parable. The stories of Jesus were puzzling for those whose loyalties and ideology was tightly connected with the public transcript of Rome, or even with alternate forms of resistance, including violence. In contrast, insiders could unpack the imagery and its meaning. The ability of the parables both to conceal and reveal is expressed by Alejandro, a Nicaraguan peasant, in the statement that introduced this chapter: "For some it's a revelation, for others it is an enigma."

Second, by referencing the historical figure of Isaiah, Jesus offers an example of an earlier prophet who was faithful to his calling to address the social and religious evils of his time. The listeners are reminded that the powerful elite of Isaiah's day were blind to what was happening and deaf to the meaning of God's message. They refused to pay attention to the message of the prophet. The failure to heed and repent eventually led to national

---

21. In Luke's Gospel, in contrast to Mark 4:10, the crowds remain with Jesus and listen to the interlude and second telling of the parable.

defeat and exile. By joining the story of the sower to Isaiah's experience, Jesus emphasizes that God's rule will not be deterred by human disregard and will not be hindered by powerful opponents.

The Second Telling (Luke 8:11–15)

> Now the parable is this: The seed is the word of God. The ones on the path are those who have heard; then the devil comes and takes away the word from their hearts, so that they may not believe and be saved. The ones on the rock are those who, when they hear the word, receive it with joy. But these have no root; they believe only for a while and in a time of testing fall away. As for what fell among the thorns, these are the ones who hear; but as they go on their way, they are choked by the cares and riches and pleasures of life, and their fruit does not mature. But as for that in the good soil, these are the ones who, when they hear the word, hold it fast in an honest and good heart, and bear fruit with patient endurance.

I refer to these verses as the second telling of the parable rather than its explanation. In the second telling, the figure of the sower is completely absent, and the seeds are the primary actors. The metaphor is slippery, because the seed is first identified with the word of God and then later represents people who respond in various ways to the mission of Jesus. However, the message of the parable is clear and forceful.

The four vignettes of the second telling describe and comment on different responses to the proclamation of God's rule. The first scene portrays opponents and disinterested listeners that reject the message of Jesus from the outset. Their immediate dismissal of his mission is attributed to the work of the devil, who takes the word from their hearts. In Hebrew thought, the heart signified a person's capacity to think, feel, imagine, and make decisions. God can speak into the heart of a person through his word.[22] Deprived of God's voice, those in the first vignette lack the faith to enter into God's transforming work in the world.[23]

The second, third, and fourth vignettes deal specifically with women and men who identified themselves as followers of Jesus.[24] The seed that fell

---

22. Sorg, "Heart," in Brown, *DNTT, Volume 2*, 180–84.

23. Salvation, eternal life, and entrance into God's kingdom function as equivalent expressions in the account of the rich ruler in Luke 18:18–30.

24. This is recognized by Justo Gonzalez, who comments that the second telling has

on rocky soil is analogous to those people that receive the announcement of God's coming rule with joy and faith. However, in a time of testing,[25] their loyalty waivers, and they fall away because they have not established deep roots. The verb *aphiemi* ("to fall away") connotes desertion from a movement, denial, and even betrayal in times of oppression and persecution.[26] The theme of testing in difficult circumstances is important in the third gospel.[27] Before the mission in Galilee, the Spirit led Jesus into the wilderness, where he was tested for forty days (4:1). He taught his followers that they would face times of hatred, shame and exclusion because of their loyalty to him (6:22–23).[28] Later, he encouraged them to pray daily that God would not lead them into testing (11:4). Before his death, Jesus issued a double warning to his disciples to pray that they would not enter into testing (22:40, 46). The term's elasticity helps us to understand that testing can range from the subtle temptation to seek a less demanding vocation right through to betrayal before violent opposition. The second vignette communicates the stark reality of adversity, where followers face threats and the disappointing defections of former friends and colleagues.

In the third scenario, the seed begins to grow but is overcome by thorn bushes competing for sunlight, soil nutrients, and water. This image portrays members of the movement who lose their vitality and make, at best, only a marginal contribution to the mission of transformation. Any sense of call is choked by anxieties, wealth, and the pursuit of pleasure. This vignette deals with the subtle, but powerful, lure of conformity to the values and structures of the dominant culture, a danger that has always threatened the movement of Jesus.[29] Later in the gospel, Jesus will contrast anxieties about the needs of life with the motivation to participate fully in God's rule (12:31). He will remind his followers that the values and motives that direct their daily lives reveal the true nature of their hearts (12:34). Unlike perse-

---

a bite because it is concerned with people who are already members of the movement. Gonzalez, *Luke*, 105.

25. Mark's gospel uses the terms trouble (*thlipsis*) and persecution (*diogmos*). Luke does not use these words in his gospel.

26. Hultgren, *Parables*, 198.

27. The Greek noun *peirasmos* carries the meanings of "test" and "temptation" while verb *peirazo* connotes "to put to the test" and "to entice to sin."

28. Although the word testing is not found in 6:22–23, it is clear that such experiences would test the commitment and resilience of disciples.

29. Jesus warns about the destructive and seductive power of anxieties (10:41; 12:22–25; 21:34) and wealth (6:24; 12:16, 21; 16:19; 18:23; 19:2).

cution that ebbs and flows, anxieties, wealth and pleasure are embedded in the very fabric of the culture in which people live.

The fourth vignette, the seed that falls on fertile soil, depicts the followers of Jesus who are deeply rooted. They have learned to stand firm in times of difficulty and to resist the temptation to compromise with the dominant culture. They are described as holding tightly to the message of the kingdom[30] and nurturing it in hearts that are good and honest.[31] I am drawn to the concluding words of the parable about endurance.[32] Endurance was an aspect of character that was widely admired and valued in the Mediterranean world.[33] Roman centurions prized steadfast endurance in battle. Soldiers trusted comrades beside them who were known to hold the line against the forces of the enemy. In the long history of Israel, courageous men and women displayed steadfast endurance by maintaining confidence in God's covenant promises even under distress (e.g., Isa 40:31; 51:5; Dan 12:2). After Jesus entered Jerusalem, he warned about coming times of hatred, betrayal, and martyrdom. He encouraged faithfulness with the words: "By your endurance you will gain your lives" (21:19). In our own time, we recognize the importance of those women and men who do not change positions based on opinion polls and upon whom we can depend in difficult circumstances.

Unpacking the description of the fourth soil that bears an abundant harvest leads us to consider two dimensions of God's transforming work in the world. There is a quiet and hidden aspect that is easy to overlook. God speaks his word into human hearts. The nurture of a good and noble heart attentive to God's messages does not happen by accident. It requires solitude, patience, humor, prayer, and a stubborn commitment to face the truth about the world and our own lives. On the public stage, steadfast endurance describes the strength of character required to maintain the course in times of fatigue, discouragement, and difficulties. Both the inner work and public activities of faithful discipleship are crucial for God's work of justice and mercy in the world.

---

30. Johnson, *Luke*, 133.

31. A good heart was the most important quality for a student of the Torah according to the first-century Jewish teacher Johannan ben Zachai. See Young, *Parables*, 274–75.

32. In Greek *en hypomonei*.

33. Falkenroth and Brown, "*Hypomone*," in Brown, *NIDNTT*, 2:772–73.

Reflection on the Parable

Readers will have noticed that I see an important shift in focus between the first and second telling of the parable.[34] The first telling emphasizes the certainty of God's rule, whereas the second telling is concerned with the demands of fruitful participation in God's work of personal and social transformation. The following reflection on the parable of the sower, seed, and soils recognizes these distinct themes along with the importance of the interlude.

I somewhat hesitantly opened this chapter with a story from the Cuban revolution. My decision to use this story might be misconstrued as a political endorsement of the revolution in some highly politicized areas of North America. However, the account of Castro on the beach conveys a moment of defiance and courage in the face of overwhelming odds, and this strikes me as a good way to introduce the theme of the sower parable. Many of us are familiar with overwhelming feelings of discouragement and failure. We may feel that our dreams of personal and social transformation lie strewn like garbage on a city street. Each new report on climate change and CO_2 levels further disheartens those of us who are committed to more sustainable patterns of living. Recent events in Ferguson and Baltimore have shattered illusions about law enforcement and racial equity. The massive movement of refugees in Europe is an alarming sign that the global community has no solution for the violence in Syria. The surveillance of western governments steadily increases their access to our lives and personal communications. Those who work for deep change in their communities often feel misunderstood and dismissed as radicals. They are discouraged by their impotency before entrenched powers that defend the status quo and offer token responses rather than transformation. It can be difficult to act as if the triumph of God's justice and mercy has already taken root in our world.

Similarly Jesus' closest followers faced uncertainties and discouragement before the entrenched powers of first-century Palestine. Those who opposed Jesus were quick to discredit his movement. They drew attention to the dubious social positions of the people around him. They criticized him for breaches of the purity code. They pointed to the dungeons of Herod Antipas, the presence of Roman troops, and the murder of John the Baptist

34. I am not alone in reading the parable in this manner. John Nolland writes that the so-called explanation is really a development of one aspect of the parable's message. Nolland, *Luke 1–9:20*, 384.

as evidence that nothing substantial was happening to prove that God was establishing his rule in Galilee. Other critics, whose voices are not recorded, might have mocked his strategy of confronting the force of violence with the counter-force of love. The sympathetic and hopeful crowds that gathered around Jesus must have been shaken by the negative comments of so-called people of influence. Perhaps even his closest associates entertained doubts about the message of God's rule.

Stanley Hauerwas writes that each of us needs a story that is powerful and truthful enough to break through the illusions that are part of our personal and social lives.[35] It seems to me that the public transcripts of our time propagate the illusion that social change only comes from above— the government, the courts, and corporate power. Our dreams of justice and equity are eroded by the sinking feeling that transformation can take place only in measured quantities and at a gradual pace dictated by the privileged minority. It matters little if we are working on water projects in rural Nigeria or a home for abused women in New York. We come up against barriers of indifference, inadequate finances, corruption, misrepresentation, personal egos that need to be massaged, and political roadblocks. The defection and abandonment of former colleagues and friends may be the hardest burden to bear. It is no wonder that so many people retreat to taking care of themselves and their families while leaving community issues to politicians and professional social workers hired by the state to put bandages on open wounds.

I propose that the parable of the sower, seed, and soils is a powerful and truthful story that addresses critical issues in the places where we live and serve. The first telling invites us to examine our faith in God's power to change individuals, communities, and the structures of evil that ensnare us. As I have emphasized, three quarters of the parable deals with failure. Those committed to the issues of people on the margins will have to deal with the disappointment and cynicism that emerge when people and projects seem unable to achieve lasting change. Critics on the sidelines, and even within our faith communities, will find fault with our project planning, the investment of time and money, and the people with whom we associate. We need to be reminded that the story Jesus told concludes with a harvest beyond all expectations. God will triumph, and his rule will prevail. When we journey through chaos and rough places, we must nourish our souls by anticipating the abundance of God's harvest and seek to participate fully and joyfully in

35. Hauerwas, *Hauerwas Reader*, 216, 218.

the everyday tasks of our callings. We hold fast to a story that is powerful and cuts through the illusions of our time.

The interlude, with its quotation from Isaiah, reminds us of our solidarity with faithful servants of the past who banged their heads against the walls of entrenched power and resistance. We can remember that the glory of God's appearance to the prophet, narrated in chapter 6 of Isaiah, transitioned quickly into the warning that people would be blind and deaf to his ministry and message. It is worth noting that Jesus did not quote the portion of the Isaiah text that pointed to the impossibility of change and social healing.[36] This deliberate omission indicates that Jesus understood the power of the public transcript, but trusted in the power of the Spirit to lead people to repentance and faith. The omission also signifies that women and men who serve God among wounded and broken people must nourish faith that even powerful people can hear God's voice and make dramatic decisions that will transform their lives, families, and communities.

I think of two people who did not give up hope that even their powerful enemies could be transformed into people of peace and justice. Dr. Izzeldin Abuelaish was a Palestinian medical specialist who worked in a Jewish hospital in Israel. In 2009, his home in Gaza was destroyed by shells, killing his three children and a niece. The Israeli Armed Forces later acknowledged this attack, but never apologized nor offered compensation. Abuelaish wrote that violence is futile, a waste of lives and resources, and only has the capacity to create further acts of retaliation. He now devotes his energy to grassroots dialogue and cooperation between Palestinians and Israelis who work for peace.[37] Similarly, after a bomb blast damaged the home of Dr. Martin Luther King Jr. in Montgomery, Alabama, an angry crowd gathered, and a shaken Dr. King addressed the people, saying that retaliation would only fire the flames of further violence. "Jesus still cries out: Love your enemies, bless them that curse you, pray for them that despitefully use you. This is what we must live by." James McClendon comments that King had the faith of an evangelist that even the most evil person could be converted and transformed.[38] I cite these two examples because we draw strength from people, past and present, who have not given up hope that people can change. They can help us believe that our labors are not in vain.

---

36. ". . . so that they may not look with their eyes, and listen with their ears, and comprehend with their minds, and turn and be healed" (Isa 6:10).

37. Abuelasish, *Shall Not Hate*, 174.

38. McClendon, *Biography*, 59–60.

The second telling of the parable addresses our personal lives as followers of Jesus who serve in the borderlands, where evil destroys life and hope in so many ways. Cornel West speaks from experience when he states that ". . . there are profound joys and unbearable sorrow that accompany being true to one's calling."[39] We cannot afford to be naïve. We will pass through difficult and lonely times. Our initial commitments to justice and compassion will, at times, lose any sense of emotional satisfaction and personal fulfillment. We will find that it is costly and draining to build relationships in places with a history of poverty, dependency, addictions, systematic racism, crime, and environmental damage. The organizations we serve will sometimes be dysfunctional. The moments of celebration and shared feelings of accomplishment will come after a prolonged period of hard work, sacrifice, setbacks, unexpected obstacles, management issues, and endless rounds of self-doubt. Expectations of good feelings will not keep us in the game!

The second telling of the parable emphasizes our response to the Spirit that speaks God's word into our hearts. The noun "word" (*logos*) and the verb "to hear" (*akouo*) are each used four times in the second telling, but they are absent in the text of the first telling until Jesus shouts to the crowds. The same combination of words is found again in 8:21, when Jesus says, "My mother and my brothers are those who *hear* the *word* of God and do it."[40] The challenge of listening to the word whispered by the Spirit in our own time requires solitude and discernment. The reference to good and noble hearts is connected to the theme of deep listening. Jesus uses this phrase to describe the inner disposition or character of people who collaborate with God in bringing transformation to the borderlands. The description points us toward the inner work required if we desire to offer our gifts and abilities with generosity, grace, obstinate determination, and love.

I wish to single out, for a moment, those readers who might describe themselves as activists. This broad category of people lives in constant tension between the exterior life of service and the inner life of the soul. They recognize that performance is measurable and easy to justify. Furthermore, they face the daily reality that they can never do enough even to satisfy themselves. They spend time with people, write reports, raise money,

39. West, *Brother West*, 88.

40. Luke Timothy Johnson observes that this incident and saying offer the perfect moral conclusion to the parable of the sower (Johnson, *Luke*, 133). Marshall likewise writes that it makes the final comment on the parable of the sower (Marshall, *Luke*, 317).

manage projects, and send off proposals to the point of exhaustion. While their work is commendable, there is a danger of burnout and voluntary martyrdom to an unrelenting schedule. Activists must be reminded of the importance of the practices of solitude and prayer so that the performance of their vocations is not compromised by imbalanced egos, undue responsibility, ambitions, hyper-sensitivity to criticism, and resentment of other people. Thomas Merton writes that action and contemplation can grow together in one's life so that they become two aspects of the same thing.[41] Spiritual disciplines will enable us to face our personal and vocational issues with the assurance that we are God's beloved, who have been uniquely called to contribute to the mission of justice, mercy, and faith. This work of the heart will also make us sensitive to our own wounds and our need for healing and compassion. In solitude, we will be given the resiliency and wisdom that is required to participate in an abundant harvest through steadfast endurance.

The next chapter leads us into a first-century description of marginalization and poverty that seems to defy any hope of transformation.

41. Merton, *Island*, 73.

CHAPTER 4

A Rich Man and Lazarus

Elites and Expendables (Luke 16:19–31)

It seems to me that here Jesus has put himself on the side of
the poor. But the Gospels can also be the liberation of the rich.
—FELIPE[1]

I think the word of God has been very badly preached, and the
church is much to blame in this. It's because the Gospel hasn't been
well preached that we have a society still divided between rich and
poor. —OLIVIA[2]

. . . there shouldn't be rich or poor, nobody should be screwed
in this life, nobody should be damned in the next life. All people
ought to share the riches in this life and share the glory in the next
one. —FELIPE[3]

Stories from the Margins

RATNAPANDI, A TWENTY–SEVEN–YEAR–OLD MAN living in rural India, supported his wife and children by climbing date palms with a tin pot in order
to tap juice from the highest parts of the trees. A typical workday was six-

---

1. Cardenal, *Solentiname,* 1:187.
2. Cardenal, *Solentiname,* 3:253.
3. Ibid., 252.

teen hours, during which he shinnied up and down trees around 150 times. The vertical distance covered would be roughly equivalent to walking up and down the stairs of a fifty-story building five times. Ratnapandi had no ladder, but used his arms and legs to press against the sharp bark of date palms. For this work, he earned less than one dollar a day. He was forced to sell the juice to a creditor, who loaned money to climbers and set the price for their product. Like other tree climbers, Ratnapandi had to pay land owners for the right to tap the date palms on their properties. Ratnapandi and other climbers suffered from muscular pains, skin diseases, occasional broken bones, and asthma. A fall could mean a debilitating injury or death. The only hope for Ratnapandi and others in his situation was social action that would break the debt cycle, give control of trees to the climbers, and establish fair prices for their product. The prospects for such transformation seemed dim because tree climbers were considered to be expendable.[4]

During trips to India, I thought about this story from the margins. I wondered if Ratnapandi's days as a tree climber had ended badly. It seemed inevitable that one day he would fall with a heavy bucket from a high tree and suffer permanent injury. I even speculated if he was among the crippled men who begged for money on the streets of Hyderabad or was sitting on the sidewalk outside my hotel asking for a few rupees. Although I do not know what became of Ratnapandi Nadar, I am certain that his poverty cannot be explained merely as the result of unfortunate circumstances. He bore the weight of an unjust system that profited from his dangerous labors, provided inadequate compensation, and would blame him if he fell from a tree. At the opposite end of the economic chain, there were parties that lived with abundance by processing and bottling the date palm juice that Ratnapandi and his associates risked their lives to harvest.

I see striking parallels between Ratnapandi's circumstances and the Lazarus parable. People in Galilee and Judea witnessed peasants who were forced to leave their rural communities to work as day laborers in urban areas. They saw men carried home from Sepphoris, Tiberius, or Jerusalem with broken bodies and broken hearts after falls from crude scaffolding on construction projects. They knew of permanently disabled men who remained in the cities to beg and live on handouts. Many of the original audience gathered around Jesus would have instinctively sympathized with

---

4. Sainath, *Good Drought*, 136–41.

Lazarus. They shared a common anxiety that they might someday descend into his marginal existence and shame.[5]

Background to the Parable

The Lazarus parable[6] is severe and uncompromising. Most pastors in North America and Europe would never consider it as a passage for their sermons or homilies. The story lacks the warm feelings of the "the prodigal son," the exemplary model of "the good Samaritan," the moral utility of the "the sower," or the optimism of "the mustard seed." Accordingly, it seldom enters into the annual preaching plan of congregations. The plot of the story offers two contrasting scenes. In scene one, a closed gate separates poor Lazarus from a lavish banquet in the rich man's villa. In scene two, a chasm separates the rich man from the banquet in the kingdom of God, where Lazarus reclines beside Abraham.[7] At first glance, it appears that God determines eternal destiny based on a criterion of socio-economic standing—an unsettling prospect for western readers since our lifestyles have more in common with the rich man than with Lazarus.

I suggest modern readers *feel* their way through the parable as well as *think* their way through the plot. It is important to refrain from theologizing too early in working with this story. Keep in mind that the Lazarus parable does not intend to present a full explanation of systematic theology regarding heaven, hell, salvation, and God's final judgment. But it does have an important message for this world with implications that extend beyond our lifetimes. If we chose to be deaf and blind to the message of the parable, our disregard will contribute to the eventual outcome of our lives when God pronounces his judgment on how we failed to practice justice and mercy in our communities.

Two perspectives may help us to enter more deeply into the narrative. First, we can remember the limited good concept of economics and honor that prevailed in first-century Palestine. This ground was covered in the second chapter of the book. Let me remind readers that most people believed that wealth and social honor existed in finite quantities. As a result,

---

5. Herzog, *Parables*, 119–20.

6. I refer to this Lukan passage as the Lazarus parable, because the poor man is named while the rich man is anonymous.

7. To be situated at the bosom of Abraham presupposes a banquet in which the guests recline on mats. See John 13:23 and Luke 13:28–30.

an individual who excelled in honor did so at the cost of other people. Similarly, a person accumulated wealth by reducing the economic assets of others in the community. If I may use a modern analogy, the size of the pie had been established. Changes in the way the pie was shared impacted all the participants at the table. The application of the limited good concept to the Lazarus parable leads to the assessment that the rich man's wealth and honor is directly connected to the poverty of Lazarus. Thus there is a moral principle at play in the parable rather than a mixture of economic forces and personal misfortune. Most people in the first century listened to the parable in this manner. The exception, of course, would have been those who had disproportionate wealth and considered it to be a sign of God's favor and their superiority.

The second perspective from which to feel and think our way into the parable is related to the contrast between individualist and collectivist cultures. North Americans and western Europeans share an individualistic cultural ethos. Environmentalist Bill McKibben describes our descent into extreme individualism and the consequences for our shared life.[8] Today, there is an almost unquestioned doctrine that people exist as independent units that define and direct their separate lives. In an individualist culture, I bear responsibility for myself and my actions based on my personal code of individual responsibility. In collectivist cultures, personal identity is formed through relationships and obligations first to families, second to peer groups, and finally to the community. In a collectivist culture, my decisions are shaped by the expectations, values, and needs of my family, peers, religious faith, and the broader community. My actions will impact the honor of others either positively or negatively because I am part of a collective rather than a free agent.

Of course, there is no purely collectivist culture, nor a totally unrestrained individualist society. But there are ways to measure a country's position on a continuum from one extreme to the other.[9] In the story of Lazarus, the rich man is a member of the collective group of elite citizens. In contrast, Lazarus' identity is with those who live in extreme poverty. The two men and the two groups are separated from each other by impenetrable boundaries. We do not need to look for character flaws or great evil in the life of the rich man. Nor do we need to speculate about the piety of

8. McKibben, *Deep Economy*, 95–128.

9. See Livermore, *Cultural Intelligence*, 92–110.

Lazarus. They represent two collective groups: those who enjoy privilege and those who live on the extreme edge of the borderlands.

The Lazarus Parable: Scene 1 (Luke 16:19–21)

> There was a rich man who was dressed in purple and fine linen and who feasted sumptuously every day. And at his gate lay a poor man named Lazarus, covered with sores, who longed to satisfy his hunger with what fell from the rich man's table; even the dogs would come and lick his sores.

The opening scene of the Lazarus parable introduces the main characters and their circumstances. The rich (*plousios*)[10] man wears purple clothing associated with royalty or those who chose to publicly flaunt their wealth.[11] There is an element of humor in the way the description includes his linen undergarments, indicating that his underwear,[12] which is not seen, is as impressive as his robes, which are visible to others. We learn that the rich man celebrates his social position with a sumptuous banquet each day.[13] It seems that his household disregards Sabbath provisions for its slaves and servants, as they are required to prepare and serve lavish meals each day.[14] The reference to the gate (*pylon*) of the rich man creates the impression of a large villa, with the gate attached to a wall that would have shielded the rich man from viewing people on the street.

There is an element of irony in the way Jesus gives the name "Lazarus" to the poor man. Poor beggars were generally nameless and expendable, whereas the rich had prominent names that were well-known in the community. But in this story, the poor man has a name and the rich man remains anonymous, suggesting that those who have been pushed into the borderlands of their communities are valued by God (16:15). A second irony is that the word "Lazarus" means "God helps." Yet the accompanying

10. The adjective "rich" (*plousios*) comes from a word group that frequently has negative or cautionary connotations in Luke's gospel.

11. Purple dye, made from sea snails, was rare and expensive. These were the garments of a man who never engaged in "real" work (Snodgrass, *Stories with Intent*, 425).

12. Only the very wealthy could afford to wear linen undergarments.

13. The Greek verb *euphraino* (to celebrate, gladden, cheer) is used in Luke's Gospel in connection with special festivities associated with the return of the prodigal son (15:23, 24) and the rich fool (12:19).

14. Herzog, *Parables*, 117.

descriptions do not reveal God helping Lazarus during the final stages of his miserable life. Friends apparently carried Lazarus to the rich man's outer gate each day, indicating that Lazarus was unable to walk.[15] From his position outside the gate, Lazarus could witness the comings and goings of members of the household and guests, and he could hear the jovial noises emanating from the banquet hall. He was covered with sores and suffered from hunger, longing to eat the morsels of bread that banquet guests used to clean their hands and then tossed on the floor.[16] His open sores were licked by guard dogs,[17] making him ritually unclean. Lazarus, the beggar, exists in a horrifying wilderness spending time each day just outside the gates of affluence.

The Lazarus Parable: Scene 2 (16:22–31)

The poor man died and was carried away by the angels to be with Abraham. The rich man also died and was buried. In Hades, where he was being tormented, he looked up and saw Abraham far away with Lazarus by his side. He called out, "Father Abraham, have mercy on me, and send Lazarus to dip the tip of his finger in water and cool my tongue; for I am in agony in these flames." But Abraham said, "Child, remember that during your lifetime you received your good things, and Lazarus in like manner evil things; but now he is comforted here, and you are in agony. Besides all this, between you and us a great chasm has been fixed, so that those who might want to pass from here to you cannot do so, and no one can cross from there to us." He said, "Then, father, I beg you to send him to my father's house—for I have five brothers—that he may warn them, so that they will not also come into this place of torment." Abraham replied, "They have Moses and the prophets; they should listen to them." He said, "No, father Abraham; but if someone goes to them from the dead, they will repent." He said to him, "If they do not listen to Moses and the prophets, neither will they be convinced even if someone rises from the dead."

15. The pluperfect passive use of *ballos* indicates that Lazarus was carried (Hultgren, *Parables*, 112).

16. Jeremias, *Parables*, 184.

17. Bailey comments that the saliva of dogs was considered to have healing power. This creates the further irony that the guard dogs show compassion, while the rich man and his guests are apathetic to Lazarus' suffering (*Jesus*, 385–86).

The opening scene sets up expectations that are shattered by the dramatic plot shift of the second scene.[18] The evangelist uses forty–five words in the narration of the first scene, whereas the plot of the second part requires 198 words.[19] The word count is a clear indicator of the importance of the second half of the story. This section begins with a brief description of the death of Lazarus. It seems that he died alone and was not accorded the dignity of a burial ceremony. Yet God, who appeared to have been absent during the last days of his life, intervenes dramatically by dispatching angelic servants to collect his body and take the dead beggar to the presence of the great patriarch Abraham. In life, Lazarus was an expendable, a non-productive nuisance. But God reverses the values of the world, and after death Lazarus is given a place of privilege amongst the faithful of past generations.

Jesus narrates the death and burial of the rich man with an economy of words, though someone of his wealth and distinction would have been buried with a pompous funeral procession, ceremony, and appropriate feasting. The public transcript of first-century Palestine communicated that wealth and honor were signs of God's blessing. The limited good worldview was not embraced by the elite who enjoyed positions of privilege. Accordingly, the rich man and his friends would have expected further reward after death. But these expectations are shattered by a great reversal. The rich man, a representative of the elite class, is condemned by God and sent to the place of eternal punishment.

Hades, the place of torment, stands in contrast with the rich man's former life of luxury. When the rich man lifts his eyes, he can see Lazarus reclining beside Abraham in a place of honor.[20] The reader will notice that the rich man, who did not speak to Lazarus while he lay outside his gate, still refuses to address him as a person after death. Instead, he cries out to Abraham as his "father," in an attempt to appeal to kinship loyalty with the patriarch of the Hebrew people. He asks Abraham to send Lazarus to attend to his needs by leaving the banquet, traveling across the chasm, and bringing him a drop of water to reduce his anguish.[21] In this way, he maintains

---

18. Resseguie, *Narrative Criticism*, 209.

19. Word count is in Greek.

20. The description "at the bosom" presumes a banquet at which people recline to eat their food.

21. The rich man tries to take charge of things even after death (Hultgren, *Parables*, 114).

his elite perspective in which Lazarus can be valuable only by serving his needs. He fails to see Lazarus as God sees him—an authentic son of Abraham and kinsman (13:16). The plea for mercy embedded in the request is blatantly hypocritical since he failed to act mercifully toward Lazarus when he lay outside the gate. Moreover, his words convey that he knew Lazarus by name and therefore could not claim that he did not know him and was unaware of his desperate circumstances.

Abraham responds to the rich man as "child" (*teknon*), recognizing his kinship with him as well as with Lazarus.[22] He then draws attention to the lifestyle disparities that separated the two men in scene one: the rich man, representing the elite, received good things in his life, whereas Lazarus, representing the poor, suffered from bad or evil experiences and forces.[23] After death, Lazarus receives comfort in Abraham's presence, while the rich man suffers on the dark side of the great reversal. Abraham's statement, "Between us and you a great chasm has been fixed that cannot be crossed," implies that God has made the divide permanent and irreversible.[24]

Having heard that Lazarus will not serve his personal needs, the rich man asks Abraham to order Lazarus to go to serve his immediate kinship group by warning his brothers[25] of the shameful fate that awaits them. The cultural code of honor, in which elite families took care of their own, further entrenched the ideologies of the public transcript and the system of inequality that left the majority of people marginalized and vulnerable. This appeal to Abraham presumes that the rich man's father and brothers will recognize Lazarus and welcome him into their homes. Unlikely as that seems, it also assumes that they will listen to his words about God's judgment regarding their lives of conspicuous consumption. Abraham refuses the rich man's request, saying that his brothers already have the testimony

---

22. Notice that this inclusive view of the people of Israel does not have divisions based on socio–economic status or compliance with purity regulations.

23. The Greek adjective *kakos* can be translated as bad, evil or harmful.

24. Outi Lehtipuu has made a thorough study of the Hebrew term Sheol and its Greek equivalent Hades. She canvasses different understandings of Sheol/Hades and concludes that in the time and context of this parable, it was the place where the unrighteous were punished and from which there was no escape or second chances for repentance. See Lehtipuu, *Afterlife Imagery*.

25. The plural form "brothers" (*adephous*) can include sisters. However, in a patriarchal society, sisters belonged to the family into which they had entered through marriage and therefore are not likely included here.

of Moses and the prophets about social ethics and faith (16:29).[26] Though Abraham does not quote a specific passage from the Torah or prophetic writings, the listeners may have thought immediately of relevant passages, such as:

> Since there will never cease to be some in need on the earth, I therefore command you, "Open your hand to the poor and needy neighbor in your land" (Deut 15:11).

> Therefore because you trample on the poor and take from them levies of grain, you have built houses of hewn stone, but you shall not live in them; you have planted pleasant vineyards, but you shall not drink their wine. For I know how many are your transgressions, and how great are your sins—you who afflict the righteous, who take a bribe, and push aside the needy in the gate. . . . Take away from me the noise of your songs; I will not listen to the melody of your harps. But let justice roll down like waters and righteousness like an ever flowing stream (Amos 5:11–12, 23–24).

> Is this not the fast that I choose; to loose the bonds of injustice, to undo the thongs of the yoke, to let the oppressed go free, and to break every yoke? Is it not to share your bread with the hungry and bring the homeless poor into our house; when you see the naked to cover them, and not hide yourself from your own kin? (Isa 58:6–7).

In his final appeal, the rich man insists that someone returning from beyond the grave will have the authority to persuade his brothers to repent. However, Abraham closes the door by stating that people who do not pay attention to the moral teaching of Israel's Scriptures will not be persuaded by the testimony of a messenger from beyond the grave.[27] This pronouncement brings the dialogue to an end. Lazarus is left in the place of consolation with Abraham, and the rich man is confined to the place of torment. God's judgment on the five brothers remains pending based on their faithful hearing of God's word in the law and prophets, as evidenced by their repentance and active participation in his rule of personal and social transformation in the community.

26. The theme of the law and prophets is previously mentioned in 16:16, where Jesus emphasizes that the proclamation of God's rule affirms rather than nullifies the demands of Israel's Scriptures.

27. There would have been some changed nuances of meaning when early Christians used this story after the resurrection of Jesus.

Reflections on the Parable

The Lazarus parable leaves us hanging. We wonder about the ongoing story of the brothers of the rich man. Did they awaken from their moral slumber? Did the reading of the law and prophets in the local synagogue lead them to repentance? Did they find freedom from the bondage of mammon and align their lives with God's coming kingdom? As readers, we may feel that there is no closure to the parable. Even in writing this reflection, I am unable to bring the chapter to a clear conclusion. I ponder that this parable requires actions rather than mere words to show that we have understood its message.

It should be clear by now that I do not interpret the Lazarus parable as a criticism of the rich man's individual moral choices. The story portrays God's judgment on his unquestioning allegiance to and participation in an economic system that disproportionately rewarded a privileged minority and pushed others to the margins. I confess that I was happier when I thought that the rich man must have committed some secret sins. Like the rich man, I live in a warm house and enjoy healthy food. I read good books, watch television, and listen to music. I am closer to the lifestyle of the rich man than the deprivations suffered by Lazarus.

I want to bring the voices of two authors into this reflection on the Lazarus parable and its meaning for our time. First, I return to Zygmunt Bauman, whose work on the underclass I presented in the introduction to the book. He describes the underclass as an alien presence in the social organism of community life. Western nations construct voluntary ghettos or protected spaces in order to exclude these people and maintain them in the margins. The dominant culture even finds ways to blame them for their failures and dependency. Bauman states that the best we can offer is individual solutions for socially generated problems.[28]

The second voice comes from Dave Diewert, a gifted biblical scholar and social activist from Vancouver, Canada. In an article for *Clarion, Journal of Spirituality and Justice*, Dave observes:

> Justice is about ensuring mutual dignity and honor, sharing resources for sustaining and nourishing life and health, and meaningfully participating in the processes of social and political decision-making. It entails the establishment of regulations that ensure adequate care and sustenance for the most vulnerable

---

28. Bauman, *Collateral Damage*, 49.

and limiting the acquisition of power and possessions, so that the community's resources are not concentrated in the hands of a few, while many go without. This means that particular attention is given to those who lack these social and material goods. A just society, therefore, would be one in which wealth and power were more or less evenly distributed, where gross inequities of resources are not sanctioned and opportunities for participation are nurtured.[29]

The perspectives of Bauman and Diewert assist us in grappling with the meaning of the Lazarus parable for our times. I am writing during the week following the drowning of over 650 refugees, who fled from their borderlands and attempted to cross the Mediterranean in order to reach Europe. An editorial in a British paper ran the headline: "Rescue boats? I'd use gunships to stop the migrants."[30] In the United States, Republican Presidential contender Donald Trump vows to build walls and barriers to keep Mexican migrants from crossing the border.[31] In Canada, we rely on temporary foreign workers, who supply the labor and skills required by our economy, but who will never be offered a place in our country's social fabric. It is another way of building walls with gates to admit foreign workers but not allow them to really leave their homelands. Within our communities, the gap between the elite and the middle class continues to grow, while the poor are left behind in measurements of education, health, nutrition, employment, housing, and public services. An analysis of Statistics Canada data from our province of Manitoba shows that 40 percent of children below the poverty line are from families in which at least one parent is employed. This corresponds with food bank client studies in the USA and Canada, which reveal that 54 percent of households in the former and approximately 20 percent in the latter have an employed adult in the home.[32] Collectively and politically, we have created an economy in which it is impossible for households to live with security and dignity on the part-time or minimum-wage employment that is a growing reality in our nations.

29. Jersak, "Interview."

30. Katie Hopkins, *The Sun,* 17 April 2015.

31. It is ironic that thirty years ago President Ronald Reagan called on the Soviet Union to tear down the Berlin Wall.

32. Weinfield et. al., *Hunger in America,* 56; Pegg and Stapleton, *Hunger Count 2014,* 10.

We live in countries that build more prisons while reducing funding for rehabilitation services. We recognize the pervasive nature of mental illness, yet support budget cuts for counseling and social workers in order to reduce taxes. I live in Winnipeg, an urban centre that has been called the most racist city in Canada.[33] We are still struggling to grasp the significance of a 2008 event at one of our city hospitals when a First Nation's man, Brian Sinclair, died in the emergency ward after waiting thirty-four hours for someone to acknowledge his presence. He had been dead for at least six hours before medical staff attended to him. In the United States, cities have been shaken by protests about the treatment of African American males by police officers. One does not need to be an expert to conclude that there is a force of evil in the very structure of our communities that affects the programs that are supposed to offer effective and impartial assistance to all people.

Dave Diewert casts an alternative vision of a community in which there is meaningful dialogue and participation in decisions regarding the shared life of its members. Resources are distributed in ways that all community members can live with a sense of security and dignity. Diewert reminds us that justice often has less to do with the courts of law than with actions to ensure measures of equity and respect, particularly for those on the margins, who live with greater levels of vulnerability. His vision has affinities with the model of Robert Chambers, a British development specialist whom I mentioned in chapter 2. Chambers writes and speaks about responsible well-being. He defines this model of development as working for the well-being of the entire community, while giving priority to those who are most in need.[34] The minority, who possess a greater share of resources and influence, have a corresponding greater responsibility to contribute to the well-being of others.

Returning to the parable, if the rich man's brothers began to listen to the law and the prophets, would they arrive at a position on social justice similar to the vision cast by Dave Diewert? Would they become dissident agents of change in their town or city? Would they discover that a personal ethic of purity and avoidance of sin was not enough when people like Lazarus were on the other side of the wall? The tragedy of the parable is that the rich man could have used his intellect, social capital, and resources as a

33. MacDonald, *Welcome to Winnipeg*, 16–24.

34. Chambers, *Reality*, 9–11; *Ideas*, 192–94, 198–207. Chambers gives attention to four particular areas: employment, skills, sustainability and equity.

force for economic and social transformation. Instead, he chose to exploit and defend his privileged position. He went to the place of eternal punishment because his version of faith was at ease with the social inequities of his time and context.

In our communities today, there is a force that traps many of us in analysis and prevents us from positive engagement. The faith heritage of individual salvation through doctrinal belief alone has made many Christians indifferent to the gospel teaching about finding creative ways to penetrate and illuminate society as salt and light. Modern families learn to "live without time," balancing the schedules of children and adults in the household, with no conceivable space for outside involvement in transformational community work. They may convince themselves that their contribution is to care for and protect their immediate family. Others become disheartened when they feel that their small efforts amount to nothing more than placing a bandage on an open wound.

Perhaps there is another factor related to our role as spectators rather than participants in social transformation. I wonder if we have lost hold of the teaching of our faith that each child is born bearing the image of God. This fundamental principle, which we share with people of Jewish heritage, has the potential to launch us into social locations where God's image is distorted and disfigured by the evils of poverty, racism, gender inequities, hunger, and violence. We meet God's image and presence in the borderlands where people struggle to hold on to their humanity. The "image of God" also means that we, along with the people we encounter, have the capacity to live as God's beloved children and to offer our creative gifts as a contribution to the lives of others in the community. The unique capacities that we received in the womb can be developed both to give us personal fulfillment and also to serve in the mission of transformation. Understanding one's place and purpose requires a sensitive discernment to the personal call that is revealed through experience and the quiet voice of the Spirit. Deprived of a sense of call, people may choose to live passively, fearfully, and acquisitively rather than as active agents inspired by a vision of transformation in which they play a role that has been shaped for them by a loving creator.

As a final observation on the Lazarus parable, those who follow Jesus into the borderlands require a broader vision than mere charity. We are in dangerous territory when good people are content with providing a few handouts without working to address the deeper issues of poverty and alienation. In the Lazarus parable, it would not have been enough for the rich man to send out his servant with a bag of cold meat and buns. The law and the prophets demanded justice, along with acts of mercy. Justice requires repentance, a turning away from the public transcripts that buttress the status quo, and a turning towards God's rule of transformation, in which the last become first.

The chapter began with the story of Ratnapandi Nadar, whose daily climbing of date palms pointed toward a catastrophic fall that would leave him like a modern-day Lazarus, carried by his friends to a begging place. The narratives of Lazarus, Ratnapandi and others whom we come to know by name through our commitments intersect with our own stories as people who live simultaneously in local communities and the global village. The Lazarus parable poses the question, how do we envision God's transformation for those on the margins as well as for those in places of comfort? How can we pray and act for social change and thereby embody God's message that is good news for the poor? The answers will inevitably bring us into conflict with aspects of the public transcripts of our own age.

The next chapter will take us into a banquet hall, where guests feast while deliberately ignoring hungry women and men who are sitting outside their gates.

CHAPTER 5

The Great Banquet

The Vision of a Common Table (Luke 14:15–24)

... it seems to me that the problem isn't that there's no food. It's that a few people have it all. If it was shared around we'd all be eating what those few who have the food are now eating, and I think we'd all have enough. —Julio Mairena[1]

In our country there are a lot of us who are hungry. Nobody would have to be hungry if everything in the country belonged to everybody. But here things are the way the devil wants them to be. The devil, who is the Evil One, wants us to be split apart, each one separated by selfishness. —Oscar[2]

Stories from the Margins

KEVIN CARTER, A PHOTOJOURNALIST, traveled to Sudan in 1993 to cover the civil war raging between the government in the north and southern secessionists. Widespread hunger threatened the lives of thousands of people. Carter visited the village of Ayod, where relief workers at an emergency feeding center informed him that that twenty people an hour were dying of hunger-related causes. Toward the end of the day, Carter walked to an open area on the outskirts of Ayod, feeling exhausted and overwhelmed. He

1. Cardenal, *Solentiname*, 2:147–48.
2. Ibid., 156.

noticed a young girl, staggering toward the town, collapse in exhaustion. A vulture landed nearby, waiting for her to die. Carter began to take photos. After a few minutes, the girl rose to her feet and stumbled towards the feeding center. Carter sat by a tree, wept, and called out to God.

Carter's photo of the Sudanese girl and the vulture won a Pulitzer Prize. But it also raised questions from the public about why he had chosen to take photos rather than to intervene to help the girl. He justified his abandonment of the girl by explaining that journalists had a professional code that precluded physical contact with famine victims. Furthermore, the girl was simply one of thousands of starving people in the region. Perhaps these responses sounded hollow, even to him. Less than a year after winning the Pulitzer Prize, Kevin Carter committed suicide. He had told a close friend: "I am really, really sorry that I did not pick up that child." His suicide note read, "The pain of life overrides the joy to the point that joy does not exist."[3]

Each of us lives with regret about decisions made at critical moments. Fortunately we seldom face interrogators who question our motives and actions. We simply have the haunting feeling that we could have done more. There are human fingerprints at every location where people have died of hunger and malnutrition over the past century. Death by hunger is not something that just happens. People were in position from where they could have acted to save lives. Amartya Sen is a Cambridge professor of economics and a Nobel Prize winner in his field. His research into famines[4] concludes that they are largely man-made, with an emphasis on the gender specific term. The two most egregious examples of the politics of starvation in the past century were the deaths of seven million people in the Ukraine under Stalin's rule (1932–33) and an estimated thirty to forty million people in China during the Great Leap Forward in 1959–61. We can also cite death tolls from other horrific hunger scenes, such as the one witnessed by Kevin Carter.

Death by hunger is morally abhorrent in a world of surplus. Our global economic system has made food a commodity that is sold for a profit rather than regarded as a basic human right. I was struck by Sen's research, which shows that food was leaving Ethiopia for export during the great famine between 1983 and 1985.[5] His evidence indicates that hunger has

3. Russell, *Hunger*, 180. See also http://worldsalbum.blogspot.com.

4. Sen, *Development*, 178–84.

5. According to the UN's Food and Agriculture Organization, 80 percent of

more to do with poverty than food scarcity. The circumstances of the poor become even more acute during times of armed conflict when deliberate political decisions are made to withhold food. When I wrote the first draft of this chapter, the UN estimated that four million people in South Sudan were in danger of death due to hunger associated with civil conflict and the displacement of people. The conflict was political in nature, based on the competing interests of different ethnic groups within the world's newest country.

Closer to home, an increased number of households in North American cities depend on the assistance of food banks for their monthly nutritional needs. As mentioned in the last chapter, a significant percentage of the clients are employed in minimum-wage or part-time jobs. They do not earn enough to supply their household food needs along with other expenses. Substandard nutritional levels in Canada and the USA can be plotted on maps that show the low income areas of our cities. Often these neighborhoods even lack adequate grocery stores that provide the fresh vegetables and fruit required for healthy bodies. Grocery chains logically prefer to locate in suburban areas where they can maximize profits. In the city where I live, the first debate in our most recent civic election was dedicated to the theme of food security. Clearly hunger and nutritional issues are no longer confined to the Global South.

Hunger was prevalent in first-century Palestine. The restructuring of the economy under Roman rule made food insecurity a reality of life for most families in urban and rural areas. As we saw in previous chapters, wealth in an agrarian economy was based on land ownership, control of production, and the power to set prices. The Herodian rulers and the elite citizens of Galilee and Judea used debt to increase their landholdings at the expense of the peasant population. Traditional farmers were forced to become day laborers or tenant producers, or they migrated to the cities in search of employment. Those who were able to retain their land struggled to feed their families, generate funds for taxes and the temple obligations, and keep seed for the next growing cycle. They lived in constant anxiety about the future.[6] In contrast, the urban elite used their rural estates to plant crops for sale and export rather than to meet the nutritional needs of local communities. Produce was transported from rural villages to the

---

undernourished children in the world live in countries that export food.

6. Oakman, "Countryside in Luke–Acts," in Neyrey, *Social World*, 156, 167.

cities, where it was sold at prices controlled by the estate owners.[7] New Testament scholar Douglas Oakman describes the cities as economic parasites that lived off the lifeblood of rural villages.[8]

Reading from positions of relative comfort and security, we have a tendency to seek some sort of figurative or spiritual meaning for gospel statements related to hunger. When we read the gospels with people on the margins, we appreciate the material urgency of these sayings. Let me provide the reader with four such sayings from the gospel of Luke. Mary sang eloquently and hopefully about a time when God would fill the hungry with good things (1:53). John the Baptist urged his followers to repent and bear fruit by sharing food with the hungry (3:11). Jesus pronounced God's blessing on the poor and the hungry (6:20–21). He taught his followers to pray for their food needs of each day (11:3). Refugees in camps, unemployed immigrants, and dumpster divers do not look for metaphorical meanings.

Background to the Parable of the Great Banquet

The original audience of the parable did not need an orientation to the story's cultural and social background. However, we enter this foreign world as outsiders who can easily miss subtleties and gestures. Accordingly, it is helpful to pay attention to the meaning and performance of banquets in first-century Palestine and the broader context of the Roman Empire. Readers will notice that the parable is embedded within the narrative of a formal Sabbath banquet hosted by a prominent citizen and member of the Pharisees.[9] Sabbath meals were prepared the previous day and eaten after the synagogue meeting.[10] If guests were included, it made the event a social occasion. In this case, Jesus is the special guest and the men present in the room are peers or kin of the host.

The social values of honor and purity that lie beneath the surface of this event and the following parable are difficult for most North Americans to appreciate. I remind readers that in first-century Palestine honor, like wealth, existed in finite quantities. A person could only increase his honor in the community at the direct expense of others who lost honor. Every

7. Ibid., 155.

8. Ibid., 156.

9. The Greek construction is ambiguous and can mean either a local leader who was a member of the Pharisaic movement, or a leader of the Pharisees (Marshall, *Luke*, 578).

10. Josephus, *Life*, 54:279.

transaction, from selling a cow to the marriage of a child, involved potential gains or losses of honor within the community. A banquet created a contest of honor at several levels. The host could gain honor based on the social rank of the guests, the quality of the food and wine, the comfort of the dining area where people reclined on mats, and the nature of the conversations during the banquet. The honor of invitees was also at stake. Would they be among other respected members of the community? Would they be seated in proximity to the host? Would their choice of garments be adequate? Would they be able to fulfill the obligation of reciprocating the invitation and offering similar hospitality to their peer group in the community? The pressure to maintain and increase honor and the corresponding abhorrence of shame is critical to understanding the entire passage of 14:1–24.

The religious motivation for purity was a further element of a social code that is distant from the values that shape our patterns of interaction. "Impurity" is different from dirt or the presence of bacteria that threatens health. "Pure" and "impure" were defined by boundaries that separated people based on rules and regulations embedded in religious and cultural traditions. Impurity was regarded as a contagious disease that threatened the well-being of those who lived by the rigorous standards of the purity code. In hosting a formal dinner, households ensured purity by cooking proper foods, using proper utensils and bowls, and ensuring that proper people shared the meal.[11] Arrangements were made for guests to wash before a meal in order to cleanse their hands from the impurity of daily interactions.[12] Full conformity to purity regulations required time and attention that would be almost insurmountable for peasants in rural areas and poor families in towns and cities. Thus the very standards of purity further pushed those on the margins to the outside of respectable community life. A further note on the purity code is important for this passage. Physical wholeness was an external sign of purity, and deformities were evidence of impurity.[13] Accordingly, individuals who were lame, blind, and suffered from other chronic conditions were considered impure.[14]

11. The regulations in the Mishnah (Tractate *Demai* 2.2) required the tithing of the harvest by the farmer who grew the food along with the merchants who sold the produce, and the use of pure cooking pots, plates and utensils.

12. Vessels carved from stone were used for washing because clay was considered a porous receptacle of impurity.

13. Pilch, "Sickness and Healing in Luke–Acts," in Neyrey, *Social World*, 207–8.

14. This view was based on an extended reading of Lev 21:16–20 and the conviction that invalids had succumbed to evil powers that attacked the well-being and health

Shared meals crossing lines of social status were rare. On such occasions, the host acted as a benefactor to those of inferior rank, who depended on his position of power.[15] At such times, the benefactor might provide clean clothing for socially inferior guests to ensure that purity was not compromised.[16] The food and wine were generally of inferior quality. Guests who accepted the invitation of a patron understood that there was an implied obligation to praise publicly the generosity of the host and to pledge loyalty and allegiance to his family.

This section has contained a great deal of cultural information. I will now show how it helps us to understand the meaning of the narrative and the parable. The story that Jesus will tell of a Great Banquet should never be treated separately from the narrative introduction, which takes place in the home of a leading Pharisee.[17] The meaning of the parable has been lost almost every time that the context has been forgotten.

Jesus as a Guest: The Preface to the Parable (Luke 14:1–15)

Introduction and the Man with Dropsy (14:1–6)

On one occasion when Jesus was going to the house of a leader of the Pharisees to eat a meal on the Sabbath, they were watching him closely. Just then, in front of him, there was a man who had dropsy. And Jesus asked the lawyers and Pharisees, "Is it lawful to cure people on the Sabbath, or not?" But they were silent. So Jesus took him and healed him, and sent him away. Then he said to them, "If one of you has a child or an ox that has fallen into a well, will you not immediately pull it out on a Sabbath day?" And they could not reply to this.

The identification of the host as a Pharisee creates the expectation that the meal will follow the strict codes of purity. The concern for purity lies behind the observation that the host and the guests are watching Jesus closely, as

---

of individuals. Neyrey, "The Symbolic Universe of Luke-Acts," in Neyrey, *Social World*, 271–304.

15. Moxnes, *Economy*, 40–47.

16. Chilton, *Pure Kingdom*, 113–14.

17. Willi Braun recognizes the importance of treating 14:1–24 as a unit. *Feasting and Social Rhetoric.*

if waiting to catch him for a violation of the code on the Sabbath day.[18] The tension is heightened when a man suffering from edema (dropsy) suddenly intrudes into the dinner.[19] His entrance introduces an unwelcome element of impurity into the banquet room. The visible symptom of edema was an accumulation of fluids in body cavities and connective tissues. The combination of a painfully swollen body and the victim's constant desire to drink fluids led to the widespread conclusion that edema was the consequence of uncontrolled consumption.[20] Modern medical specialists recognize that edema is related to hunger and malnutrition. We know that edema was common in the Warsaw ghetto during World War II, when food supplies were restricted for the Jewish residents surrounded by the Nazi troops.[21]

Jesus responds to the anxiety in the room by asking the lawyers and Pharisees for their interpretation of the Torah regarding healing on the Sabbath. A deliberate silence falls on the guests. In the hush of the banquet room, Jesus heals the man by drawing near to him and touching him, daring to make contact with impurity on the Sabbath.[22] Jesus then mercifully dismisses him from the gathering, where his presence was not welcome.[23] The words and actions of Jesus challenge the guests' interpretation of the Mosaic Law, a way of reading that builds a wall between those who follow the law and the people of the borderlands. Then Jesus asks if anyone in the room would hesitate to rescue a child or a farm animal that had fallen into a well on the Sabbath.[24] The silence confirms that they would break the purity

18. See also 6:7 and 20:20 for the same kind of vigilance in seeking to trap Jesus (Johnson, *Luke*, 223).

19. This sudden and unexpected presence is representative of Luke's literary tendency to drop someone from the borderlands into the social setting of a narrative. See 5:18; 6:6; 7:37; 8:27, 43; 10:39; 13:11; 17:12.

20. Braun, *Feasting and Social Rhetoric*, 38.

21. Jewish doctors in the ghetto studied the effects of malnutrition and death by hunger. Edema was common with clear symptoms including repulsive swelling, distension of body parts, and unquenchable thirst.

22. The participle *epilabomenos* suggests that Jesus physically touched the man who was considered impure.

23. The fact that the man was sent away indicates that he was indeed an intruder whose name was not on the guest list. My friend Blair Taylor, an astute lawyer, proposes that the host deliberately staged the crisis by arranging for the man with dropsy to enter the banquet area. His hostile intent was meant to force Jesus to define his position publicly in regard to the purity laws, including the Sabbath provisions.

24. An interesting point of comparison is that the Qumran community permitted the rescue of people on the Sabbath, provided that no equipment was used to save them.

of the Sabbath, even to rescue a farm animal. The question challenges the honor of the host and his guests by publicly critiquing their interpretation of Torah and the cultural code of purity in favor of Jesus' own position based on the primacy of human need.

Instruction on Humility (14:7–11)

> When he noticed how the guests chose the places of honor, he told them a parable. "When you are invited by someone to a wedding banquet, do not sit down at the place of honor, in case someone more distinguished than you has been invited by your host; and the host who invited both of you may come and say to you, 'Give this person your place,' and then in disgrace you would start to take the lowest place. But when you are invited, go and sit down at the lowest place, so that when your host comes, he may say to you, 'Friend, move up higher;' then you will be honored in the presence of all who sit at the table with you. For all who exalt themselves will be humbled, and those who humble themselves will be exalted."

The second section of the banquet interaction begins with an observation about the competition for seating, based on the motivation to recline in the proximity of the host.[25] Jesus responds by giving a piece of wise advice.[26] At a wedding banquet, guests should deliberately choose the humble places in the room in order to avoid the shame of being re-seated to an inferior location by the host. Similar counsel had been given by other people in previous times.[27] If the narrative ended here, the section would be a rather banal expression of cautionary social etiquette. However, Jesus goes on to introduce the theme of the great reversal. The use of passive verbs indicates that God is the chief actor in a process that will bring humiliation to those who are proud and protective of their honor. In contrast, those who are

---

They did not allow for animals to be pulled from a well (CD 11:13–17).

25. Scott Bartchy's comment is helpful. ". . . men who sought the best seats and the places of honor were behaving precisely the way that their mothers and fathers had raised them to behave. . . . such behavior was proper and manly; it made their families proud of them." Bartchy, "Historical Jesus and Honour Reversal," in Stegemann, Malina, and Theissen, *Social Setting*, 179.

26. The word parable used in 14:7 means proverb in this context.

27. Examples from Jewish sources include Prov 25:6–7; Sir 3:17–20; *Aboth de R. Nathan* 25.

humble by birth or by choice will receive honor from God.[28] In the following verses, Jesus makes clear that orienting one's life toward humility rather than status inevitably requires solidarity with those who live on the margins.

Inviting the Poor to Banquets (14:12–14)

> He said also to the one who had invited him, "When you give a luncheon or a dinner, do not invite your friends or your brothers or your relatives or rich neighbors, in case they may invite you in return, and you would be repaid. But when you give a banquet, invite the poor, the crippled, the lame, and the blind. And you will be blessed, because they cannot repay you, for you will be repaid at the resurrection of the righteous."

Given the existing social order, where hospitality was based on balanced (equivalent) reciprocity, Jesus' advice is scandalous and unsettling. He informs the host that he should exclude peers, friends, and kinship members from future formal banquets and replace them on the guest list with the poor, the crippled, the lame, and the blind.[29] Here, Jesus attacks the accepted practices of social etiquette in favor of extending welcome to people from four socially excluded groups.[30] He acknowledges that these alternate guests will not be able to meet the expectations of reciprocity. However, God himself will reward acts of hospitality for their benefit at the resurrection of the righteous.

At this point, I want to suggest that readers place themselves imaginatively in the position of guests in the banquet room with Jesus. You find yourselves among religious men who are grudgingly aware that the scriptures collide with the social practices of culture. The scroll of Deuteronomy has instructed them to relate to the poor with an open hand. The prophet Isaiah told them to invite hungry people into their homes for meals.[31] The featured guest, the prophet from Galilee, brings the message of the Law and

---

28. This saying is also found in Luke 18:14, where the attitudes of a Pharisee and tax collector are contrasted. The antithesis is expressed in 16:15, where Jesus addresses a different group of Pharisees.

29. The host would rightly infer that Jesus was publicly criticizing his choice of guests for the dinner (Gonzalez, *Luke*, 180).

30. Fitzmyer, *Luke X–XXIV*, 1045

31. Deut 15:7–11; Isa 58:7.

Prophets into their banquet room, calling them to a radical transformation of values and practices by opening their homes to those who live beyond the social borders of respectability and honor. It is precisely into this social situation of discomfort and tension that Jesus tells a story about a man who invited hungry people to his home for a banquet.

The Parable of the Great Banquet (14:15–24)

One of the dinner guests, on hearing this, said to him, "Blessed is anyone who will eat bread in the kingdom of God!" Then Jesus said to him, "Someone gave a great dinner and invited many. At the time for the dinner he sent his slave to say to those who had been invited, 'Come; for everything is ready now.' But they all alike began to make excuses. The first said to him, 'I have bought a piece of land, and I must go out and see it; please accept my apologies.' Another said, 'I have bought five yoke of oxen, and I am going to try them out; please accept my apologies.' Another said, 'I have just been married, and therefore I cannot come.' So the slave returned and reported this to his master. Then the owner of the house became angry and said to his slave, 'Go out at once into the streets and lanes of the town and bring in the poor, the crippled, the blind, and the lame.' And the slave said, 'Sir, what you ordered has been done, and there is still room.' Then the master said to the slave, 'Go out into the roads and lanes, and compel people to come in, so that my house may be filled. For I tell you, none of those who were invited will taste my dinner.'"

The interjection of a dinner guest is unexpected and puzzling.[32] His pious statement takes God's blessing out of the dangerous context of social relationships with the poor and casts it into a more comfortable and ambiguous eschatological future.[33] The speaker completely misses the reality of God's rule that is breaking into towns and villages of Palestine by transforming social patterns and practices. Eating together in God's kingdom is not an abstract hope consigned to an indefinite future, but rather a present possibility that can be experienced by sharing a common table with people from the margins.

32. He is the only person other than Jesus who speaks in the entire literary unit of 14:1–24).

33. Snodgrass, *Stories with Intent*, 311.

Jesus responds to this misconception about the kingdom of God by telling a story. The plot is about a rich man from elite social circles who invites to his home the poor, the crippled, the lame, and the blind. This action of justice and compassion is done under strange circumstances and offers a sign of the presence of God's transforming rule. The story adds to the theme of the great reversal that was introduced in the saying about humility and honor.

The introduction to the parable creates the scene of a prominent citizen living among his peers in a city. His elite position is indicated by the capacity to stage a "great" dinner and to invite "many" people to his large villa.[34] We notice that he uses a slave to deliver invitations, and thereby surmise that there are other slaves who live and work within the household. The delivery of invitations at the time of the banquet might strike us as unusual and even presumptive. The original audience would have understood that the slave is communicating the second of two invitations to the banquet. The first invitation had provided the date and essential information about the event, giving invitees time to investigate questions related to honor and prestige. In essence, they would have wanted to know the identity of other guests, the anticipated dress code, the menu, and the nature of the inherent obligation of reciprocity. The second invitation, on the actual day of the event, assures invitees that all the preparations have been made and the appointed time has come to gather in the home of the host.[35] The audience listening to the story would assume that the host has done everything required by a man of his position.

At this point there is a shocking turn in the plot. The invited guests show that they have conspired as a group (*apo mias*)[36] to reject the invitation to the great banquet, telling obvious lies intended to shame and humiliate the host. The first asks to be excused because he has purchased land[37] and feels compelled to inspect it. No one would buy land without previously assessing it for the quality of soil, availability of water, slope, access to sun-

34. The word householder (*oikodespotes*) indicates a large residence, perhaps best expressed by the English language word villa.

35. Marshall refers to a statement from Philo (Philo, Opif. 78) that the summons to dinner is not made until everything has been prepared for the banquet (Marshall, *Luke*, 588).

36. The Greek expression means "unanimously" or "with one accord." See Arndt and Gingrich, *Lexicon*, 88.

37. Notice that such a purchase implies surplus capital that can be invested in property.

light, and clear boundary markers.[38] The second man informs the slave that he has acquired five pair of oxen and must now put them to the test.[39] Such an investment would have required previous due diligence in inspecting and field-testing the animals. Moreover, a man of honour would not soil his reputation by getting his hands dirty ploughing a field. The third man claims that his marriage obligations preclude acceptance of the invitation. In crass terms, this may mean that he values the pleasure of an evening with his wife above his relationship with the host. Alternatively, the excuse may be related to the custom of arranged marriages that involved the payment of a dowry and "bridewealth."[40] There may be outstanding negotiations to conclude the agreement between two families.[41] The slave does not need to go the homes of other men on the guest list. It is clear that the peers of the host have conspired to shame him collectively on the day of his great dinner. There is no explanation for their scheme to damage his honor. Perhaps such betrayals and reversals were part of the intense competition for honour among the elite. The audience of the parable is expecting to hear of the rich man's revenge and attempts to regain his status in the community.[42]

The second half of the story relates the dramatic and decisive actions of the host. The nature of his reaction is even more surprising than the humiliating rejections he received from the invitees. In effect, the host decides that he will no longer participate in the competition for honor among his peers, but will overturn the social code by which he has conducted his life. At this point it is essential for Western readers to suspend their logical concerns about time and space in the banquet room. There is a literary element of magic realism akin to a Gabriel Garcia Marquez novel in which temporal and spatial limitations are suspended. The principal character sends his slave into the streets and lanes of the city to invite the poor, crippled, blind, and lame to come to the banquet room and share his great dinner.[43] These,

38. Bailey, *Jesus*, 314.

39. Five pair of oxen implies a consider outlay of money and extensive landholdings. Ten oxen would have been capable of ploughing an estate of 110 acres under cultivation (Jeremias, *Parables*, 177).

40. Hansen and Oakman, *Palestine*, 30–35.

41. Braun, *Feasting and Social Rhetoric*, 76–79.

42. Malina and Neyrey, "Honour and Shame in Luke-Acts," in Neyrey, *Social World*, 38.

43. Note that he invites those who are hungry to his home rather than packaging up food and sending it to them in the streets.

of course, are the groups on the margins that Jesus just mentioned in his instructions about which guests should receive priority at a common table.

To follow the master's instruction, the slave must leave the gated area protecting the elite neighborhood and enter into the narrow streets and lanes of the city.[44] After the slave reports that he has carried out the master's orders, there is still room in the banquet room. Accordingly, the master sends him outside the city gates to the roadways and hedges[45] where the outcasts could be found.[46] The slave must compel these people on the excluded margins of the city, because they would never believe that a wealthy man would invite them to a banquet in the space of his home.[47]

The story's depiction of a common table shared by a rich man and the hungry poor tears down the walls of exclusion and addresses the disparities of food consumption. The shared table is a powerful symbol of diverse people who receive an invitation to eat ample food and drink good wine, to be treated with dignity, and to be freed from shame. Their patron does not demand obligations of loyalty and mandatory displays of public gratitude. They have become his preferred social group. In regard to the former peers, there will be no going back. He has breached the codes of honor and purity by inviting unwanted and socially contaminated people into the enclosed neighborhood.[48] This action will taint his household with permanent shame. The extension of a preferential welcome to the poor signifies the host's repentance from the policies and structures of the public transcript that has divided people in the community. Through painful and humiliating circumstances, he has embraced Jesus' teaching about transformation in God's kingdom.[49]

We can understand the host in this story as the antithesis of the rich man in the Lazarus' parable. When he states, "None of those men who were

---

44. The internal city walls were built to hide those who lived in the margins from the view of the elite.

45. Hedges were places where beggars and the homeless could find shelter. They acted like fences to enclose fields and the immediate areas around peasant homes (Hultgren, *Parables*, 338).

46. People excluded from living within the city walls represented the lowest ranks of Palestinian society and included beggars, sex-trade workers, escaped slaves, tanners, butchers, and exiles (Braun, *Feasting and Social Rhetoric*, 93–94).

47. Gonzalez, *Luke*, 181.

48. The host violated the boundaries of their gated residential area (Rohrbaugh, "Pre-Industrial City in Luke-Acts," in Neyrey, *Social World*, 145).

49. Braun, *Feasting and Social Rhetoric*, 126.

invited will ever taste my dinner," he acknowledges that his new orientation toward the poor will require further acts of generosity that will cumulatively deplete and redistribute his resources and further diminish his honor in the community. His economic position will move closer over time toward those who form his new peer group.[50] Yet he will have the satisfaction of being rich toward God (12:21) and living with the hope of joining Abraham at the shared table in God's kingdom (13:28–30).

What did the parable mean for the guests at the table? For me, the most satisfying answer draws again on Sallie McFague's idea of a wild space or Chris Hedges's concept of sublime madness.[51] The story encourages listeners to imagine radically different patterns of social interaction, in which the wealthy reject the exclusionary values of the public transcript that has held them captive to the unending competition for peer honor and the marginalization of others in the community. They can contemplate the freedom of embracing people from the borderlands as equals and opening their homes to attend to their needs for physical and social nourishment. The foundational truth is that people must imagine the world differently in order to act in ways that promote justice, equity and human dignity.[52]

This chapter began with comments from two Nicaraguan campesinos who believed that the power of evil separated people. They speculated that a spirit of sharing would ensure that there would be enough food for everyone in their country. The parable of the great banquet helps us to see God's work through the symbol of a common table. I realize that alternate interpretations propose that this story relates to the plan of salvation moving from beyond Israel to the Gentiles. This allegorical reading presumes that Jesus was a religious teacher who debated abstract theories of theology rather than acting as an agent of social change in his context. In the dialogue that precedes the parable, Jesus challenges the leading men of the city to reject their practice of social reciprocity and replace it with a form hospitality that embraces the poor, the crippled, the lame, and the blind. The double use of the phrase "the poor, the crippled, the lame and the blind" in 14:13 and 14:21 is conclusive for me. The story of the Great Banquet issues a challenge to those who are drawn to God's work of transformation in the world. There is no place for spinning theories in the safety of seclusion. It

---

50. I owe these insights to personal conversations with Dave Diewert, who was mentioned earlier in this book.

51. See chapter 1.

52. Giroux, *Giroux Reader*, 185.

calls on us to ensure that the hungry receive food and care through personal involvement and the building of relationships that cross social boundaries.

Reflection on the Parable of the Great Banquet

I referred to earlier to the work of the Nobel-Prize-winning economist Amartya Sen. The following statement from Sen lived with me during my years as a board member of the Canadian Foodgrains Bank (CFGB).[53]

> The contemporary age is not short of terrible and nasty happenings, but the persistence of extensive hunger in a world of unprecedented prosperity is surely one of the worst. . . . What makes this widespread hunger even more of a tragedy is the way we have come to accept and tolerate it as an integral part of the modern world, as if it is a tragedy that is essentially unpreventable (in the way ancient Greek tragedies were).[54]

Most readers will agree with Sen's observation that the Global North has come to tolerate hunger as some sort of inevitable consequence of life in the borderlands, rather than as a reality caused by human decisions and priorities. I began the chapter with the tragic story of Kevin Carter, who wished that he had picked up a Sudanese girl and carried her to a feeding station. Unfortunately, the past decades have witnessed squandered opportunities that align with the narrative of Carter in Sudan. Hunger is a daily reality for one in every nine people with whom we share the planet. The alleged success of the Millennium Development Goals is perhaps more a matter of definition than of substance. Our way of counting hungry people only begins after they have survived twelve months of substandard nutrition. Furthermore, nutritional standards are based on a sedentary lifestyle (like writing a book) rather than the energy needs of rural farmers or manual laborers. The way statistics are compiled masks the reality of hunger in the borderlands.

It is estimated that the world's population will reach between 9 and 9.5 billion people by 2050. The World Economic Forum's 2014 Global Risk

---

53. CFGB is a Canadian NGO composed of board members from fifteen Christian denominations. The Foodgrains bank asks supporters and the general public to imagine a world without hunger. Its international work consists of emergency food assistance, nutrition programs, and long–term food security projects. I served on the board of CFGB between 2006 and 2015.

54. Sen, *Development*, 204.

Assessment recognized widespread hunger as a high probability and high impact threat to our common security. The parable of the great banquet challenges modern readers to make hunger a priority, to seek ways to share a common table symbolically and literally with the poor, and to redistribute resources to benefit those who are most vulnerable. Food justice goes beyond soup kitchens and sandwiches handed out at street corners. We have seen that low standards of minimum wages and welfare rates have an impact on local hunger. Internationally, countries of the Global North have steadily reduced foreign aid to agriculture since the 1980s.[55] Simultaneously, subsidies to our farmers have distorted markets to the detriment of producers in the Global South. The policies and practices of major transnational companies that control seed patents and market inputs can be predatory and destructive. One way we can express solidarity with the poor is by actively encouraging our governments to increase development assistance for farmers with small landholdings in the global south.[56] Additionally, we can take meaningful collective action by supporting international projects that create local seed banks, utilize green manures and bio pesticides, experiment with rain water harvesting, restore depleted soils, assist farmers to adapt to climate change, and establish new networks for post–harvest marketing. Coming together to a common table includes innovative combinations of hospitality, partnerships, advocacy, research, and extension services to farmers with small landholdings in rural communities.

I have been inspired by the example of local churches in North America and the Global South. Farming groups in Canada participate with CFGB by growing crops that are sold to provide funds for the alleviation of global hunger. Urban churches support these groups by paying the cost of land rental and inputs. They join together at harvest time to celebrate this good work at a community dinner and worship service. A few years ago, unexpected snow at harvest time threatened the crops of farming families in Brownfield, Alberta. They made the costly decision to take their equipment first to the Lord's field and consequently reduced the value of their own harvest. Each family lost thousands of dollars.

55. For example, in the closing decades of the past century, World Bank grants to agriculture shrank from 17 percent to 3 percent of annual budgets (Thurow and Kilman, *Enough*, 30).

56. The Good Soil campaign, supported by a number of Canadian Christian denominations, is attempting to raise a collective voice requesting government funding to increase agricultural research and aid for farming families in the developing world. See http://foodgrainsbank.ca/campaigns/good–soil/.

In India, my friend Judson Pothuraju belongs to a church in Hyderabad. Judson is a world-recognized entomologist who left his university position to work with farmers in small communities in Andhra Pradesh. Supplementing Judson's personal commitment, his church supports projects that assist farmers to grow organic rice, vegetables, and cotton. The church property is used on Saturdays as a market that allows producers to sell at a fair price to urban consumers. A generous donation from a congregation in North America provided resources for Judson's church to establish a dry land agriculture research and training center outside Hyderabad to work with poor farming families.

These people and congregations, from both the Global North and South, provide models for how committed groups can metaphorically celebrate a common table by addressing hunger and promoting food justice. Over the past decade, Wendell Berry has been a prophetic voice representing a dissident approach to food and agriculture. He differentiates exploiters from nurturers in their attitudes toward both farming and the purchase of food.[57] Exploiters are usually specialists in making land produce quickly and efficiently. Their goal is short-term return on investment at the expense of long-term sustainability. At the consumer level, the purchase decisions of consumer-exploiters are based on the simple criteria of price and convenience without asking further questions. Farmers who are nurturers are likely to be generalists. They work with the end objective of health—healthy soil, produce, communities, and consumers. Nurturers hope to achieve a decent standard of living while investing in the complex work of protecting soils, biodiversity, and the lifestyle of working with creation. We who live in cities can ensure that we share a common table with those whose farming methods nurture rather than exploit. We can be wise and thoughtful consumers that support local sustainable agriculture in our areas. We can take symbolic action by planting urban vegetable gardens and inviting others to share in the production. We can be attentive to issues that affect local farmers and find ways to support their interests.

The story of the Great Banquet leaves us with the symbol of a common table that encourages us to take action in a world of hunger. We have the capacity to make choices about supporting good projects and raising our voices to advocate about local and international issues that impact the food needs of other people. The story also invites us to restructure our friendships in order to include people from the borderlands. We may find

57. Berry, *Unsettling*, 3–14.

unexpected joy and grace by sharing hospitality and conversations with people whose life experiences are markedly different from our own.

The following chapter on the parable of the Good Samaritan will lead us further into the struggle to overcome the boundaries and borders that divide us.

CHAPTER 6

A Man Left to Die on the Jericho Road (Luke 10:30–37)

We no longer considered the Tutsis as humans or even as creatures of God. We had stopped seeing the world as it is, I mean as an expression of God's will. So we found it easy to wipe them out. That's why those of us who prayed in secret did so for ourselves, never for our victims. —LEOPOLD[1]

We left the Lord and our prayers inside (the church) to rush home. We changed from our Sunday best into our workaday clothes, we grabbed clubs and machetes, we went straight off to killing. —ADALBERT[2]

They are importing forgiveness to Rwanda, and they wrap it in lots of dollars to win us over. There is a Forgiveness Plan, just as there is an AIDS Plan, with public awareness meetings, posters, pretty local presidents, super–polite Whites in all-terrain turbo vehicles. . . . But when we talk among ourselves, the word forgiveness has no place; I mean that it's oppressive. —INNOCENT[3]

---

1. Hatzfeld, *Antelope's Strategy*, 25.
2. Ibid., 177.
3. Ibid., 17–18.

Stories from the Margins

Michael Ignatieff visited conflict areas of the former Yugoslavia in 1993 while doing research for his book *The Warrior's Honor*.[4] He writes about an evening when he goes to the front lines to join members of a Serbian militia, with the opposing Croat soldiers about two hundred yards away. In conversation with the Serbian combatants, Ignatieff learns that the fighters on both sides were once friends and neighbors and about one–third of marriages in the area are of mixed ethnicity.

As the two sides exchange small arms fire and blasts from a bazooka, Ignatieff is struck by the radical change of identity from friends to deadly foes. He tells the Serb combatants that he cannot visually distinguish Serbs from Croats and asks them to explain the differences that provoke such violence. A man laughs at his question, then takes a cigarette and holds it up as a symbol of all that divides Serbs from the Croats. "See this! These are Serbian cigarettes. Over there they smoke Croatian cigarettes." Ignatieff replies, "They are both cigarettes." The man walks away in disgust, muttering, "Foreigners don't understand anything." Later, the same soldier approaches Ignatieff and says, "They think they are better than us. Think they are fancy Europeans. I'll tell you something. . . . We're all just Balkan shit." Ignatieff observes that this short conversation reveals three different attitudes. Everything about them is different. They think they are better than us. We are all the same.

Ignatieff's story has become lodged in my inner library. I recalled the combatant's final analysis during conversations with rural farmers in Bolivia, women's self-help groups in India, students in Kenya, and business executives in North America. I thought about this story when I read the painful account of Cornel West as a high school athlete in Oakland. His track coach invited him to train in the swimming pool of an apartment complex where he lived in a Caucasian area of town. Residents abandoned the pool the moment that West entered the water. When he finished swimming, maintenance workers began to drain the pool in order to replace the water.[5] I thought of the story when a first nation's leader told me that parents in his area had told their children not to have an Indian as a friend in high school. His son had been left hurt and confused. I thought of Ignatieff's story when Romeo Dallaire, former head of UN troops in Rwanda, shared about his

4. Ignatieff, *Warrior's Honour*, 25–36.
5. West, *Brother West*, 37–38.

brokenness and the residual trauma resulting from the 1994 genocide. The UN had intervened in the former Yugoslavia to save lives, but he was given orders that prevented him from stopping the slaughter in Rwanda. Dallaire commented: "All people are born equal, but it seems that some have a lot more equality than others."

In spite of the cultural and racial diversity of the world, there is a fundamental element of "sameness" that is expressed in our ability to think, feel, laugh, cry, analyze, dialogue, and determine future action. I return to the fundamental principle of our faith—individual women and men are created in the image of God. Unpacking this doctrine, we arrive at the minimal conclusion that every life should have dignity and meaning. To bear God's image is not a privilege accorded to a restricted minority. This understanding of human life is critical for our consideration of the parable of the man left to die on the Jericho road (Luke 10:30–35). In this story, the heroic figure emerges from a social group that most people surrounding Jesus would have defined as an enemy. The modern story from the Balkans and the ancient narrative from Palestine bring to light the pervasive human evil of creating social categories that divide people into in-groups and out-groups. These borders and barricades endure for generations and shape the way people think and interact with one another.

In the opening story, the ethnic categories of Serb and Croat render as inconsequential alternative ways of considering and relating to people on the basis of vocation, abilities, moral character, family life, and common interests. Distorted historical memories, alleged differences, and gross generalizations come to dominate the public discourse, erasing any sense of shared humanity. People who are called to invest themselves in borderland regions of conflict become sensitive to the alienation, fear, anger, suspicions, and stories that separate social and ethnic groups, even within the same communities.

Rwanda and Palestine: Hutus and Tutsis, Hebrews and Samaritans

Emmanuel Katongole, a Ugandan theologian who teaches at the Kroc Institute for International Peace Studies at Notre Dame University, has provided personal and theological insights that can help us navigate the darkness of ethnic violence.[6] Katongole was born to Rwandan parents—one Hutu

---

6. Katongole's writings on Rwanda include *A Future for Africa* and *Mirror to the Church*.

and the other Tutsi. After their marriage, his parents decided to live in Uganda because of the ethnic divisions in their home country. Accordingly, Katongole was raised in a foreign land with a painful awareness of ethnic hatred and violence. Now, as a scholar, he joins most other researchers in arguing that the Belgium colonizers imported concepts of racial superiority to Rwanda. Their so-called scientific theories of race became part of the colonial transcript of power. The Tutsi minority of Rwanda were elevated as being genetically superior and favored with greater opportunities for education and government positions. Previously, the categories of Hutu and Tutsi had been fluid and based on vocation. Under Belgium rule, the boundaries became permanently fixed on identity cards, using technical criteria such as measurements of stature and the length of noses. The "pseudo science" of ethnic superiority received the support of the Roman Catholic Church, which developed a theology of the Tutsis as descendants of Noah.[7] By the late 1930s, ethnicity had become the defining feature of ordinary life in Rwanda, destroying the country's previous sense of collective identity, shared language, and culture

Katongole observes that Rwanda's independence in 1961 took power away from the Belgium colonizers without challenging the racist myth embedded in the public transcript. Ethnic quotas, policies of exclusion, and government-sanctioned violence relegated the Tutsi minority to a precarious existence and resulted in a refugee movement to neighboring countries. The power of the colonial story was evident in 1994, when the rally cry of the Interahamwe Hutu gangs was to kill Tutsis and throw their bodies in the river so that they would float back down the Nile to where their ancestors had originated. Tutsi people were tied up, placed in potato sacks, and thrown in the river in order to save bullets.[8] Katongole concludes that the violence of Rwanda proves that stories have the power to kill.

My partner Regine has personal experiences that shed further light on Rwanda's tragic story. In grade one, teachers encouraged Hutu students to call their Tutsi classmates "cockroaches" and "snakes." Her father died

---

7. The line of ancestors moved from Noah through his son Ham to the Tutsi people in Rwanda. For an explanation of the Hamitic myth, see Bjornlund et al., "The Christian Churches and the Construction of a Genocidal Mentality in Rwanda," in Rittner, Roth and Whitworth, *Genocide in Rwanda*, 148–52. The Hutu composed the majority of Rwandans, estimated to be approximately 85 percent of the population. The Twa were a small group who had traditionally lived in the forests. They amounted to about 1 percent of the population.

8. Survivor's testimony (Winnipeg, 2015).

under mysterious circumstances. She was denied access to university, even though her secondary school grades were among the highest in the country for her year of graduation. Later she was granted acceptance into teacher training rather than medicine. During the 1994 genocide, neighbors were instructed to kill her and open her head to expose the brains of an educated Tutsi woman.

There are connections between the barricades that have been erected to separate Hutus from Tutsis in our time along with Jews from Samaritans[9] in the first century and countless other people in diverse places throughout history where groups have engaged in practices of exclusion, suspicion, lies, and propaganda. The deep antagonism between Jews and Samaritans first appears in Luke's Gospel as Jesus embarks on his long trip from Galilee to Jerusalem (9:51–56). At the outset of the journey, he sends an envoy ahead to a Samaritan village to request hospitality for the night.[10] The community leaders refuse the petition. Their denial of a social obligation indicates that the walls of separation were maintained by people on both sides. Angry at this insult to the honor of their leader, two disciples ask for approval to call on God to send fire to destroy the village and its people.[11] Their request needs to be read for what it is—a statement of religiously sanctioned genocidal intention. Jesus censures the two disciples, and the group passes on to another village.

We might ask what lies in the background of such hostility. As in Rwanda and the former Yugoslavia, the desire simply to "get rid" of another group does not appear suddenly and catch people by surprise. In the context of this chapter, there is only space to make note of two significant landmarks that may help us to comprehend that the ethnic and racial hostilities between Samaritans and Jews had deep historical roots, which were deliberately fostered. Those readers who wish to pass directly on to the discussion of the parable can skip the following excursus.

---

9. John P. Meier provides a helpful introduction to the "Samaritan problem." He notes that even the term "Samaritan" is slippery because it can be defined in terms of geography, ethnicity, and/or religion. He observes that ". . . not everyone who was geographically a Samaritan was ethnically or religiously a Samaritan." Meier, *Marginal Jew*, 3:532–34.

10. Galileans often chose to travel by a longer route to Jerusalem in order to avoid passing through Samaritan territory.

11. The symbol of fire from heaven is taken from 2 Kings 1:9–12, where the prophet Elijah calls on fire from heaven to destroy the troops of Ahaziah, King of Samaria (Israel).

Excursus on the Samaritans

We find what I call the first landmark embedded in the accounts of the forced deportations of Hebrew people under the Assyrian and Babylonian Empires and the return of some of their descendants under the Persian Empire in 537 BCE. The deportation of the ten tribes of the Northern Kingdom (also known as Samaria) took place in stages around the years 740 to 720 BCE. The Babylonian deportation also happened in intervals after the fall of Jerusalem in 587 BCE. The Book of Kings contains the biblical accounts of these exiles. Readers must remember that the traditions were put in final written form long after the return from Babylon and the stories were reshaped to address issues of that time.

The accounts of the two deportations in 2 Kings stress that "all" the population was taken, except for the poor (2 Kings 17 and 2 Kings 25). The impression is deliberately made of mass forced evacuations, which left the territories open for re-settlement by neighboring people with pagan deities. (One such group was identified as people from Cuthah or Cuth (2 Kings 17:24, 30), a significant detail because Samaritans were often called Cuthites.) The deportation accounts were clearly exaggerated to serve the agenda of the returnees from Babylon, who enjoyed the support of the Persian Empire. They established themselves as the new elite, the guardians of the ruins of the temple, and the only people with authenic bloodlines. It served their interests to maintain that the land was neither ethnically nor religiously pure. The returnees consolidated their positions of power by excluding people who had remained in the land (Ezra 10:9–15; Neh 13:25–27). Since this line of interpretation may be contentious for some readers, I will quote from a standard reference work by the biblical scholar John L. McKenzie: "The group of exiles asserted that they and only they were the 'holy seed,' the remnant of the true Israel, the living heirs of the chosen people. . . . In this dispute we see the antecedents of the Samaritan schism."[12] The peasant population that remained in towns and villages of Galilee and Judea, including Samaritans, were marginalized, driven into poverty, and suffered the loss of properties (Neh 5:1–13). Isaiah 55–66 reflects some of the social tensions of this period. There is a poignant saying from a group of people who retain faith in Yahweh, but are not counted as members of the nation of Israel and as descendants of Abraham (Isa 63:16). This is the complaint of people who found themselves excluded by the new

12. McKenzie, *Theology*, 260.

elite that had returned from Babylon. I suggest that a similar statement could have been made by Samaritans in the time of Jesus.

The second landmark is less controversial, because it does not originate in scriptural texts. The Jewish historian Josephus (37–100 CE) relates a story that is a prime piece of anti-Samaritan propaganda. The alleged incident is found in his twenty-one volume history of the Jewish people, which he entitled *Antiquities*. His objective in writing such an extensive work was to present the history, culture, and faith of his people in a manner that elicited sympathy and support among powerful people of the Roman Empire during the volatile rule of Domitian. Readers will recall that after the rebellion culminating in the fall of Jerusalem (66–70 CE), Romans viewed the Jewish people as troublemakers and threats to national security. In *Antiquities* 12.257–264, Josephus relates the story of a Samaritan delegation sent to the Seleucid ruler Antiochus Epiphanes during the period in which the Greeks ruled Palestine and Egypt. Josephus claims to quote from the official letter presented on behalf of the political and religious leaders located in Gerizim. In the letter, the Samaritan leaders offer to pay increased taxes to the Seleucid officials and to rename their temple after the Greek deity Apollos. They also affirm that Samaritans are not related to the Jewish people in any way and only desire to live in peace. It seems evident that Josephus drew on a narrative that was used by people in circles of power in Jerusalem to foment hostility against Samaritans. I reiterate that there is no historical evidence that syncretism was practiced in the temple in Gerizim. Furthermore, it is highly improbable that Samaritans would have volunteered to increase the level of taxation paid to a foreign oppressor. It is likely that Josephus repeated a narrative slur that was useful for stigmatizing Samaritans as foreigners, idolaters, and insincere opportunists. The story would have been useful for denigrating their temple on Mount Gerizim, which actually competed for funds with the Jerusalem temple among Jews in parts of the diaspora.

With the passage of time, the walls of separation, suspicion, and enmity became firmly established. Josephus expressed the conclusion that Jewish people had no reason to expect any kindness from Samaritans.[13] Sharing food with a Samaritan could be equated with eating the flesh of pig.[14] Documents signed by Samaritans were regarded as untrustworthy.[15]

13. See *Ant.* 12.257–64.

14. *M. Sebi'it 8.10.*

15. *Gittin* 10.

Places where Samaritans had been seated were considered impure.[16] Some people argued that the murder of a Samaritan should be exempt from legal punishment.[17]

I am certainly not alleging that people in Galilee and Judea were particularly evil or extreme racists. We should all be aware of the horrible record of anti-Semitism during the past century and leading into our own day. In the final section of this chapter, I will encourage readers to engage in critical analysis of our time and place in history. Here, I simply wish to observe that ethnocentrism and racism are an endemic evil of humanity. The stories used to maintain and justify barricades and boundaries between people are useful tools in supporting policies of exclusion and the rationalizations of violence. In the following pages, I will argue that Jesus told the story of a man left to die on the road to Jericho to challenge the social enmity and ethnic tensions that permeated Palestine—including the attitudes of some of his closest followers.

The Confrontation with a Lawyer and the Jericho Road Parable

I want to begin this section by addressing the dangerous tendency to treat this parable as a piece of polite encouragement toward responsible citizenship. It seems important to state at the outset that the Samaritan parable was not intended to promote random acts of kindness or to make the audience resolve to be nicer people. Readers who are familiar with this line of interpretation might wish to consider N. T. Wright's statement that the Samaritan parable encapsulates much of the significance of Jesus' mission, redefines the rule of God for the audience, and contains themes of deep significance.[18] His assessment supports my contention that the parable is not a "light read" and that it offers a radical vision of transformation for a broken and wounded world.

16. *Niddah* 4.1.
17. *B. Sanhedrin* 57a.
18. Wright, *Jesus*, 305.

Conversation with a Lawyer (10:25-29)

> Just then a lawyer stood up to test Jesus. "Teacher," he said, "what must I do to inherit eternal life?" He said to him, "What is written in the law? What do you read there?" He answered, "You shall love the Lord your God with all your heart, and with all your soul, and with all your strength, and with all your mind; and your neighbor as yourself." And he said to him, "You have given the right answer; do this, and you will live." But wanting to justify himself, he asked Jesus, "And who is my neighbor?"

The parable flows directly out of the conversation between Jesus and a lawyer. It seems certain that the introduction and the parable were combined in the pre-Lukan tradition. Lawyers belonged to the broad category of scribes—men who could read and write documents. Scribes often served within government administration, maintained tax records, kept records for the military, and assisted the wealthy with their commercial ventures. In Palestine, certain Jewish scribes had additional functions of copying sacred documents and interpreting the Torah.[19] Accordingly, the word "lawyer" is often used as a synonym for "scribe" in the gospels. As a Torah expert, the lawyer in this narrative has a vested interest in maintaining the public transcript of ritual purity and the temple cult. Thus there is an alignment of the lawyer with the priest and the Levite in the parable.

At the outset of the account, Luke draws attention to the fact that the lawyer takes a standing position before he addresses Jesus, a posture which suggests that it is not a friendly conversation. The use of the verb "to test"[20] underlines the tension of the exchange. The lawyer has deliberately come to challenge the honor and authority of Jesus as an interpreter of the Torah.[21] In his first question, he asks Jesus to state his position about the entrance requirements for eternal life—or membership in God's kingdom.[22] He demands that Jesus speak with clarity about the border that separates those on the inside from those who are beyond God's saving action. The riposte of Jesus shifts the weight of the question to the lawyer. How does this Scripture expert read the Torah?

19. Meier notes that different religious movements in Palestine had their own scribes (*Marginal Jew: Vol. 3*, 550–55).

20. 10.25. Greek *ekpeirazein*.

21. Nolland, *Commentary Luke 9:51—18:34*, 585.

22. I draw attention again to the way in which eternal life, entrance to the kingdom and salvation are used interchangeably in 18:18–30 (the rich ruler passage).

The lawyer responds by quoting the teaching of Jesus, which combined Deut 6:5 and Lev 19:18 into the double-love command. The first text was part of the Jewish Shema, the prayer that was repeated twice daily by people of faith. The second text belonged to the Torah's holiness code. John P. Meier's extensive research led him to conclude that these two texts had not been joined as a summary of the Torah prior to Jesus.[23] This means that the lawyer is deliberately throwing Jesus' teaching back in his face in order to get to the real matter of controversy. The second statement of Jesus is an attempt to end the conversation and dismiss his adversary. "You have answered right; do this and you will live."

The lawyer has steered the conversation precisely to this point. He now wants Jesus to take a public position on the question: Who is my neighbor? Who are the covenant people who will inherit the promises? To whom do I owe obligations of solidarity? The question expresses an implicit understanding that the social justice commitments of the Torah do not extend to all the people of the community. The reduced scope is consistent with the emphasis on purity obligations and regulations that separated people into in-groups and out-groups. It is certain that the lawyer was aware of Jesus' friendship with so-called sinners, outcasts, women, and even Gentiles.[24] He views Jesus' association with these people on the margins as a point of vulnerability which can serve to discredit his mission and message.

The Jericho Road Parable (10:30–37)

A man was going down from Jerusalem to Jericho, and fell into the hands of robbers, who stripped him, beat him, and went away, leaving him half dead. Now by chance a priest was going down that road; and when he saw him, he passed by on the other side. So likewise a Levite, when he came to the place and saw him, passed by on the other side. But a Samaritan while travelling came near him; and when he saw him, he was moved with pity. He went to him and bandaged his wounds, having poured oil and wine on them. Then he put him on his own animal, brought him to an inn, and took care of him. The next day he took out two denarii, gave them to the innkeeper, and said, "Take care of him; and when I come back, I will repay you whatever more you spend." Which of these three, do you think, was a neighbor to the man who fell

23. Meier, *Marginal Jew: Vol. 4*, 490–528.
24. Snodgrass, *Stories with Intent*, 353.

into the hands of the robbers? And he said, "The one who showed mercy toward him." And Jesus said to him, "Go and do the same."

The parable of the man left to die on the Jericho road shifts the audience's attention from an intense theological debate to a gritty story about human need. The formulaic expression "a certain man" is used to introduce seven other Lukan parables.[25] The words provide a minimalist description of the only figure who is present in the narrative from the beginning to the end—the wounded man. The distance from Jerusalem to Jericho was approximately twenty-nine kilometers over a route that passed through hills where bandits were known to hide. The traveler is vulnerable because he walks alone.[26] The robbers beat him, strip off his clothing, and presumably take his possessions.[27] The wounds inflicted suggest a fierce struggle.

The central character remains an enigma throughout the remainder of the parable. The audience wants to know more about his identity, the purpose of his journey, and the people waiting for his arrival, but the beating has rendered him silent throughout the story. The theft of his clothes makes it impossible to determine his home region, social class, and even ethnicity.[28] The term "half dead" (*hemithanes*) suggests that he either seemed to be dead or that death was imminent apart from some intervention. In this condition, he represents a threat to people concerned about maintaining personal purity, as contact with a dead body rendered a person impure until ritual cleansing and sacrifices had been performed.[29]

Modern readers should not assume that the audience of the parable was sympathetic to the plight of the wounded man. People on the margins might have viewed the assailants as social bandits who attacked retainers employed by the elite. Their violent actions were an expression of political resistance and an ideology of redistribution of wealth by force.[30] Peasants in rural areas provided support for social bandits. This perspective is another reminder that we are challenged to enter into the social world

25. 10:30; 12:16; 14:16; 15:11; 16:1, 19; 19:12.

26. In fact, all four characters on the road share the common danger of traveling alone.

27. Robbery is not mentioned. However the use of the Greek word *lestai* to designate the assailants leads to this conclusion.

28. Circumcision was widely practiced by Semitic people.

29. People who maintained strict purity regulations held that contact with a cadaver rendered a person impure (Lev 21:1–3; Num 5:2; 19:10–22; Ezek 44:25–27).

30. Richard Horsely with John S. Hanson, *Bandits*, 48–77.

of the parables before we attempt to find meaning for our own time and circumstances.

The chance arrival of a priest offers potential relief to the tension caused by a man lying near death at the side of the road. He is returning from duties in Jerusalem to his residence in Jericho.[31] This character's identity as a priest is significant. He is a representative of the public transcript of faith that stands for Torah obedience, sacrifice, and purity. He benefits personally from the temple system and its economic wealth.[32] The wording of the narrative is precise. Having seen the victim, he makes the deliberate decision to pass by on the other side. Although no explanation is provided, listeners are left to suspect that human need has second place to purity laws here at the side of the Jericho road.

The next traveler on the road is a Levite. The social and economic position of Levites was similar to that of the priests, whom they assisted in the temple. The temple system—with its taxes, tithes and offerings—sustains this man's life and provides him with a respectable identity. The parable repeats the same vocabulary of "having seen" and "passed by on the other side." As with the priest, no explanation is given for the Levite's moral decision. He simply abandons the man at the side of the road. The shadow of the public transcript of the temple and purity code falls on the place where the priest and Levite divert their steps.[33] Their refusal to provide assistance has an ironic twist in that they become potential accomplices of the social bandits in the death of the man left beside the Jericho road.

The story to this point has created a narrative need for a third character to intervene in some manner. The original audience might have anticipated the arrival of a devout Pharisee, a Jewish peasant, or a heavenly angel sent by God.[34] The entrance of a Samaritan into the story is abrupt and jolting. He represents an unwelcome, alien presence on a Judean road. The audience gathered around Jesus would have expected no solidarity from

31. Many priests and Levites lived in Jericho. The fact that the priest was traveling toward Jericho means that his temple duties had been completed. Priests were superior to Levites because they could trace their line of descent to Aaron, the first priest of Israel. Priests presided over the temple sacrifices while Levites served as their assistants.

32. Priests were granted the privilege of living from the tithes collected from the people. They were obligated to live by higher standards of purity associated with the temple. Later in Luke's gospel, Jesus will call the temple a den of robbers (19:46), draw attention to its cruel demands on the poor (21:1–4), and predict its destruction (21:5–6).

33. Snodgrass, *Stories with Intent*, 354.

34. Nolland, *Commentary Luke 9:51—18:34*, 594.

such a person. The first words that describe his appearance link him with the priest and the Levite. Like the two men before him, the Samaritan sees the wounded victim by the side of the road.

Yet unlike the two men before him, the Samaritan responds to what he has seen by allowing his heart to be moved with compassion.[35] The use of the verb "to be filled with compassion" marks the turning point in the story,[36] for the compassion or mercy of the Samaritan moves him to subsequent actions, which are costly, dangerous, and time consuming. Jesus identifies seven ways in which the Samaritan engages with the man who was left to die on the road to Jericho.

First, the Samaritan draws near the man instead of passing him by. He stops his journey in order to enter the space of the wounded man, thereby placing himself at risk on a dangerous road. Second, he bandages the man after using oil and wine to cleanse his wounds.[37] Third, he places the wounded man on his own animal, thereby giving preference to the man in need. Fourth, he takes the wounded man to the safety of an inn located in a nearby community. Once again, this implies certain danger to the Samaritan, as he is in an alien context characterized by suspicion and prejudice against his ethnic group. Fifth, the Samaritan detains his journey to care for the wounded man for one night at the inn. Sixth, he gives two denarii to the innkeeper the following day. This amount is sufficient to provide board and lodging for two weeks. This generosity signifies that the Samaritan is not content to offer some immediate assistance and then withdraw from further obligations. Seventh, he tells the innkeeper to care for the wounded man and promises to repay any additional funds required when he returns. This commitment recognizes that the time of recovery is uncertain and also demonstrates the Samaritan's refusal to shift the responsibility to others. By making this commitment, the Samaritan leaves himself vulnerable to the arbitrary "running up of the tab" by the innkeeper, who might take advantage of a despised foreigner.[38]

35. The text uses the Greek verb *splagnizomai* which means "to be filled with compassion." Earlier in the third gospel, Jesus sees and has compassion on a widow who lost her only son and, accordingly, will henceforth live without male protection (7:13). The same combination of "to see" and "to have compassion" occurs when the father of the prodigal sees his son returning home and has compassion on him (1:520). In all three cases (including the Samaritan parable), compassion leads to action.

36. Hendrickx, *Gospel for the Third World, (Luke 13:22—17.10)*, 68.

37. Olive oil was used to soften wounds and wine was a mild disinfectant. These details suggest that the Samaritan was a merchant.

38. Innkeepers had tarnished reputations because of the association of inns with

Readers of this book are challenged to set aside their familiarity with the parable in order to hear it in a fresh manner. A member of an ethnically marginalized group intervenes to save another person's life in a messy situation in which the victim could be blamed for being foolhardy for traveling alone. Two respectable pillars of the public transcript choose not to get involved. The Samaritan's actions seem ill-advised and excessive. Negative reciprocity (abandonment) would have been the accepted cultural standard for strangers and enemies.[39] The Samaritan's actions convey a radical position, which rejects social categories and simplifies morality. One person's life hangs in the balance. One man, motivated by compassion, has the courage to cross social, cultural, economic, and ethnic boundaries to save him.

Jesus concludes the parable with a carefully crafted question that does not allow the conversation with the lawyer to be redirected toward a theoretical discussion of the limits of the Torah commandment to love one's neighbor (Lev 19:18). He pointedly asks the lawyer, "Which of these three became the neighbor to the man who fell among the bandits?" This question would have made the entire audience uncomfortable, because the scribe, the disciples, and the crowds around them were all caught up in practices of ethnic exclusion. In replying to the question, it is striking that the Torah expert is unable to bring himself to say the words, "the Samaritan." Instead, he uses the impersonal designation, "the one who showed mercy." Jesus' final response is: "Go and do the same!"

Reflection

This chapter opens with a story from the former Yugoslavia, where ethnicity could be a matter of life or death during the years of conflict. The combatant's graphic statement, "We are all Balkan shit!" has been confirmed by scientific evidence. DNA analysis at mass grave sites in Bosnia has shown that there are no genetic differences that distinguish Serbs, Croats, and Bosnian Muslims. Ethnicity is something learned in homes, schools, and social institutions (including places of worship). Thus the creation of barricades and borders to separate people is human work rather than a matter of genetics.

Miroslav Volf, a theologian who teaches at Yale Divinity School, was born in the Balkans and lived through the ethnic hostility that engulfed the

---

prostitution. In colloquial language, innkeepers were often viewed as pimps.

39. Oakman, *Peasants*, 175.

region. Volf observes that violence is rooted in attitudes and actions that categorize and marginalize people who are deemed to be different.[40] The dominant culture explicitly and implicitly encourages tight lines of separation in regard to members of out-groups. As a result, there is a socially shared evil behind individual acts of discrimination and violence. Unfortunately, churches have often participated in attitudes, policies, and practices of exclusion and intolerance, rather than modeling a prophetic vision of the new creation. We have acted as if some people were created in the image of a lesser god. At an extreme, we might consider the statements of Leopold and Adalbert at the beginning of this chapter, who attended church each Sunday morning and in the afternoon became killers in the Rwandan Tutsi genocide. Leopold prayed for his own needs and was not troubled by his conscience because he did not consider his victims to be creatures of God.

Visits to genocide sites in Rwanda have left me emotionally and spiritually shaken. The stories told by survivors portray the evil acts of ordinary people in ways that are terrifying, even twenty years removed from the events. Two authors have shaped my understanding of ethnic violence and the way in which I read the Jericho road parable. In *The War of the World: Twentieth-Century Conflict and the Descent of the West*, Niall Ferguson describes the past century as the bloodiest in human history, thereby making a convincing case about the collective sinfulness of humanity.[41] Ironically, this period was also unparalleled in economic and technological progress. Fergusson expresses amazement at the ability of leaders in diverse settings to motivate and unleash the murderous instincts of their followers (including prominent intellectuals) against people of minority groups. Women and girls were often subjected to cruel and degrading abuse. Fergusson's work encompasses the geography of the planet and in this manner shows that ethnic prejudice and violence is a fundamental human problem. Paul Collier, professor of Economics and Social Policy at Oxford, has shown the connection between poverty and civil violence in his book *The Bottom Billion, Why the Poorest Countries are Falling Behind and What Can be Done about It?*[42] Seventy-three percent of the bottom billion are either caught in a violent conflict or have been through one in the past ten years. He observes that when civil conflicts come to an end, they are usually followed by periods of increased violent crime and murder. The personal and economic

---

40. Volf, *Exclusion*, 57–98.
41. Ferguson, *War of the World*.
42. Collier, *Bottom Billion*.

costs of civil violence are staggering. Recent research by the Institute for Economics and Peace shows that the cost of conflicts in 2014 amounted to 13 percent of the world's GDP. A 10 percent reduction in violence would be worth more than 10 times the entire amount of development assistance that flows from rich to poor countries.[43] Paul Collier has convinced me that activists concerned with poverty must invest attention, money, and time in the work of peace-making and reconciliation.

I recognize that Volf, Ferguson, and Collier draw attention to dramatic cases of ethnic violence that may seem removed from our daily lives in North America. However, we should not be blind to the evil of ethnic divisions that prevail within Canada and the USA. Regine and I live in a city in Canada that has a significant percentage of First Nations residents, a social group that suffers from the highest rates of poverty, homelessness, unemployment, health issues, and imprisonment in our area. The legacy of the residential school project of assimilation is still an open wound in our country. The number of unsolved crimes of violence against First Nations women is a tragic scandal. The news from the USA over the past months has been dominated by stories of differential treatment of African American males by the police. We have seen race riots in cities where anger boiled over into wanton destruction. In addition, a recent Senate report revealed that the CIA, with the support of psychologists and medical specialists, used torture against people of other ethnic groups in the name of national security. There is a disturbing link between this report and the shameful abuse of Middle Eastern prisoners at Abu Ghraib prison in Iraq and illegal detentions in Guantanamo Bay of prisoners who are known to be innocent. It is impossible to deny elements of racism and to attribute the blame to a few bad actors. Racialization and ethnocentrism are deeply rooted in the cultures of our countries, a fact that is revealed in the stories we are told and the stories we tell about people from the borderlands. The barricades and boundaries are maintained, at least in part, by stories of fear rather than narratives of engagement.

I made reference earlier to Katongole's conclusion that stories have the power to kill. In our North American cultures, we hear stories about drunken Indians, dangerous black youth, and Moslem terrorists, and then use these stories to make unfair representations of entire social groups. A story told by First Nations author Thomas King illustrates our reluctance to examine and abandon stories of division and exclusion. According to King,

43. Institute for Economics and Peace, *Global Peace Index Report*, 64

the sons and daughters of the Idaho pioneers erected a plaque dedicated to the memory of three hundred settlers killed in an Indian massacre in 1861. Later historians proved that the event had no historical reality. The story had been fabricated to justify violence against Native People and the seizure of their land. Despite protests, the plaque remained in place as part of local culture and history.[44] This account illustrates that stories of enmity do not easily move off the stage. They continue to be dangerous, even when exposed as lies. Such stories have the capacity to close the door to the common places of meeting where we can enter into dialogue with one another. As a result, alienation grows and the walls of the borderlands become even more impenetrable.

Social transformation requires that new stories be placed within the inner libraries of the people of a community. These stories must nurture a vision of renewed patterns of relationships based on the values of justice, mercy, and faith. These stories must be strong enough to create wild spaces or a spirit of sublime madness (to use again the expressions of Sallie McFague and Chris Hedges), in which group members can critique the dominant discourse of suspicion and fear, and take Spirit-led actions that point toward the new creation. The parable of the man left to die on the Jericho road created such a wild space for the first followers of Jesus, inviting them to imagine a world in which determined actions of compassion could overcome ethnic borders and barricades. In the next chapter, we shift our attention to the theme of faithful service as a form of slavery. But before turning to these slave parables, I offer the following excursus on compassion and historical forgiveness.

Excursus on Compassion and Historical Forgiveness.

My treatment of the Jericho Road parable has been extensive because ethnic and racial divisions are so deeply entrenched in our communities. During the final edits to this chapter, a young male Caucasian entered an African American Church in South Carolina, sat in a prayer meeting, and then killed nine members of the congregation. The horror of this act of racial violence was immediately countered by the statement of forgiveness issued by two children of a slain mother. In the following days expressions of forgiveness were repeated by members of the congregation. There was an element of hope that emerged out of the deep pain of the moment. I offer

44. King, *Inconvenient Indian*, 4–7.

the following excursus on compassion and historical forgiveness to readers who can bear with me for a few more pages, as I did not want to distract from the main theme.

Compassion or Mercy[45]

We have all encountered people who carry out their professional duties without really engaging others in a personal way. Such people fulfill job descriptions without a driving sense of passion and compassion. As a result, people become statistics for reports, and projects are referred to as "interventions" rather than community initiatives. One of the lessons of the Samaritan narrative is the importance of working from our hearts rather than simply completing the requirements associated with our positions.

The theologian Jon Sobrino wrote about compassion and mercy after his home country of El Salvador was shaken by two major earthquakes in 2001.[46] He observes that compassion is an emotional reaction to human suffering that enables us to identify personally with people whose lives are marked by pain and injustice. Compassion motivates us to know strangers by name and to cross cultural boundaries in order to enter into their stories. Compassion convicts our hearts and stirs us to take concrete actions of mercy and justice on behalf of people who are brought into our lives. Sobrino's comments have helped me to grasp the importance of the compassion that penetrates the heart of the Samaritan on the Jericho road. His example encourages those who work for social transformation to feel the pain of others and to take the time to build deep and loving relationships. Our vocations can become an outworking of the heart, in which our emotions sustain our connections with borderland friends and issues. When we fail to nurture compassion, we run the risk of becoming cold professionals with skills but no warmth.

45. My friend Rupen Das has written a book on compassion and mission while serving among Syrian refugees and Lebanese Baptist churches in the Middle East. *Compassion and the Mission of God: Revealing the Invisible Kingdom.* My understanding of compassion was shaped by conversations with Rupen that took place in various parts of the world.

46. Sobrino, *Where is God*, 12–13, 29. See also Sobrino, *Mercy*, 10–11, 16–19, 39. I am grateful to Pastor Miguel Castro of Emmanuel Baptist Church, San Salvador, for explaining the preference for the term "mercy" in Latin America because of paternalistic connotations associated with the word "compassion."

Historical Forgiveness

The circumstances on the Jericho road push the Samaritan to come to terms with a history of grievances, insults, and mistreatment. He could easily have justified passing by on the other side. Historical forgiveness is tricky. It requires us to deal with attitudes and actions that were either inflicted on victims with whom we identify, or by perpetrators associated with our ethnic or racial group. Often we wonder if forgiveness is desired, appropriate, and even supported by the broader community. Canadian Prime Minister Stephen Harper apologized to First Nations people in 2008 for the residential school system that had sought to "kill the Indian in the child" through assimilation. He spoke for the government of Canada. Did he speak for the people of Canada? Who was authorized to accept his apology on behalf of parents whose children were forcefully taken from their homes? Dealing with history is difficult.

Yet without faltering confessions of evil and expressions of forgiveness, personal and community transformation is impossible. We are left with resentment, suspicion, and fear. I recently heard Amanda Lindhout speak about her experience as a hostage of Somali insurgents for over 450 days, during which time she was treated brutally as her captors bargained for the price of her release.[47] Lindhout describes how she became consumed by anger and self-pity. She reached a turning point when she decided that she would attempt to nurture compassion for her captors and make forgiveness a daily practice. She discovered that acts of forgiveness were expressions of her own freedom and determination to live with dignity and humanity. Lindhout's testimony is reminiscent of Miroslav Volf's statement that forgiveness is the only force that can overcome the evil of ethnic and social divisions.[48] This is not a simple process. There are times when specific attitudes and injustices must be acknowledged and confessed. The words of confession uttered by perpetrators of violence are important. Victims and survivors of mass violence, on the other hand, may find that repentance and forgiveness are communicated most strongly when enacted by deeds rather than words. A tearful embrace, a shared meal, attempted reparations, or assistance in a difficult situation may say more than the repetition of phrases that seem forced and insincere. As we move between victims,

47. Lindhout's experiences and convictions about the power of forgiveness are found in Lindhout and Corbett, *House in the Sky.*

48. Volf, *Exclusion,* 121.

bystanders, and perpetrators, some of us will be required to serve as guides and encouragers in the whole process of confession, forgiveness, and reconciliation. In these moments, we will be required to walk with the Spirit, to examine our own attitudes and pain, and to enter humbly with others into God's healing process.

As a family, we have learned some of the hard lessons of the struggle to participate in God's new creation. My brother-in-law, Theoneste, was called to present his testimony in a community genocide trial in Rwanda a few years ago. He had been attacked in 1994 by men with machetes, who cut his tendons, inflicted wounds on his head, stole his clothes, and left him for dead. In the months leading up to his appearance at the tribunal, he struggled with the tension between demanding justice and offering forgiveness to the leader of the mob that had attempted to kill him. He reached the difficult decision that he would extend forgiveness to this former neighbor. At the hearing, the accused listened to Theoneste's testimony and then presented a counter-narrative, in which he was the virtuous figure who only wanted to protect the neighborhood from a robber. Members of the audience—from the accused man's own ethnic group—were angered by his lies. They informed the tribunal that the accused had participated in other murders the same night. As a result, he was sentenced to serve time in jail as a convicted genocide perpetrator, rather than receiving freedom for a full confession and apology.

Theoneste's story does not reach a satisfying conclusion. The prophetic mission of bringing down walls of separation and enmity will, unfortunately, have many stories without warm and wholesome endings. Theoneste, along with thousands of other people like him, serve as examples of what it means to find comfort in solidarity with the crucified one and to take up the struggle against evil by following Jesus' example. We are called in different ways to enter compassionately into the deep pain of vulnerable people with a message of confession, forgiveness, and reconciliation. The Samaritan provides a model of courageous action that demonstrates that love is stronger than enmity and violence.

CHAPTER 7

Five Stories About Slaves
(Luke 12:35–48; 17:7–10)

My whole life, I have been treated like a donkey. All I want is that one son of mine—at least one—should live like a man. —Vikram Halwal[1]

The jails of Delhi are full of drivers who are there behind bars because they are taking the blame for their good, solid middle–class masters. We have left the villages, but the masters still own us, body, soul and arse. —Balram Halwal[2]

The hands [slaves]are required to be in the cotton field as soon as it is light in the morning, and, with the exception of ten or fifteen minutes, which is given to them at noon to swallow their allowance of cold bacon, they are not permitted to be a moment idle until it is too dark to see. . . . After weighing [the cotton] follow the whippings; and then the baskets are carried to the cotton house. —Solomon Northup[3]

Stories from the Margins

Aravind Adiga's award-winning novel *The White Tiger* tells the story of Balram Halwal, an indentured worker who lives in conditions of slavery

1. Adiga, *White Tiger*, 30.
2. Ibid., 170.
3. Northup, *Twelve Years*, 135–36.

in modern India. His father Vikram, a rickshaw driver in a rural village, dreams that one of his sons will live with the dignity that he has been denied throughout his life. Poverty forces Vikram to make arrangements for Balram to become a servant in the household of a local landholder. As he grows older, the boy learns to drive vehicles and, with this new skill, becomes more useful to his master. After a few years, the landholder takes Balram to Delhi to serve in the family's city residence. Balram sees the exteriors of mansions, shopping centres, offices, and restaurants that he is never allowed to enter. When not driving, he works long hours sweeping floors, cleaning, and performing other services. At night, he sleeps in a small basement room of a luxury condominium with the servants of other masters, along with cockroaches and mosquitoes.

As an indentured servant, Balram endures false accusations, deprivations, and beatings. When the master's wife strikes a child while driving the car, Balram is forced to sign a confession indicating that he is responsible for the child's death. One fateful night, the master arranges to pay a bribe of seven hundred thousand rupees to a local politician. Balram feigns a flat tire while driving to the meeting place. Then he kills the master, steals the money, and flees to another city. Although he lives under the constant fear of recognition and arrest, he expresses no regrets for the violence that has allowed him to experience freedom for the first time in his life. He reflects, " . . . even if they make me walk the wooden stairs to the hangman's noose— I'll never say I made a mistake that night in Delhi when I slit my master's throat. I'll say it was all worthwhile to know, just for a day, just for an hour, just for a *minute*, what it means not to be a servant."

The fictional story of Balram Halwal has been described as a parable of the modern India that contrasts the country's economic growth with social issues of inequality, poverty, and corruption.[4] It is a fitting introduction to this chapter, which treats five short slave parables in the third gospel. Slavery was as cruel and demeaning in the Roman Empire as it has been at other times and places in world history. Most modern readers who are familiar with the gospel parables have lost the sense of shock felt by the audiences of Jesus when he used stories about slaves to describe faithful service in God's kingdom. In our own time, the analogy of God with a first-century slaveholder is particularly disturbing for those whose ancestors suffered as slaves, as well as for social activists who work to preserve human rights and dignity. Anyone who watched the Academy Award-winning movie, *Twelve*

4. Kapur, "Secret of His Success."

Years a Slave, will feel a sense of revulsion about suggestions that equate God with a slaveholder. The slave parables exemplify Arthur Frank's concept of narrative ambush in a strange and objectionable manner.

This chapter was difficult to write, and it may be challenging to read. In the initial section, I will focus on the oppressive nature of slavery in the Roman Empire and Palestine during the time of Jesus. Then I will examine the Hebrew tradition of the slave/servant of Yahweh, which stands in the background of the slave stories of Jesus. The rest of the chapter will be devoted to reading and interpreting five short slave parables from Luke's gospel.

Background to the Slave Parables: Slavery in the Roman Empire

It is important to recognize that the existing historical documents on slavery in the Roman Empire were written from the perspective of slaveholders rather than slaves. The list includes informal papyri documents found in Egypt through to comprehensive historical annals, such as the writings of Tacitus. There is a consistent social bias that accepts the institution of slavery as an unquestioned economic and social reality. Accordingly, these documents must be used with discernment in order to shed light on the general nature of slavery and the lives of most slaves around the time of Jesus.[5]

Slaves were considered to be property, much like animals, buildings, and land.[6] People of wealth listed slaves as part of their estates to be distributed to heirs upon death. Slaves were categorized as bodies to be used, sold, or traded. The dehumanizing terminology of "bodies" even enters into the New Testament, where in the Revelation of John, the seer envisions the merchants of the earth mourning because no one will purchase their cargos of gold, silver, pearls, linen, wood, ivory, bronze, iron, marble, spices, olive

---

5. Jennifer Glancy's research and writing was foundational for my comprehension of slavery. She states that conditions of slavery changed little over the centuries beginning with the early Roman Empire and ending in late antiquity. Furthermore, the treatment of slaves was virtually indistinguishable through the empire including Palestine. Glancy, *Slavery*, 3–7. See also Horsley, *Slave Systems*, 19–66. Horsley criticizes academics in the field of classics for treating slavery as a humane institution rather than recognizing its cruel and inhuman nature.

6. Goodman, *Rome and Jerusalem*, 237.

oil, wheat, cattle, chariots, and bodies. His discomfort with this designation for slaves is revealed by the additional phrase "and human souls."[7]

Slaves were forced to display their naked bodies for inspection at the time of purchase.[8] Slaveholders had the right to abuse their slaves physically and verbally virtually without limitations. The corporal punishment of slaves took place in public to produce shame and pain, and to deter further acts of disobedience or insolence in the household.[9] It was impossible for female slaves to protect their bodies from the sexual abuse of the master, his family, and his guests.[10] An infant born to a slave mother had no legal paternity. The slave mother had no right to raise her child. She might see the infant or young child sold to another slaveholder. Slaves were sometimes used for public entertainment, either as prey for wild beasts, or forced to fight to the death as gladiators in the ring. In summary, slaves lost all control over their bodies. They lived in perpetual shame and powerlessness.

The trade in slaves was immense, and the institution of slavery was built into the economic structures that maintained the elite class. The Roman Emperor Augustus imposed a tax of 2 percent on the sale of slaves in order to raise money for his military ambitions.[11] Slave markets sold prisoners of war, members of defeated populations, debtors, abandoned children, and kidnapped victims of slave traders. Some women and men were born into slavery and from birth were part of their master's property. Fortunate slaves might work for freedom through the process of manumission. However, even after legal release, they lived with a stigma of dishonor and shame that was passed down to their children.[12]

There might be reason to hope that the treatment of slaves was significantly more humane in Palestine, since the Torah reminds the Hebrew people that they suffered as slaves in Egypt and were liberated by God, who heard their cries. Slave owners were instructed not to use harshness in treating their Jewish slaves. Male and female slaves were to be released after six years of labor and provided with provisions to establish a new life

---

7. Rev 18:11–13.

8. Glancy, *Slavery*, 86.

9. Slaveholders could hire professionals that specialized in whipping and torture in order to inflict pain and shame (Ibid., 102).

10. Ibid., 17–23.

11. Goodman, *Jerusalem and Rome*, 238. He cites Cassius, *Dio*, 55.31.

12. Rabbi Johannan advised against trusting the descendants of a former slave until the sixteenth generation after attaining freedom. Quoted in Jeremias, *Jerusalem*, 337, note 106.

in freedom.[13] In addition to the ancient Exodus tradition, there were more recent memories of the horrors of slavery. People in post-exilic Palestine feared slave traders from Tyre and Sidon, who abducted people and sold them in Greece.[14] Peasants felt threatened by wealthy members of their own communities, who could require them to give up their daughters and sons as slaves as payment for defaulted loans.[15] At the beginning of the Roman occupation of Palestine, after the siege of Jerusalem in 63 BCE, the general Pompey transported thousands of Jews to Rome as slaves. Approximately twenty years later, another Roman general, Cassius Longinus, sold the people of Gophna, Emmaus, Lydda, and Thamna into slavery because they were tardy in remitting tribute to the empire.[16]

Unfortunately, neither Torah provisions nor bitter experience modified the treatment of slaves owned by Jewish masters. The Wisdom of Sirach, written in the second century BCE, advised slaveholders that rest for a slave would give rise to thoughts of liberty, whereas fetters, racks, and torture would ensure productive obedience.[17] The apocryphal work known as Pseudo-Phocylides[18] took for granted the use of women slaves as concubines.[19] Philo recognized that Jewish masters followed the compulsions of nature and were likely to impregnate female slaves.[20] Women who had been freed from slavery were regarded as prostitutes by rabbis because of the virtual certainty of sexual exploitation during their enslavement.[21] This survey suggests that slavery should not be confused with modern ideas of the role of voluntary, paid servants.

·One final point needs to be made before moving to the next theme. Slave owners lived in constant anxiety about armed uprisings of slaves. Sparticus led a rebellion of almost seventy thousand slaves that threatened the Roman Empire in 72–70 BCE. After the death of Herod the Great, his palace in Jericho was plundered by former slaves who gained access to

---

13. Deut 15:12–18; Exod 21:2–6.

14. Joel 3:4–6.

15. Neh 5:1–5.

16. After the fall of Jersualem in 70 CE, slave markets were so glutted by Jewish slaves that a woman or man was worth no more than a horse.

17. Sir 33.25–30.

18. This document is dated between 100 BCE to 100 CE.

19. *Sentence* 181.

20. *Spec. Leg.* 2.233.

21. Jeremias, *Jerusalem,* 336.

weapons.[22] Later, in the Jewish War of 66–70 CE, slaves formed a significant portion of the rebel army motivated by the promise of emancipation.[23] It seems that a significant number of slaves did not accept "their status" without questioning the existence of slavery. In all probability, their attitudes were much closer to the feelings of Balram Halwal, who killed his master in order to experience, however briefly, liberation from servitude.

The Hebrew Tradition of the Slave as a Servant of Yahweh

First-century Palestinian audiences were also influenced by their faith traditions as they listened to the stories of slaves told by Jesus. Scriptural descriptions of the covenant relationship between Yahweh and his people often employ the vocabulary of servants and slaves to express their different positions and roles.[24] An early example is found in the Song of Moses, which describes the newly liberated slaves as God's servant/slaves who stand under his care (Deut 32:43 MT). Though Yahweh freed Hebrew slaves from the Empire of Egypt, they were to exercise their freedom as slaves of his household.

The image of the servant/slave of Yahweh found in Isaiah 40–66 is particularly important for the slave parables. On one hand, the nation and its leaders are presented as servants who are blind and deaf.[25] However, God's mission is accomplished by another slave/servant who establishes his rule and acts to save the oppressed.[26] The slave/servant of Yahweh becomes a light to the Gentiles so that God's salvation may reach to the ends of the earth.[27] This mission is costly. The slave/servant of Yahweh suffers marginalization, rejection, suffering, and death. In Isaiah 40–66, the slave/servant's faithfulness exposes him to humiliation and violence at the hands of powerful people intent on defending the status quo. It would have been

---

22. Josephus, *Ant* 17.273–76; *Wars* 2.57–59.

23. Josephus, *Wars* 5.443; 503–13

24. The term *'bd* and its cognates conveyed the idea of relative powerlessness before a superior who could require loyalty and service. The *'bd* word group is often translated into English with nouns such as "slave," "servant," and "service" and the verb "to serve." The word group can be used of the nation as a whole or individuals, such as patriarchs, kings and prophets who owe loyalty and obedient service to God.

25. Isa 42:18–20.

26. Isa 40:9–11; 42:1–9; 49:1–7; 50:4–9; 52:7; 52:13—53:12.

27. Isa 49:5–6.

natural to connect Jesus' message of God's rule and his stories of slaves with the slave/servant tradition from the book of Isaiah.

I propose that these two streams, the culture of slavery and the image of the slave/servant of Yahweh, provide the historical frame of reference for the slave parables. We can assume that the mention of slavery would have evoked emotions of fear and shame among Jesus' listeners. Slaves were dehumanized and suffered physical and psychological violence from slave-holders and their families. No one dreamed of being a slave any more than Vikram Halwal aspired for his son to be a bondservant in the household of a wealthy family. The motifs of the slave/servant of Yahweh would have connected God's transforming work of justice and mercy with the rejection, persecution, and even violent death of his slave/servant.[28]

Slave Parables in Luke's Gospel

Nine parables of the third gospel feature slaves in either major or minor roles.[29] The slaves of these narratives perform menial tasks, work long hours, and are subject to violent abuse. A small minority have been promoted to managerial responsibilities for absentee masters. Five of the nine slave parables will be examined in the remainder of this chapter.[30]

Before entering the text, I want to touch on two objections that modern readers may raise in regard to the slave parables.[31] The first is that the role of the slaveholder has frequently been understood as a representation of God. The second is that historically the church has used these biblical passages to justify the institution of slavery. I have been aware of these concerns in my research and hope that they are addressed in the treatment of the narratives. Here, I merely want to emphasize that the slave analogy was useful in first-century Palestine precisely because it was shocking and

28. This is an important point of Lukan theology. Joseph Fitzmyer has demonstrated that motifs associated with the slave/servant of Isaiah are used in Luke–Acts to describe Jesus and Paul (*Luke I–IX*, 211–13).

29. The parable of the unjust steward (16:1–13) could possibly be added to this list. However, the relatively light punishment for his misbehavior suggests a free man who was hired to act as manager rather than a slave who would have faced at least the whip.

30. This book does not treat two parables in which slaves play a minor role: the prodigal son (15:11–24) and the tenants of the vineyard (20:9–18). The great banquet (14:16–24) and the slave who defies a king (19:11–27) are each given a complete chapter, although the slave's role is incidental in the first narrative.

31. Schottroff, *Parables*, 171.

powerful enough to create a wild space in which members of the movement could contemplate the costly dimensions of loyalty and obedience to God. The comparison of discipleship with slavery encourages a present sense of solidarity with those who are oppressed and a past connection with the slave/servant of Yahweh. These stories remind us that there is no room for motivations of personal honor, wealth, power, and privilege in the movement of Jesus. His followers are called to be models of humility and service.

A Cluster of Four Slave Parables (12:35–48)

This composite passage created by the evangelist can be likened to four snapshots or photos of slaves in first-century Palestine. The scenarios are narrated without detail.[32] The four images are brought together by the evangelist in a way that allows the theme of each parable to enrich the others and provoke thought about what it means to serve God in a broken world. These plots are located in households where slaves live and work under the uncontested authority of a single male figure.[33] The variety of terms used for slaves and the brief descriptions offer insights into their positions and experiences in first-century Palestine

Snapshot One:
Slaves Waiting for Their Master's Return (12:35–38)

Be dressed for action and have your lamps lit; be like those who are waiting for their master to return from the banquet,[34] so that they may open the door for him as soon as he comes and knocks. Blessed are those slaves whom the master finds alert when he comes; truly I tell you, he will fasten his belt and have them sit down to eat, and he will come and serve them. If he comes during

32. It may be helpful to remember that the Hebrew term *mashal* and the Greek word *parabole* were flexible and their meanings included proverbs, aphorisms, similitude, metaphors, and stories. The parables in this section are not narratives in the usual sense of the word.

33. The senior man of the household (*paterfamilias*) exercised authority over family members, salaried servants, and slaves.

34. The Greek word *gamos* could be used for formal banquets that were not associated with weddings.

the second or the third watch[35] and finds them so, blessed are those slaves.

As the first in the series of four parables, this story functions as a defining lens through which the others are meant to be read. It begins with a command, addressing the listeners as if they were slaves under orders to remain awake and prepared to serve, even during the third watch of the night (02:00–06:00 hours). The wealthy slaveholder has left his home to participate in a formal banquet that may last until dawn. The slaves of the household must remain alert with their lamps lit in order to serve the needs of the master when he returns and knocks on the outer door.

The demand for slaves to stay awake strikes one as a cruel display of power illustrating the authority of a slaveholder. The audience is ambushed by how the rest of the story unfolds. There is an astonishing twist at 12:37 when a blessing is pronounced on the slaves.[36] The blessing is introduced with the solemn words: "truly, I say to you,"[37] because the pronouncement and the subsequent actions of the slave owner are counter-intuitive to the master-slave relationship in the social world of the audience. The blessing is not that slaves are privileged to lose sleep and serve the slaveholder when their bodies crave rest, but that the master returns from the banquet and prepares for work by fastening a belt around his robe. He then takes up the duties of a slave and treats the slaves as if they were the masters. In this reversal, the slaves are invited to recline in the dining room of the villa while the master serves them food and wine.[38] The last become first. By treating his slaves as superiors worthy of service, the slave owner tramples upon the prevailing code of honor and class distinctions.[39] This amazing story takes the whip from the master's hand and replaces it with trays of food that he carries to serve to his waiting slaves, who are reclining in the dining room.

---

35. The translation departs from the NRSV in order to retain the original reference to the second and third watches of the night found in the Greek text.

36. Slaves, living at the bottom of the social order, were not considered to be recipients of God's favor.

37. The phrase draws attention to a surprising or difficult saying (Marshall, *Luke*, 536).

38. Slaves would have entered the dining area only to clean or to serve food to the master and his guests.

39. Herman Hendrickx observes that such an inversion of roles would threaten the institution of slavery and the whole social structure in which it existed. Hendricks, *Third Gospel, Volume Three*, 237.

Luke's motif of the social reversal of God's transforming rule figures in this opening snapshot. Unfortunately, our familiarity with the story often negates the shock of the master's actions, which turn the culture of slavery on its head. The story invites members of the movement to imagine themselves as slaves who owe duties of obedience to God. Yet the relationship between God and those who serve under his authority is not the typical master-slave relationship, for the slaveholder's scandalous humility accords extraordinary dignity and honor to his slaves.[40]

Snapshot 2: A Slave Responsible for His Master's Household (12:39–40)

"But know this: if the manager of the household[41] had known at what hour the thief was coming, he would not have let them them dig through the walls of the house.[42] You also must be ready, for the Son of Man is coming at an unexpected hour."

This snapshot features a slave whose duties include ensuring the security of his master's household.[43] We should probably think of several buildings on a property. The thieves may be social bandits supported by the local population and perhaps assisted by slaves on the inside of the compound who have nothing to lose.[44] The danger to the estate owner is not an armed attack, but rather robbery expedited by the quiet excavation of the mud-brick walls of the household buildings. The slave who manages the security of such a property needs to exercise constant vigilance because he is held responsible for all losses.

40. The theme of the master who serves is found again in a saying unique to the third gospel. "For which is the greater, the one who sits at the table, or the one who serves? Is it not the one who sits at the table? But I among you as the one who serves" (Luke 22:7).

41. The NRSV translates *oikodespotes* as owner of the house. While this is possible, a more probable meaning is the head steward or manager of the household. See Hendrickx, *Third Gospel, Volume Three*, 238.

42. The translation, "dig through," attempts to express the literal meaning of the Greek verb *diorusso* (BADG, *Lexicon*, 198).

43. Slaves often rose to positions of significant responsibility within a household because they were less expensive than paid employees and feared the retribution of their master (Schottroff, *Parables*, 176).

44. Hanson and Oakman, *Palestine*, 87.

The parable exhorts the audience gathered around Jesus to be vigilant about the coming of the Son of Man. In Luke's gospel, the Son of Man is linked with the arrival and establishment of God's rule.[45] Just as a slave who serves as manager of a household must be prepared for the threat of thieves, so also must members of the movement conduct their lives with the awareness that God's sovereign judgment is at hand. Earlier, the parable of the seed and soils warned about the distractions of cares, riches, and pleasures (8:14). This slave story simply repeats, in a different way, the theme of hearing, obeying, and living productively. Members of the movement cannot simply drift through life. They are required to be attentive to the demands of God's rule and their duties within his service.

Snapshot 3: The Ration Manager (12:41–46)

> Peter said, "Lord, are you telling this parable for us or for everyone?" And the Lord said, "Who then is the faithful and prudent manager whom his master will put in charge of his slaves, to give them their allowance of food at the proper time? Blessed is that slave whom his master will find at work when he arrives. Truly I tell you, he will put that one in charge of all his possessions. But if that slave says to himself, 'My master is delayed in coming,' and if he begins to beat the other slaves, men and women, and to eat and drink and get drunk, the master of that slave will come on a day when he does not expect him and at an hour that he does not know, and will cut him in pieces, and put him with the unfaithful."

This snapshot, like the former, features a slave who is given significant responsibility within the household of a master.[46] In both stories, the master is absent from the household and, accordingly, the slave is entrusted with duties under conditions of minimal supervision. Readers might imagine a rural estate, with the slaveholder making occasional visits. The central concern in this parable is the nutritional needs of fellow slaves, rather than the protection of assets from thieves. Apart from some stylistic variations,

---

45. The association of the son of man and the kingdom of God already existed in Dan 7.13–14. The son of man sayings in Luke are connected with the themes of the mission of Jesus (5:24; 6:5, 22; 7:34; 9:26, 58; 11:30; 12:8–10)) and his sufferings (9:22, 44; 18:31). Significantly, after chapter 12 the emphasis falls on the coming of the son of man as judge (17:22, 24, 26, 30; 18:8; 21:27, 36; 22:69).

46. This parable and the former can be attributed to Q. The Matthean parable is found in Matt 24:45–51.

Luke's account differs from its Matthean counterpart in the question posed by Peter (12:41) and the vocabulary of slavery. The evangelist introduces four terms for slaves that are not found in the parallel text. An *oikonomos* is a slave who manages the work and needs of other slaves in a household.[47] The noun *therapeia* refers to domestic slaves whose primary duties involve catering to the needs of the master and his family. The use of this term suggests a significant number of slaves in the household.[48] Later, in 12:45, the slaves of the household or estate are classified by gender as male slaves (*paides*) and female slaves (*paidiskai*). This division recognizes the place of women both among slaves in Palestine and within the membership of Jesus' movement.

Peter's question in 12:41, "are you telling this story for us [apostles] or for everyone?" casts him in the position of the leader or spokesperson of the group. Jesus responds with a counter-question, "Who proves to be the faithful and prudent manager who will be appointed by his master over the other slaves with the purpose of ensuring that they are given appropriate rations for each day at regular times?"[49] This question creates the transition to the snapshot of a slave who has been granted privileges and responsibilities that distinguish him from his peers. As ration manager, he is entrusted with the duty of ensuring that adequate food is served to other slaves. This position elevates an ordinary slave to a place of power in the household of an absentee slaveholder, for food was a precious commodity for slaves who labored long hours under adverse conditions.

The blessing pronounced in 12:43 reiterates in form and content the blessings found in the first slave parable (12:37–38). Once again, the announcement of God's blessing upon a slave is unexpected and jolting. Listeners capture the point of comparison between slaves and disciples as an answer to Peter's question. The master's favor rests upon the household manager, who is faithful in his absence by caring for the needs of other slaves. Certain members of Jesus' movement are given positions that require them to be attentive to and serve the needs of others in the community. The storyline is that service to fellow slaves will be noticed and rewarded with a promotion within the household. The clear implication is that God takes

---

47. It is likely that the evangelist substituted *oikonomos* for *doulos* in 12:43 (compare Matt 25:45). See Fitzmyer, *Luke X–XXIV*, 989.

48. Hultgren, *Parables*, 165.

49. The Greek word *sitometrion* (measured amount) is found only here in the New Testament. Matthew has the more common word *trophe*, which means food.

note of humble and attentive concern leaders take in regard to the needs of other followers of Jesus.

The parable takes a decidedly negative turn in 12:45–46, which portrays a slave who reasons that his master will be delayed for an extended period. Taking advantage of his position of authority without immediate accountability, the ration manager breaks the code of solidarity among slaves in order to dominate and abuse them.[50] He deliberately disregards both the directions of his master and the needs of his fellow slaves in order to enjoy the temporary privileges of power through eating, drinking, and intoxication. The description corresponds with the aspirations of the rich fool in 12:19 and the fate of the seed that falls among the thorns in the parable of the sower. It is clear that Jesus views an excessive and self-centered lifestyle as a dangerous character flaw and a threat to his movement.

The arrival of the slaveholder at an unknown date and time creates a link with the previous two parables, which portrayed the return of a master from a banquet and the appearance of robbers. The judgment is severe. The slaveholder orders the death of the abusive ration manager, the desecration of his body, and the placement of his remains with the body parts of other disobedient slaves. Such drastic punishment of slaves was not unknown in ancient Mediterranean settings.[51]

The message of this parable is related to the social responsibilities of disciples in positions of leadership within the movement of Jesus. The twelve apostles would have been viewed as people entrusted with special privileges and duties in the early stages of the post-resurrection mission. As the movement expanded in the apostolic age, other men and women were given positions of leadership and responsibility. Faithfulness to God requires attending to the needs of vulnerable people with an attitude of humility that recognizes that those who serve are not fundamentally different from those who are served. Abuses of authority, the self-serving use of resources, and the failure to act responsibly toward others will not be tolerated by God. The consequences will be severe for members of the movement who abuse their positions of power and live in arrogant disregard for the dignity and needs of others.

---

50. Sexual violence may be implied in this description. His actions imitate the customary practices of slaveholders in his cultural world. In other words, he aspires to dominate in the manner that he has witnessed and experienced domination.

51. Marshall, *Luke*, 543.

Snapshot 4: Slaves Informed of Their Master's Intentions (12:47–48)

> That slave who knew what his master wanted, but did not prepare himself or do what was wanted, will receive a severe beating. But one who did not know and did what deserved a beating will receive a light beating. From everyone to whom much has been given, much will be required; and from one to whom much has been entrusted, even more will be demanded.

Nolland appropriately describes this section as a mini-parable with a double proverb,[52] as it builds on the previous three slave stories and brings them to a conclusion. The first slave hears the orders of his master, but intentionally makes no preparations to carry out his duties. The master will inevitably authorize a severe whipping for this negligent slave. In the second case, a slave inadvertently does something that merits punishment. The master orders a reduced penalty, while still establishing an example. These scenarios from the social world of masters and slaves do not imply that God is like a slaveholder who uses a whip. The analogy simply makes the point that knowledge creates accountability.

The emphasis of this section falls on the principle of God's rule expressed in the final verse. Those who have been entrusted with comparatively greater resources live under a corresponding obligation to render a higher level of service. More is expected from those who have been given special gifts. Comparisons with the accomplishments of others are neither meaningful nor helpful. The role of the slave/servant of Yahweh in Isaiah points us toward one who poured out his life in bearing the infirmities and evil of the world around him (Isa 52:17—53:12).

In summary, the slave parables of Luke 12 draw upon social practices in first-century Palestine and Isaiah's tradition of the slave/servant of Yahweh. The abhorrent abuses associated with slavery create a sobering perspective on the meaning of living fruitful lives and participating in God's work of transformation. The four slave stories do not define evil as breaches of regulations and conventions surrounding purity and sacrifices. Rather, judgment falls on slaves who fail to fulfill the demands of their masters—and, by analogy, on disciples who do not put into practice the teaching of Jesus. The third parable emphasizes the social dimensions of caring for the needs of those who are most vulnerable as a service to God. The image

52. Nolland, *Commentary, Luke 9.21—18.34,* 704.

of the slaveholder who carries food to his slaves reclining in the banquet room contrasts starkly with the socially accepted practices of masters who compelled obedience through public beatings and humiliation. In this way, the first story creates an image of God who is not ashamed to act as a slave and who calls us to lay down our lives in service to his rule. He sustains us through the grace that flows into our lives when we receive provisions from his hands in the dining room where we recline in his presence.

The Fifth Parable: A Faithful Slave Who has Earned No Special Rewards (17:7–10)

> Who among you would say to your slave who has just come in from ploughing or tending sheep in the field, "Come here at once and take your place at the table?" Would you not rather say to him: "Prepare supper for me and, after you dress appropriately,[53] serve me while I eat and drink; later you may eat and drink?" Do you thank the slave for doing what was commanded? So you also, when you have done all that you were ordered to do, say, "We are worthless slaves; we have done only what we ought to have done!"

I agree with Kenneth Bailey's comment that this parable's significance far outweighs the attention it usually receives from commentators and preachers.[54] The story is drawn from one of Luke' special sources containing sayings and events not found in Matthew and Mark. Commentaries offer discussion about the evangelist's role in shaping the tradition for use in his gospel. The storyline is straightforward. A slave returns from his duty in the fields at the end of a normal workday. He is not allowed to rest or eat before he prepares dinner for his master, dresses appropriately to enter the dining area, and serves the food and drink until the master completes his meal. The details depict slavery as it existed in first-century Palestine. Slaveholders demanded unchallenged obedience and long hours of work under the constant threat of the whip. The personal needs of slaves were given little attention in comparison with the requirements of the master and his family. Slaves existed to work for those who owned them, and their only legitimate aspiration was to render diligent and faithful service.

53. The Greek verb *perizonnumi* means literally to fasten one's belt around the outer garment in order to work. However, it can also have a more figurative meaning of dressing appropriately. The second meaning seems more likely here. See ibid., 842.

54. Bailey, *Poet and Peasant*, 114.

This parable also provides insight into the pervasive nature of slavery in Galilee and Judea. The setting is not an elite household, such as those depicted in the slave parables of Luke 12 or in the story of the great banquet (14:15–24). This household is rural and of modest means, with a single slave who performs both farming and domestic duties. The acquisition of the slave was likely an economic decision that saved the property owner from paying wages to day laborers.

The structure of the parable is formed by three rhetorical questions posed by Jesus to the audience.[55] The first question asks about the probability of the master issuing an invitation to a slave returning from the fields to recline in the dining room and enjoy a meal.[56] The direct nature of the question engages members of the audience who are familiar with the working conditions of slaves. The very idea of such an invitation to slaves would threaten the economic and social system built around slavery. Thus the answer to Jesus' question is obvious, and we can imagine the ripples of laughter in the audience.

The second question is a logical response to the first: Will the master not order the slave to prepare dinner in the kitchen, dress appropriately, and serve the master his food and wine before attending to his own needs?[57] The Greek verb *deipneo*, used for eating in 17:8, often carried the connotation of formal banquets.[58] The use of this verb in relatively humble circumstances, along with the demands of the master, emphasize the social distance that separates the slaveholder and his slave. Each and every day, the slave is expected to work in the fields during daylight hours. In the evenings, he is required to prepare a formal meal and serve it to his master. The slave is allowed to take care of himself only after his duties are completed.

The third question concerns the obligation of the slaveholder to express gratitude to his slave. Once again, the audience hears a ludicrous idea that elicits smiles and laughter. T. W. Manson's comment is apt: "Even

---

55. Rhetorical questions with obvious answers are sometimes used by speakers because they have greater power than simple direct statements. Resseguie, *Narrative Criticism*, 60.

56. The reader may note the resonance with the shocking parable of the master who serves in Luke 12:35–38. The phrase, "who of you," is used at the beginning of other Lukan parables to attract the attention of the listeners (11:5, 11; 14:28; 15:4).

57. The grammatical construction of the sentence with *diakonei* in the present imperative tense suggests a translation such as: "Prepare the food, dress properly, and serve me continuously while I eat and drink (BADG, 335).

58. Marshall, *Luke*, 647.

when he has done all this, he has not put his master under any obligation to him. He has not given anything that the master was not already entitled to demand."[59]

A dramatic shift takes place at 17:10, when the duties of slaves are compared with the reality of serving God in the movement of Jesus. Discipleship and faithful service require humility, uncompromised loyalty, and simple hard work. People engaged in God's work of transformation do not negotiate terms of service and rewards. Faithfulness to one's sense of call will inevitably lead to periods of intense demands and sacrifices. There are times when we need to recall that Jesus offered his followers the graphic image of a person who carries a cross following behind him.[60]

Reflection

I begin this reflection by noting that several people advised against including the slave parables in my research and writing. They felt, quite correctly, that the history of slavery was abusive, cruel, shameful, and inhuman. I was cautioned that the association of slavery with faith was open to misunderstanding and objections from people with a history of marginalization and oppression. I want to be sensitive (along with my readers) to these concerns. I am afraid that my justification for this chapter was seldom well-articulated in early discussions. The truth is that I found them meaningful in my vocation as a leader of a Christian community development team, whose members were called to work in the marginal areas of their countries. The pressures were intense. Budgets were tight and our colleagues served in places that most people would chose to avoid. At times, I was privileged to join them in those locations and to witness the costly nature of their work. I ask the readers for tolerance in allowing me to make this section personal in nature.

The first point of this reflection deals directly with the analogy that links service in God's rule with first-century slavery. The comparison forcefully reminds us that the call to work for personal and social transformation is never easy. The challenges of the vocational choices we have made can leave us confused, exhausted, wounded by betrayals, and misunderstood. It is impossible to establish boundaries that cannot be broken. Hours of work

59. Manson, *Sayings*, 302.

60. It should be remembered that the cross was a symbol of the ultimate power of the Empire over slaves and rebels.

are not easily confined to a schedule. Budgets and resources are strained, requiring additional sacrifices and creativity. I used to find myself inwardly laughing when young idealists commented on the fulfillment and satisfaction that they imagined I felt on a daily basis. Such naïve comments reveal ignorance about the painful reality of needing to reduce project budgets to match resources, the disappointment of the loss of gifted staff members, the agony of questions about the integrity of partners in the field, difficult discussions about initiatives that under-perform and fail to reach expectations, or the desperation of lying sick in hotel rooms in foreign countries. In my darkest moments, I needed the light of the slave parables to remind me that my responsibilities and tasks were given to me by a master who rules a kingdom and holds me accountable to perform small tasks. He expects me to be faithful and dedicated to the work he has given me. There were times when I needed to consider myself less as the employee of an organization and more as a slave of the king.

The second point of reflection requires more explanation because of its importance for the life of organizations that work in the margins of communities. Leaders and managers of these organizations are entrusted with special responsibilities in their relationships with beneficiaries, colleagues, and supporters. They may have been appointed to their positions because of higher levels of training and experience. The organizations believe that they have specialized knowledge about what needs to be done and a strong sense of how the work should be accomplished. Leaders usually receive a higher level of compensation than other members of their teams because of the weight of their duties. They are accorded privileges that come with authority and responsibility. The slave parables remind us that managers and leaders are required to maintain solidarity with the members of their teams while discharging their special responsibilities with attention to detail.

The story of the ration master is particularly meaningful in thinking about the way leaders manage themselves and care for their colleagues. The slave becomes intoxicated by the temporary authority he has been given and mistreats his peers, who depend upon him. The violent and merciless conclusion of this story, whiles shocking, stresses the importance of the way leaders handle human relationships. It can seem that some board members and senior leaders of faith-based organizations struggle with a sense of inferiority in comparison to management models and corporate executives from the business world. They can be attracted to myths of "kick-ass" CEOs, vice-presidents and directors who claim to achieve dramatic results.

Christian leaders may pay attention to the hype but miss the details that can include the bullying of employees, the wholesale dismissal of workers, and the reorganization of entire departments in order to slash costs and achieve a quick turn-around. Too often, the human cost is immense and the results are disappointing. Most of us know of Christian churches and ministries that have been severely damaged by arrogant and assertive leadership. The business models that exist in a competitive context of short-term profits are often not appropriate for transformational change in the borderlands.

I want to be careful about what I say here. Leaders are accountable for results. Organizations and employees need periodic renewal. There are times when managers must make changes in the composition of their teams. The reluctance to make such decisions may prolong the agony and extend the damage of poor performance. However, team members deserve to be treated fairly and compassionately, even when difficult decisions are being made. Most employees will go to the wall for leaders who treat them with dignity, respect, and understanding. Building these relationships takes time and energy.

I have thought about two contrasting stories while writing this reflection. In the first, sixteen senior executives left a college during a president's four-year term. Eight of these people were fired, including three that had been personally hired by the president. One of those who allegedly chose to leave reported that he was told: "You are no longer welcome here, and here is your offer." The cost of severance payments pushed the college into a serious deficit. The personal damage cannot be calculated. Ironically, the crisis leading to the president's departure was related to abuses of his personal expense account rather than the treatment of senior employees. Evidently, money was more important than people to the board members of the college. In the second story, a staff member of a small international organization had disappointing results in her fundraising responsibilities. She and the director of the department spoke several times about the bottom-line issues and eventually reached a joint decision that it would be best for her to leave the organization. In my conversation, I could sense this woman's deep sense of disappointment about leaving the organization. I was surprised about her concern for the well-being of the director who had been her superior. She had deep respect for his genuine interest in the lives of his team members and the fairness with which he treated people. She hoped he would continue in his position. This second story gives me hope that leaders and managers can attend to the bottom line and also care for the needs of colleagues that serve in their departments.

The third point of my reflection concerns the compulsion for recognition that threatens to compromise the service of some men and women who work for transformation in the margins. The public face of service can become a mask that conceals the inner need to be seen and acknowledged. Perhaps we fear being taken for granted like a cog in a machine. We may feel discouraged or resentful when other colleagues are praised or promoted while our contributions seem to be overlooked. We may find ourselves voicing our opinions in team meetings, even when we have nothing important to contribute, simply because we want our presence to be noticed and recognized. The story of the slave returning from the field to serve his master dinner has led me to moments of regret and repentance. I share the weakness of desiring recognition, and I have noticed this same tendency among other women and men on the teams in which I have served, whether secular or faith-based. The story of the slave returning from the field challenges us to build regular "gut" checks into our spiritual practices that will purify our motives and aspirations. In the end, we are expendable women and men who can only aspire to accomplish faithfully the tasks to which God has called us.

My fourth and final reflection is connected to the first parable in this chapter. Like most of my readers, I have worked long days without ever completing the work on my desk. Most nights, I have taken home a briefcase along with my laptop in order to accomplish a few more tasks that needed attention. I have regularly spent weekends speaking in churches or meeting with groups and then reported to the office on Monday morning. People engaged in transformational work are seized with a passion and a mission. They understand the reality of long hours. Yet this labor is not always joyful. There can periods of resentment in which we question our choices. There are times when we experience deep fatigue and disappointment. In such times, I find it helpful to visualize myself as a slave who, along with others, waits with my lamp lit for the return of the master. Our bodies want rest, but we are under orders to remain attentive and prepared. I share the surprise of my ministry colleagues when the master arrives, smiles, and graciously leads us into the dining room. He tells us to recline and rest. He puts on work clothes and serves us the best food and wine of the household. In my imagination, he calls each of us by name and talks with us one by one. We cannot believe that the master of the household is serving us and taking an interest in our lives. We feel valued and loved by this man, to whom we belong. Memories of the long night are replaced by the warmth of his presence, which we share in community. The parable of the master who acts like a slave reminds us that our compensation for faithful service in a broken and wounded world is to know that we are loved and served by God whose grace is beyond all comprehension. We draw our strength from the times when God draws near to grant us rest, feed our hearts, and restore our spirits.

In the next chapter, we will consider the actions of a slave who publicly exposes the cruel ambitions of a king.

CHAPTER 8

A Slave Who Defies the Orders of a King (Luke 19:11–27)

... one of the biggest problems in any revolution isn't the rich at all: it's the poor people. They've taken everything away from the poor. And among the things they have taken away is the sense to understand their situation, or, using the Gospel words, they've taken away their ears. —ANTIDIO[1]

... the priest and bishops keep prudent silence in the face of the crimes that happen in this country, because they say that it's not proper for them to get involved in politics. —FELIPE[2]

It's clear that for the sake of justice we have to risk even our bodies. They can kill the body but they can't kill the cause for which we fight. —ALEJANDRO[3]

Stories from the Margins

WHILE TRAVELING IN RURAL Rwanda with my colleagues, Gato Munymasoko[4] and Bruno Soucy, we stopped the truck along the road at the site of the Nyange Girls' Secondary School. Gato shared that in 1997, he

1. Cardenal, *Solentiname*, 3:232.

2. Ibid, 1:255.

3. Ibid.

4. Gato Munyamosoko was the recipient of the 2015 Baptist World Alliance Congress Quinquennial Human Rights Award.

had been principal of another boarding school in the same region. There had been frequent incursions of armed Interahamwe soldiers from camps across the nearby border in the Democratic Republic of Congo.[5] The survivors of the 1994 Tutsi genocide lived in constant fear of attack by Hutu militants, who remained committed to continuing the work of ethnic cleansing.

The Nyange Girls' School was run by the Catholic Church, and many of the students lived in dormitories on the school property. One night in 1997, Interahamwe troops seized the school compound, forced seventeen students from their beds, and told them to assemble in the school cafeteria. Hutu girls were then ordered to separate themselves from their Tutsi classmates. When no one moved, the militia leader repeated the order. The girls remained together as a group. The order was repeated a third time. One girl replied, "There are not Hutus and Tutsis at this school. There are only Rwandans." The commander responded to her defiance by ordering that all the girls be beaten and killed along with a nun from Belgium. Two days later, a man confessed to authorities that he had been among the killers, and he related the story of the girls' courage.[6]

As Bruno, Gato, and I continued our journey in silence, I reflected on great courage of adolescent girls in developing a "hidden transcript" of resistance ('we are all Rwandans") in seclusion (a rural school) and using it to confront a " public transcript" of exclusion (Rwanda should be ethnically pure). The young woman's words of solidarity unmasked the cruel and perverse violence of the genocidaires, who had traded their humanity for the power of weapons and an ideology of death. The students' refusal to comply with the orders of those who temporarily held ultimate power cost them their lives. I hope that few of my readers will face such life and death decisions. However, the call to transformational work in the margins requires us to deal with the structures of violence and oppression that build walls that force people to remain in the borderlands. Faithfulness to God's rule creates conflict with the powers that maintain the status quo of disparity and injustice.

5. The Interahamwe movement was composed of young Hutu men who had been indoctrinated by the Hutu power movement and trained by the Rwandan army to kill. The frightening rage of the Interahamwe is described in Romeo Dallaire's book, *Shake Hands*, 179, 186, 234, 367, 392, 456, 521.

6. Philip Gourevitch, author of a prize-winning book on Rwanda, recounted the story of the Nyange Girls' Secondary School as the singular event that gave him hope for the future of Rwanda. Gourevitch, *We Wish to Inform You*, 352–53.

Critiques of Power in the Hebrew Scriptures

The previous chapter considered the theme of the slave/servant of Yahweh whose ultimate loyalty is to God's justice. I want to return to the Hebrew Scriptures to explore the relationship between a commitment to God and confrontations with political power. I remind readers that the conflict between prophets and rulers was part of the cultural heritage of Jesus and shaped his understanding of the mission to which God had called him.

Kings in Israel and Judah were required to keep a copy of the Torah in their presence as a sign that they, like all citizens of their rule, lived under the authority of God. However, monarchs frequently abused their power and oppressed their subjects. The priest Samuel warned the Hebrew people that the popular demand to be led by a monarch would mean that young men would owe compulsory military service, young women would be taken to work in the palace, farm produce would be required for the royal banquet tables, and the kings' estates would be cultivated by forced labor.[7] Samuel's speech culminated with the dire prediction of a new form of slavery that would be imposed by the political and military power of the nation's kings: "*You shall be his slaves*. And in that day you will cry out because of your king, whom you have chosen for yourselves; but the Lord will not answer you in that day."[8]

The biblical story of Jeremiah illustrates the conflict between a powerful monarch and a prophet who critiques his abuses of royal power. In the sixth century BCE, the throne of Judah was passed from Josiah, a righteous king, to his son, Shallum (also known as Jehoahaz).[9] The country was caught in a prolonged crisis due to its position as an insignificant nation in a strategic location threatened by the empires of Egypt, Assyria, and Babylon. The danger did not deter Shallum from demanding increased tributes (taxes) from the population and reintroducing forced labor to extend and upgrade the royal palace. Jeremiah publicly criticized the king for building a house by means of oppression, shedding innocent blood, and failing to protect the poor and needy.

> Woe to him who builds his house by unrighteousness,
>
> and his upper rooms by injustice;
>
> who makes his neighbors work for nothing,

7. 1 Sam 8:11–17.

8. 1 Sam 8:17b–18. Italics added.

9. 2 Kings 23:31.

and does not give them their wages;

who says, "I will build myself a spacious house

with large upper rooms,"

and who cuts out windows for it,

panelling it with cedar,

and painting it with vermilion.

Are you a king

because you compete in cedar?

Did not your father eat and drink

and do justice and righteousness?

Then it was well with him.

He judged the cause of the poor and needy;

then it was well.

Is not this to know me? says the Lord.[10]

Shallum was removed by the Egyptians, who installed his brother, Joiakim. Under Joiakim's reign, the policies of oppression and exploitation increased to new levels. Jeremiah's message and actions challenged the monarchy, the temple, and the leading families who profited from the system of forced servitude. As a result of Jeremiah's loyalty to the Torah's vision of social justice, he was marginalized, accused of being a traitor, suffered from periods of intense depression, stared down threats, and endured beatings and forced confinements.[11] Jeremiah's story reveals how a loyal and robust commitment to Yahweh places those who serve him in positions where they feel compelled to speak into the political, military, and economic power of the state.[12] Jeremiah reminds us that it is dangerous to advocate for justice by critiquing a public transcript of power. As we move into the gospel account, we need to keep in mind the tension between those who hold power and prophets who speak for God.

10. Jer 22:13–16.

11. Jer 20:1–2, 7–18; 26:7–11; 37:11—38:6.

12. Callender, "Servants of God(s) and Servants of Kings," in Callahan, Horsley, Smith eds., *Semeia, 83–4, 77.*

The Jericho Interlude (Luke 18:35—19:27)

The city of Jericho, which was located within walking distance of Jerusalem, was the site of a summer palace built by Herod the Great.[13] A disproportionate number of priests and Levites lived in Jericho because of its relative proximity to the temple. Thus Jericho was firmly fixed in the public transcripts of empire and religion. The arrival of Jesus to Jericho creates an interlude prior to his entrance to Jerusalem. Three significant events occur before Jesus enters Jerusalem: the healing of the blind beggar (18:35–43), the conversion of Zacchaeus (19:1–10), and the parable of the slave who confronts a king (19:11–27). These three components of the Jericho interlude build on one another in preparing the gospel's audience for the final days of Jesus in Jerusalem. The interpretation of the story of the dissenting slave requires attention to the two preceding narratives of this Jericho interlude.

The Blind Beggar (18:35–43)

The blind beggar represents a social group that lives in extreme poverty at the margins of Palestinian society. He cries out to Jesus for help, using the epithet, "son of David," a title that conveys the popular anticipation that Jesus will defeat the nation's enemies and establish a rule of righteousness and peace. The crowd attempts to silence the blind man so that the march toward Jerusalem is not interrupted. However, Jesus stops to give his attention to the beggar, thereby showing his fidelity to the mission announced in the Nazareth synagogue, where he quoted from Isaiah 61.[14] With Jerusalem on the horizon, Jesus continues to speak and act in ways that bring good news to the poor, freedom to prisoners, recovery of sight to the blind, release to the oppressed, and the proclamation of the time of God's favor.

Attentive readers will notice that the theme of blindness connects this healing narrative with the final passion prediction that precedes it. Jesus clearly states that humiliation, beatings, and death at the hands of the Gentiles await him in Jerusalem. Yet the meaning of this saying is hidden from the twelve so that they do not understand (Luke 18:31–34). The deliberate

---

13. Archelaus, the son of Herod the Great, had lived in this palace prior to his father's death in 4 BCE. At that time he traveled to Rome in order to formally request that Caesar Augustus grant him the throne of his father.

14. See Luke 4:18–19.

crafting of the Lukan narrative connects the physical blindness of the beggar with the inability of the disciples to see what will happen in the coming
days.[15] The restoration of sight to the disciples will occur after the resurrection (Luke 24:31).

The Repentance of Zacchaeus (19:1–10)

The healing of the blind man heightens the enthusiasm of the crowd
(18:43). Their fervor and expectancy quickly turn to negative murmuring
when Jesus interacts with Zacchaeus, a chief tax collector, who is described
as wealthy and too short in stature to see over the people who line the road
(19.3). Zacchaeus has gained his wealth by collaborating directly with the
Roman authorities and exploiting his own countrymen. As a result, he has
been socially marginalized for his dishonorable profession. When Jesus
asks Zacchaeus for hospitality, the crowd reacts because it seems discordant
for the son of David, on whom the dreams of national liberation rest, to
share table fellowship with someone who represents Roman oppression.
The surprising nature of the hospitality that Jesus requests leads to further amazement when, after dinner, Zacchaeus states that he is ready to
renounce his participation in the economic policies of the empire. As an act
of repentance, he makes the costly decision to give half of his possessions to
the poor and make four–fold restitution to those he has cheated.

The story of Zacchaeus contrasts starkly with the earlier account of a
member of the elite class who could not part with his possessions in order
to enter God's kingdom (18.18–30). Zacchaeus moves from profitable collaboration with the Roman Empire to the position of a dissident, whose
new life orientation might accurately be described as the love of God and
justice (11.42). Accordingly, Jesus announces, "Today salvation has come
to this house," reaffirming the mission of the Son of man to seek and heal
the lost.[16] The themes of collaboration with power, dramatic repentance,
redemption, and dissident discipleship prepare the audience for the parable
of a slave who challenges the economic policies of a king.

---

15. Fitzmyer, *Luke X–XXIV*, 1214.

16. I understand the Greek verb *sozo* ("to save") here as signifying personal, social
and spiritual transformation in the same way it is used in healing stories.

The Parable of a Slave who Defies the Order of a King (Luke 19:11–27)

Narrative Preface (19:11)

> As they were listening to this, he went on to tell a parable, because he was near Jerusalem, and because they supposed that the kingdom of God was to appear immediately.

This parable is the third and final component of the Jericho interlude before Jesus enters Jerusalem. The crowd is comprised of committed disciples, sympathizers, onlookers, and even opponents. The majority are united in the hope that Jesus will challenge the power of Rome and bring liberation to the Jewish people of Galilee and Judea. Even the surprising announcement of salvation in the home of Zacchaeus could be construed to mean that God is at the point of acting to establish his rule and vanquish the nation's enemies.

I made the observation in earlier chapters that most parables would have been repeated numerous times in varying forms as Jesus adapted his material to different teaching situations and discussions with local audiences. This parable may be the exception, as it is rooted in a specific context that is unique in its nature and importance. The story brings to conclusion the travel narrative that has been an important section of Luke's Gospel (9:51—19:17) in which the disciples are prepared for the coming events in Jerusalem.

The anticipation of a revolutionary showdown in Jerusalem is in the air and reaches an apex of public enthusiasm during the triumphal entry. Gospel readers are aware that Jesus has sought to temper this enthusiasm throughout the journey from Galilee. On the eve of his departure from Galilee, Jesus warned his disciples that powerful people in Jerusalem would kill him and that his followers would need to face the prospect of violent death at the hands of Roman soldiers (9:21–24). The theme of violence is emphasized several times during the journey. Jesus criticizes scribes for their tacit approval of the actions of their ancestors, who murdered the prophets. He states that God will send more prophets and apostles,[17] who will be persecuted and killed (11:47–51). Jesus encourages the crowds not

---

17. The Matthean parallel does not have the word "apostles." The use of this word creates a link with 6:12–16, where the apostles were chosen from a broader group of disciples.

to be intimidated into subservience by armed soldiers and rulers who have the imperial authority to inflict the death penalty. This particular saying reflects a social setting of repression, in which powerful leaders consider members of Jesus' movement to be a threat to national stability. Jesus challenges the disciples to give their ultimate loyalty to God, who values their lives so much that he counts the hairs on their heads. He promises that the Spirit of God will come to their assistance when they are brought before synagogues, rulers, and authorities (12:4–12).

When Jesus is warned that Herod Antipas has issued orders for his death, he states that death threats from Herod's court will not provoke him to seek personal safety. He will press on to Jerusalem because other prophets died in that city (13:31–35). At one point he warns a crowd of painful divisions and betrayals that will take place, even within households. He goes on to link the theme of commitment to his movement with the resolve to face state violence symbolized by the cross, upon which Rome killed escaped slaves and rebels who resisted the power of the empire.[18] He then offers a double parable about a tower builder and a king going to war who must determine if they can pay the cost of their ambitions (14:25–35). Finally, as we have just seen, before entering Jericho, he warns his followers again about betrayal and his impending death at the hands of the Roman procurator and his troops (18:31–24).

A responsible interpretation of the parable must take into account both the apocalyptic expectations of the moment and the theme of violent opposition emphasized in the travel narrative. These two elements provide the context into which Jesus tells a narrative about the defiance of a slave and the horrific execution of citizens who challenge the rule of an exploitive and cruel despot appointed by the emperor in a distant country. Thus the parable offers a warning about the forces that will be unleashed against Jesus and all those who choose to resist rather than to collaborate with the ruling powers of the state, the economy, and the temple.

The Parable: Act 1 (Luke 19:12–14)

So he said, "A nobleman went to a distant country to get royal power for himself and then return. He summoned ten of his slaves,

---

18. The demand to pick up the cross and follow Jesus cannot be tamed down to exclude or minimize the possibility of violent death instigated by men in positions of power.

and gave them ten minas,[19] and said to them, 'Do business with these until I come back.' But the citizens of his country hated him and sent a delegation after him, saying, 'We do not want this man to rule over us.'"

The central figure of the opening scene is a man of noble birth who travels to a distant land to have his right to rule confirmed by a higher power. For members of Jesus' audience, Rome was the only place where such authority could be conferred, and the emperor was the only person who could make this kind of an appointment. A journey to a distant destination implies a prolonged and indeterminate period of absence.

Prior to his departure, the nobleman summons ten of his slaves[20] and entrusts each with one mina.[21] A mina is a sum of money estimated to be roughly equivalent to the wages of a laborer for one hundred days of work.[22] This was not a substantial amount for a person of prominence among the elite minority.[23] A mina represented an appropriate amount to test the performance of a slave with an eye to future duties.[24]

The slaveholder commands the slaves to do business with his money while he travels. To understand what this order entails, it is important to recall that agrarian economies were based on land ownership and farm production.[25] Wealth was acquired by gaining more land, often through foreclosure on defaulted loans. Land that was held by the wealthy could be farmed by day laborers and slaves or leased to peasant farmers, who gener-

---

19. The NRSV employs the translation "pounds." I prefer the original term "minas."

20. I translate *doulos* here as slave rather than servant. Jennifer Glancy has shown that Roman emperors, their appointed territorial rulers, and elite families preferred to use slaves to manage their business interests because they served under submission to the whip and could be motivated by aspirations of manumission as a reward for fruitful service (Glancy, *Slavery*, 114–15). There is a contrast in the story between free citizens, who oppose the prospects of the nobleman's rule, and slaves, who serve under orders.

21. Compare with Matt 25:15, where differing amounts are given according to the ability of each slave.

22. Snodgrass, *Stories with Intent*, 258.

23. A mina was worth one-sixtieth of a talent (Fitzmyer, *Luke X–XXIV*, 1235). Accordingly, the amounts in the Matthean parable of the talents are much more substantial. Snodgrass concludes that Matthew and Luke have two independent parables (*Stories With Intent*, 523, 531).

24. Manson, *Sayings*, 315; Nolland, *Commentary Luke 9:21—18:34*, 914.

25. David A Fiensy, "Ancient Economy and the New Testament," in Neufeld and DeMaris, *Social World*, 194–206. The alternative of investing in shipping and trade entailed high risks and was not favored by the elite families.

ally paid one-quarter to one-half of their production to the landowner. This economic system was oppressive for peasant families, who were burdened with debts to the wealthy, taxes and tributes to Rome, along with temple taxes and tithes. As I have shown in previous chapters, they struggled to survive at a subsistence level. Accordingly, the order to do business entailed finding productive ways to further dominate and squeeze the rural population, with the objective of increasing the wealth of the master. The nobleman's goal is to add to his personal holdings at the expense of the poor. Readers note that the nobleman's ambition is diametrically opposed to Luke's vision of vertical redistribution in favor of the poor, as exemplified by the conversion of Zacchaeus.

The story transitions from the interior of the nobleman's villa to the territory he plans to rule. An influential group of citizens[26] detest the nobleman and seek to thwart his scheme by sending an official delegation to the distant land to present a case against his reign. Their unified message is simple: "We do not wish this man to rule over us." This section of the narrative is grounded in a dangerous political reality. After the death of Herod the Great, his son Archelaus traveled to Rome to make a case for receiving the throne of his father. An official delegation of fifty elders from Jerusalem was commissioned to meet Augustus Caesar and argue that Archelaus was unfit to rule because he was violent, corrupt, and oppressive. As a result of their intervention, the emperor gave Archelaus a diminished title (ethnarch) and restricted the territory under his rule to Judea. Archelaus returned from Rome to Jerusalem and settled score with those who opposed him through beatings and state executions.[27] This allusion to Archelaus and the Roman Emperor clearly establishes the parable as a critique of imperial power. Moreover, it is told immediately before Jesus will enter Jerusalem, where forces of Roman soldiers have been deployed to maintain law and order during the Passover.[28]

26. The Greek construction *hoi de politai*, without the adjective *pas*, means some rather than all (Nolland, *Commentary Luke 9:21—18:34*, 914).

27. See Josephus, *War*, 2.6.1–3; 2.7.3

28. "... the parable is alluding to the political realities of the time, and the cruel and vindictive king of the parable is not an outlandish figure of fiction" (Gonzalez, *Luke*, 223).

The Parable: Act 2 (Luke 19:15–27)

> When he returned, having received royal power, he ordered these slaves, to whom he had given the money, to be summoned so that he might find out what they had gained by trading. The first came forward and said, "Lord, your mina has made ten more minas." He said to him, "Well done, good slave! Because you have been trustworthy in a very small thing, take charge of ten cities." Then the second came, saying, "Lord, your mina has made five minas." He said to him, "And you, rule over five cities." Then the other came, saying, "Lord, here is your mina. I wrapped it up in a piece of cloth, for I was afraid of you, because you are a harsh man; you take what you did not deposit and reap what you did not sow." He said to him, "I will judge you by your own words, you wicked slave! You knew, did you, that I was a harsh man, taking what I did not deposit and reaping what I did not sow? Why then did you not put my money into the bank? Then when I returned, I could have collected it with interest." He said to the bystanders, "Take the mina from him and give it to the one who has ten minas." (And they said to him, "Lord, he has ten minas!") "I tell you, to all those who have, more will be given; but from those who have nothing, even what they have will be taken away. But as for these enemies of mine who did not want me to be king over them—bring them here and slaughter them in my presence."

The second act of the parable commences with the return of the nobleman, who now enjoys official authority to rule with the support of the empire's army. Literally, he has received the kingdom! The newly installed king immediately orders an officer of his court to summon the slaves to whom he entrusted the minas so that they can report the return on his investment. The king is not interested in hearing about their activities. He only wants to be informed of the results. One by one, each slave renders an account. The first slave reports that he used one mina to make ten for his master, an increase of 1,000 percent on his investment.[29] The king immediately congratulates the slave for producing such excellent results and appoints him to administer his rule over ten cities of his territory. The second slave reports a 500 percent increase. Because the results are not as impressive, the king does not offer the same verbal commendation. Nevertheless, the profit merits an appointment to serve the king's interests over five cities.

---

29. Nolland comments that the profit was not unreasonable: "Ancient business knew very high returns, but also spectacular failures" (*Commentary Luke 9:21—18:34*, 915).

The story skips over the accounts rendered by the other seven slaves and passes to the final slave, leaving the audience to assume that they had produced mixed results and were rewarded with different levels of responsibility.[30] The tenth slave breaks the pattern. With no profit to report, he boldly informs the king that he chose to disobey the orders he had received by concealing the mina in a sweat cloth (usually worn around the neck). He explains this shocking action with a startling public critique of the king. He states that he lived in perpetual fear[31] of his master because he knew him to be an exacting man who demanded a disproportionately high return on his investments[32] and seized harvest production from peasant farmers. In a few words, the last slave publicly unmasks the character of the ambitious nobleman-turned-king.[33] By refusing to act as an agent of his unjust master, he has courageously chosen to follow his moral compass and express his solidarity with the oppressed members of the kingdom. At a critical moment, he has confronted the king with the nature of his rule.[34] Through these actions, the tenth slave communicates that he is serving under an authority higher than that of the local king and the emperor who appointed him.

The role of the dissenting slave in this story differs from the slave narratives of the preceding chapter. The former stories treated diligence and humble obedience as a virtue of discipleship. The central figure of this parable is like a prophet of Yahweh who speaks for God against political and economic leaders. He displays a commitment to justice rather than submission to the coercive power of the regime in which he lives. Accordingly, like the prophet Jeremiah, he must anticipate marginalization and retribution. The audience of the parable now expects the king to react decisively against the dissenting slave and the citizens who opposed his rule.

30. One may note that the Matthean parable of the workers in the vineyard (Matt 20.1–16) concentrates on the laborers hired first and last and thereby passes over three groups contracted at different times during the day.

31. The verb to fear is used in the imperfect tense, implying a habitual attitude of intimidation.

32. This is the most likely meaning of the phrase, "you take what you have not placed down." Marshall refers to this terminology as a proverbial complaint. He cites Josephus (*Against Apion*, 2.30) as providing a similar example. The present tense can indicate a common and repeated action. See Marshall, *Luke*, 707.

33. Herzog, *Parables*, 164–68.

34. To his credit, the slave hid the master's money rather than attempting to escape with it.

Readers will notice that the king neither refutes the allegations of the tenth slave with political "spin" nor attempts to argue that his rule offers security and peace to the people of his kingdom. He publicly describes the slave as "evil" (rather than lazy) because of his refusal to participate in the business of generating profit. He continues his condemnation of the slave by saying that he should have at least invested the mina at a money lender's table and allowed someone else to do the dirty work. The king commands that the money be taken and given to the first slave who garnered the most profit. This action should not be interpreted as a personal reward for the first slave; it is a calculated move to give his money to someone who will produce results. The tenth slave, who was given an equal opportunity to serve his master's ambitions, now has no hope for future advancement. The audience assumes that he will be punished physically and demoted to backbreaking duties in the king's household or on his farms. Thus the story of the tenth slave functions as a warning about the cost of dissent and provides a sobering message on the eve of Jesus' entry into Jerusalem.

At this point in the narrative (19:26), Jesus interjects a solemn pronouncement: "I say to you that to the one who has, all things will be given and from the one not having, even what he has will be taken." In the socioeconomic world of this parable—and I dare to say the current contexts in which so many people live—rewards are distributed to those who serve the personal agendas of people who hold positions of power. Challenges to the system result in measures that marginalize and punish dissenters. Jesus' words offer a realistic warning to those who oppose "the powers" as an expression of their faith in God, who works for transformation in a world of inequitable wealth and power.

The parable reaches its conclusion by shifting back to the drama of the citizens and the king. The ruler categorizes those who opposed his reign as state enemies. He orders his security forces to bring them to the palace and slaughter them in his sight. The final gruesome details of the plot underline yet again that the king is a brutal despot who will not tolerate challenges to his power from slaves or citizens.

There should be no attempt to create an analogy between God or Jesus and this king! This is not a parable about the delay of the parousia and the rewards of faithful service to the church. It is a political parable that seeks to dispel the revolutionary illusions of the moment with the violent reality that Jesus anticipates in the coming days.

Reflections on the Parable

I spent over forty years reading this parable in a way that portrayed God (or Jesus) as a demanding and severe boss who counted results—and I continue to hear sermons that follow this line of interpretation. The connection is sometimes drawn that God's "profit" is measured in souls saved, churches planted, number of congregants, and the size of the church budget. Often there is an exhortation that in God's business there is no room for the timidity or sloth exemplified by the tenth slave, who hides his gifts and removes himself from the playing field. Of course, this line of interpretation also implies that God (or Jesus) will return to demand accounts, reward successes, and violently crush those who oppose his rule.[35] Yet such images of God do not line up with the teaching of Jesus. This traditional way of reading the parable encourages pastors to move to comfortable suburban parishes or mega–churches. It motivates social activists to invest their energies in popular projects with prospects for quantifiable and secure results. And this is what many people are doing—much to the detriment of transformational work in difficult places. They judge the Spirit's call to work in the margins as unrewarding and impractical.

Dave Diewert, whom I have mentioned in previous chapters, first introduced me to the reading of the parable that I have developed in the preceding pages. Dave convinced me that this approach to the story liberates the reader from the mental gymnastics of trying to balance God's grace and justice with the calculated and harsh actions of the king. The tyrant in the story represents the way that the world works. The plot is violent and destructive—a mirror of the social world that we encounter so often in the borderlands. Those who defend the weak and resist the powerful are classified as evil or enemies of the state.

The comments from the Nicaraguan peasants at the beginning of this chapter were made during the brutal Samoza dictatorship, which ended with the Sandanista revolution in 1979. Though almost fifty years have passed, the residents of Solentiname offer a sober assessment that transcends their particular time and location. Antidio recognizes that the public transcript, which is disseminated through the official media, has

---

35. Note N. T. Wright's comment: "Even granted that Jesus' hearers did not always grasp what he said, it strains probability a long way to think of him attempting to explain, to people who had not grasped the fact of his imminent death, that there would follow an intermediate period after which he would 'return' in some spectacular fashion, for which nothing in their tradition had prepared them" (Wright, *Jesus*, 635).

the power to deceive ordinary people and keep them from understanding the systemic evil in which they live. Felipe is discouraged that educated bishops and priests—who can see what is happening—choose to remain silent rather than risking dissent. Alejandro highlights the costly nature of a commitment to social justice.

If we return to the story of the courageous students of the Nyange Girls' Secondary School in Rwanda, we see that young women at a critical moment had the capacity to understand the deadly nature of ethnic hatred. They made the moral choice to die rather than to follow the orders of the men with guns. Each time I think of them, I am inspired by their solidarity with one another and their vision of social equality. I am shamed by my compromises with the seductive power of *Realpolitik*,[36] which compels us to navigate life without challenging the powerful interests that maintain the status quo. Faithful service to God in a world of inequitable power and wealth is costly, and this parable challenges us to take our stand among those on the margins in order to speak and act truthfully about compassion, justice, and love.

Christopher Hedges has a degree in theology, worked for twenty years as a foreign correspondent in war-torn areas, and in recent years has become a social activist and a Presbyterian pastor. Hedges warns us that we live in a time of crisis that will impact the well-being and even survival of our children and grandchildren. Environmental destruction has reached the point of no return, with rising sea levels, the degradation of oceans and lakes, the loss of biodiversity, alarming CO_2 levels in the atmosphere, and severe storms threatening human life throughout the planet. The global economy is creating entrenched inequalities, with national governments failing to address these issues as they concentrate on increased internal surveillance of their citizens. Ongoing political repression and ethnic violence continue to force the mass migration of people, as we see in Europe at the time I am completing this manuscript.

With a thoughtful and determined voice, Hedges beckons us to new forms of resistance and civil action in order to reverse the trends that are pushing the human race toward self-destruction. He comments that St. Augustine, who lived through the fall of Rome, believed that hope had two beautiful daughters—anger and courage. Righteous anger does not accept

---

36. *Realpolitik* is a term that describes the practice of making decisions based on the situation, the needs of the moment, and the personal ambitions of leaders, rather than on principles of justice and community solidarity.

things the way they are; courage enables us to take action for a more humane and just world.[37] Hedges advocates that we must take sides rather than cover ourselves with a false blanket of objectivity that ultimately leads to paralysis.[38] He encourages us to use forms of communication that appeal to emotions as well as to reason.[39] We need to find ways to speak to both the heart and the head about the dangers that face us in a fractured and broken world.

I want to bring this chapter to a conclusion by focusing on the economic crisis of 2008, an egregious situation about which Christians in the Global North have remained willfully ignorant and intentionally silent, even as people on the margins—in our own countries and internationally—have been pushed into deeper poverty. In North America, the economic crisis resulted in falling stock prices, the closure of factories, rising unemployment, foreclosures on family homes, and heavy government borrowing to prop up industry and provide bailouts for financial institutions. Internationally, the rapid rise of food commodity prices in global markets led to hoarding and hunger riots in various parts of the world.

I was fortunate to be shielded personally during the worst years of this period. My employment remained secure, and we were able to maintain mortgage payments as Regine continued her PhD studies. However, our organization—along with most others in the international sector—found it much more difficult to raise funds from the public. Supporters felt insecure about the future, and there was a new urgency about the needs of individuals and families in our North American communities. I have painful memories of slashing the budgets of development projects by an average of 28 percent so that our organization could weather the recession. A church partner in Bolivia sent me a message of protest in which the development director had calculated the number of lives that would be lost because of the reduction of funds for a community health project. This analysis was neither melodramatic nor exaggerated—the economic recession cost lives!

The 2008 recession was neither a freak accident, nor a so-called "act of God," such as a typhoon or earthquake, but was rooted in the greed and the immoral pursuit of wealth of financial institutions in the Global North. Joseph Stiglitz, a Nobel Prize winner in economics, wrote an illuminating book about the global economic crisis, observing that corrupt dictators

37. Chris Hedges, *World As It Is*, 84.

38. Ibid., 34.

39. Ibid., 31.

and officials in southern countries stand in awe of the unethical and highly profitable activities of senior executives of financial institutions in North America and Europe.[40] He connects the 2008 global recession with the unrestrained greed and unethical behavior of multinational institutions in the financial sector.[41] The government made massive financial transfusions to save major banks and investment houses, thereby increasing the national debt. At the same time, millions of people in the working class suffered from loss of their employment and homes. Internationally, more than 250 million people moved into the ranks of the hungry because they could not afford higher food prices. Spokespeople of the finance industry and political leaders in the United States argued that they had been working together to pursue the noble vision of extending home ownership to millions of citizens. Yet in secluded offices, the investment industry had created complex loan products with multiple levels of built-in fees and decreased levels of transparency for borrowers and government regulators at a time when the income of the working class was falling and property values were rising. These covert activities generated money for large financial institutions (and their shareholders) that sold bundled mortgages.[42]

Professional economists were largely silent about the dangers caused by this relentless drive for profit. According to Stiglitz, the study of economics had been reduced to a training program for capitalist cheerleaders taught by professors that had been blinded by their faith in the infallibility of self-regulating free markets.[43] Disturbingly, the very executives who created the financial crisis were rewarded with bailouts for their companies and retention bonuses to maintain their positions.[44]

Since the 2008 recession, we have struggled to move toward economic recovery and reasonable levels of full-time employment in the United States, Canada, and Europe. Yet there has been no substantial restructuring of the financial system. Ordinary tax payers have been left with massive

40. Stiglitz, *Freefall*, 225–26. Stiglitz is not a left-wing theorist. He was awarded the Nobel Prize in economic sciences in 2001, has been a senior vice-president of the World Bank, and has advised several US presidents on economic policies.

41. Ibid., xviii.

42. Ibid., 161.

43. Ibid., 238, 244.

44. Nine US banks that received $175 billion in bailout money used $33 billion to pay bonuses to executives. Over 5,000 executives received bonuses in excess of $1 million. In November 2009, the average Wall Street trader received a bonus of more than $900,000 (Ibid., 80, 56).

debt burdens, which we will pass on to other generations. Perhaps the most shocking outcome has been the lack of accountability. Four years after the publication of Stiglitz's book, a respected business journal published an article which noted that substantial fines had been paid to the US treasury by some companies implicated in the 2008 recession.[45] The author observed that no high ranking financial executive had been imprisoned or even charged with criminal activity. The fines were paid by shareholders as a cost of doing business, rather than taken from the personal income of individuals in key positions, who oversaw predatory lending with subprime mortgages, credit card abuses by banks, and the payment of six and seven figure bonuses to executives at the height of the recession.

These ethical issues became more personal while I was on a flight from Toronto to Washington DC in 2010 in order to attend meetings of the Baptist World Alliance. My seat mate was an economist who had been asked to make a presentation to the Internal Revenue Service about proposed changes in taxation policies. He was familiar with Stiglitz's book and agreed with the general thrust of his analysis. At one point in the conversation, he expressed dismay that his church had said nothing about the ethical issues of the recession. He then asked me, as a Christian leader, about the position of my congregation and denomination. I was forced to admit that our church network had eased the burden of some of the victims, but had remained silent about the issues of calculated greed and evil in the economic system. I spent the next weeks thinking about this conversation. My theological education had taught me to parse verbs of the Greek New Testament, yet not equipped me to interpret the signs of the times in which we lived. Along with most other Christians, I had been silent before the massive and systematic evil at the heart of the 2008 recession and the ongoing structures of the global economic system.

The Spirit of God has led some of us to serve in the borderlands, where we build relationships and participate in community among the poor. We know some of their heartbreaks and personal stories. Those on the margins seem destined to live on the outside, seeing from afar the security enjoyed by other citizens on the inside. The economic and social systems of our countries do not serve their interests. According to a 2015 Oxfam Report, the richest 1 percent of people in the world own 48 percent of the global

45. The Bank of America paid $16 billion; JPMorgan Chase paid $13 billion; Citigroup paid $7 billion. Reguly, "Crime and Punishment," in *Globe and Mail Report on Business (October 2014)*, 26.

wealth, whereas the bottom 80 percent of the world's population holds only 5.5 percent of global wealth. If current trends continue, by the end of 2016, the top 1 percent will have more wealth than the remaining 99 percent of people in the world.[46]

Some critics might wish to dispute these numbers, but there has been sufficient analysis to confirm that our economic system benefits a small percentage of people, while the middle class is increasingly stressed, and people on the margins are sinking into deeper poverty. We no longer live under an empire with a reigning emperor, regional despots, and legions of troops. Power today is generally more subtle and diffused. Some of the principle rulers of our time sit in corporate offices from where they send highly paid representatives to lobby elected officials.[47] They make campaign contributions that will ensure the election and loyalty of people who will support their political and economic agendas.[48] It is questionable whether democracy in the United States and Canada serves the well-being of local communities, and in particular of the people who live on the margins.

Women and men who respond to the call of God to serve in the borderlands cannot avoid clashes with social and economic systems that sustain a privileged minority and exclude large portions of the population. When we try to maneuver within structures of inequity and oppression without challenging them, we fail to serve and honor both the poor and the God of justice and mercy. There are times when we must respond by offering a critique of the status quo and a vision of the new creation. Like the unjust ruler in the parable of the dissenting slave, those in power may dismiss us as "radicals," "enemies of stability," or even "evil." In Canada, the the office of our former Prime Minister distributed a list of the enemies of the government to new cabinet appointees. Names on the list included environmental advocates and leaders of not-for-profit organizations that challenged government policy. A number of these "enemies" were Christians dedicated to social change and environmental protection. Other

---

46. The Oxfam analysis draws on data from Credit Suisse. Hardoon, *Wealth*, 2

47. Currently there are four lobbyists from the financial sector for every elected official in the US Congress. Five of the seven largest lobbying organizations are run by pharmaceutical companies and medical insurance corporations. Micklethwait and Wooldridge, *Fourth Revolution*, 200, 239.

48. The cost of the 2012 presidential and congressional elections was $6.3 billion. Micklethwait and Woolridge, editors of *The Economist*, write that observers are left with the impression that democracy is for sale and the rich have the most power and influence (Ibid., 257–58).

Christian leaders have been silenced by legislation that threatens to revoke the charitable status of organizations that take a public stand on issues of sensitivity to the government. And this is Canada!

In the introduction to this book, I presented Arthur Frank's concept of stories that have the capacity to act as dangerous companions. Some stories compel us to take great risks and to act with bold determination. The parable of the dissenting slave is such a story, and it belongs in the inner libraries of people who are committed to God's rule of transformational change. The dissenting slave encourages us take our place alongside those who live in the borderlands and to raise our voices on their behalf. May we be strengthened as we remember that God identifies with people who have been pushed to the margins, and so it is our great privilege to be called to serve where Jesus has gone before us.

The following chapter introduces us to a vulnerable victim of power living in the borderlands of a first-century city.

CHAPTER 9

A Widow Who Demands Justice
(Luke 18:1–8)

There was one invasion after another. Once a number of helicopters and planes dropped bombs right on our village. . . . They
say that we help the subversives when they come to our villages.
That's why the Army cuts down our cornfields. But if we don't have
enough food for ourselves to eat, how are we going to help others?
We cannot endure any more suffering. I pray to God that a change
will come, and end this injustice. —LUISA[1]

The poor are the ones who tell us what the world is and what service the church must offer to the world. —OSCAR ROMERO[2]

The church cannot be silent before these injustices in the economy,
politics, and society. If the church chooses to be silent, it will be an
accomplice. —OSCAR ROMERO[3]

Stories from the Margins

IN 1989, I WAS appointed to serve a five-year term as a member of Canada's
Immigration and Refugee Board. The global context included Tiananmen
Square in China, armed conflicts in Lebanon, Sri Lanka, and Somalia, state
persecution in Iran, torture chambers in Libya, and repressive governments

---

1. Wright et al., *El Salvador*, 22–23.
2. Romero, *Violence of Love*, 189.
3. Personal translation, Romero, *Dia y Dia*, 20.

in Latin America. Many of the testimonies we heard from refugee claimants were heartbreaking and at a broader level revealed the pervasive evil of people in positions of power.

A woman, whom I will call Teresa, gave testimony at a hearing before the refugee board. She fled a Central American country where she had worked in a garment factory (sweat shop) on the edge of the capital city. Like other women, Teresa needed the employment, but working conditions were oppressive and salaries were minimal. Employees worked long hours in an uncomfortable environment with constant pressure to meet production quotas. Teresa joined a union and became an organizer among other female employees. Tensions rose in the garment factory when the union threatened a strike for improved pay and working conditions.

Teresa testified that one evening, as she was leaving work, a paramilitary group abducted her at gunpoint, blindfolded her, and took her to a secluded building. They pulled off the blindfold and threatened to kill her if she resumed union activities. Then they gang-raped her and left her lying on the floor. Teresa was a credible witness, and her story matched information from human rights reports from her country. It was easy to reach a positive decision and grant her refugee status. Yet in her testimony, Teresa mentioned one detail that has haunted me for years. She stated that two English-speaking Caucasian men stood by and witnessed the threats and the rape. Over the past two decades, I have retained a sense of horror and outrage about these men who saw, heard, and were accomplices in the violence because they chose to remain passive spectators. Were they protecting the "rights" of a company to pursue profit? Were they military advisors? What did they say when they reported to their corporate headquarters or base? Did they tell their superiors what had happened to Teresa?

The chapter begins with the statement of Luisa, a woman from El Salvador, who was forced to move to a camp for displaced people during the presidencies of Jose Napoleon Duarte in her country and Ronald Reagan in the United States of America. The rhetoric of the public transcript justified military, political, and economic action to promote freedom and save El Salvador from communism. Luisa's personal narrative mentions disappearances, bombings, land mines, military incursions, and the destruction of crops by government forces. She states that her community cannot endure further suffering and prays that God will bring change to El Salvador and end the injustice.

The accounts of Teresa and Luisa have the capacity to provoke compassion and anger. Women in the borderlands suffer disproportionate injustice and indignity, particularly in locations of conflict, because they lack protection and are often denied venues in which to share their stories. Teresa's and Luisa's accounts intersect with the gospel story of a widow who will no longer tolerate the powerless situation in which she has been trapped. This parable has affinities with the preceding chapter, which depicted a slave who refused to carry out the orders of a king. However, the slave was placed in a position where, for at least one moment, he could speak directly to the centre of power. Teresa, Luisa, and the widow represent women whose voices are suppressed and whose stories are seldom told.

Introduction to the Parable (Luke 17:20–37)

The parable of the widow who demands justice is frequently domesticated into a tame lesson to encourage daily prayer.[4] This dumbed-down reading overlooks the vocabulary of justice,[5] the social oppression and inequities that form the social background of the narrative, and the clear identification of the widow with people who cry out to God day and night for his intervention. These initial observations indicate that we need to seek a deeper meaning for this parable.

As with other parables, we must consider the narrative setting in which the story has been placed. The journey which began in Galilee (9:51–52) is now drawing near to its end. Jerusalem is almost in sight, and Passover is approaching, when the Jewish nation will recall God's deliverance from their slavery in Egypt. The two discourses immediately preceding this parable emphasize the presence of God's sovereign rule in a world marked by evil and injustice. In the first (17:20–21), a group of Pharisees confront Jesus. Their inquiry could be rendered in a colloquial manner along the following lines: "You are always talking about God's kingdom. So when are we going to see him take real control by liberating us from foreign domination?"[6] Jesus' reply dampens listeners' expectations of cataclysmic

---

4. Mental gymnastics are required to suggest that the judge represents God, because the judge bears no resemblance to what Scripture reveals about God. I appreciate Herzog's comment: "It is difficult to leap from the judge in the parable to the assurance that a gracious God will hear the anguished cries of disciples in the midst of tribulation and respond to soothe their anxiety and comfort their grief" (Herzog, *Parables*, 218).

5. The verb "to grant justice" is used in 18:3 and 5; the noun "justice" is found in 18.7.

6. This expanded paraphrase is not too much a stretch. Consider Malina's comment: "The proclamation of the kingdom of God meant at least that the God of Israel would be taking over control of the country soon" (*Social Gospel*, 1).

signs by emphasizing that God is already active in their social locations. He has begun to establish his reign in their midst.

Jesus directs the second discourse (17:22–37) to his disciples, changing his theme from the reign of God in the present to the days of the Son of Man on the future horizon. Though the disciples will long for the present period of history to be brought to an end by the appearance of the Son of Man in glory,[7] they must concentrate on living faithfully within the violence and pervasive evil around them. Jesus refers to the lifetimes of Noah and Lot, which were remembered as epochs when wickedness and aggression reached such an extreme point that God was stirred to intervene dramatically. Jesus' words dampen expectations of imminent glory by challenging the disciples to live as dissidents in places of evil, violence, and suffering.

These two discourses prepare the reader to enter into the widow parable by emphasizing that God is already establishing his rule of transformation in the midst of the daily lives of individuals and communities. There is a sober warning about a prolonged period in which the destructive powers of evil will distort and damage human life. These two themes are central to a faithful interpretation of the parable of the widow.

The Parable of a Widow Who Demanded Justice (18:1–8)

The story of the widow (18:2–5) is enclosed by an introduction (18.1) and an application or conclusion (18:6–8). I have chosen to treat each section separately. There is a strong consensus that the introduction was written by the evangelist and that the parable is authentic to Jesus. There is no such broad agreement regarding the conclusion (18:6–8). I will approach the text as a complete literary unit, rather than attempting to dissect its various layers.[8] The evangelist clearly wanted his readers to understand the passage as a coherent piece.[9]

---

7 The connection between the kingdom of God and the Son of Man, which was present in Daniel 7, is maintained in Luke's Gospel. See 9:26–27 and 21:27–31.

8. This is the approach of narrative criticism (Resseguie, *Narrative Criticism*, 19).

9. It is worth noting that Jeremias (*Parables*, 156) and Snodgrass (*Stories with Intent*, 455–56) argue for the unity of 8:2–8.

Introduction to the Parable (18:1)

> Then Jesus told them a parable about their need to pray always and not to lose heart.

The introduction functions as a bridge, connecting the parable with the previous section that treats the presence of God's rule within the social context of enmity and malice (17:20–37). The verse explains the twofold intent of the story that Jesus is about to tell his followers. First, he wants his disciples to maintain the practice of faithful prayer.[10] Second, he encourages them to cultivate resilience for those times when they feel overwhelmed and drawn toward despair.[11] The conditions of weariness and loss of heart presume circumstances that generate discouragement, fatigue, and doubt. These debilitating emotions stand in contrast with the attitude of steadfast endurance, which characterizes members of the movement whose lives bear abundant fruit for the rule of God.[12]

Please allow me to comment that some readers of this book may have passed through dark moments of despair and overwhelming fatigue. They may recall feelings of abandonment, misunderstanding, and loss of direction. There are times when evil seems entrenched, personal limitations are painfully evident, and even our friends have lost confidence in us. When we are able to pray, our half-formed petitions seem to drift off into some undefined space. If some of these phrases resonate with your experience, then you know what it means to lose heart.

The Parable (18:2–5)

> He said, "In a certain city there was a judge who neither feared God nor could be shamed by people. In that city there was a widow who kept coming to him and saying, 'Grant me justice against my opponent.' For a period of time he refused; but later he said to himself, 'Though I have no fear of God and people cannot shame

---

10. The adverb *pantote* means consistent rather than continuous or perpetual (Fitzmyer, *Luke X–XXIV*, 1178).

11. The verb *enkakeo* means to become weary, to lose heart, and to enter into a state of passivity in regard to the future. See BADG, 214 and the usage in 2 Cor 4:1, 16; Gal 6:9; Eph 3:13; 2 Thes 3:13.

12. Luke 8:15. See chapter 4.

me, yet because this widow keeps bothering me, I will grant her justice, so that she may not give me a black eye.'"

The double use of "city" suggests that the location is important. In earlier chapters we saw that the wealthy minority of the Palestinian population lived in enclosed neighborhoods of urban areas. The influence and interests of the elite dominated the city and surrounding rural villages.[13] Cities also contained the homes of scribes, tradesmen, merchants, day laborers, domestic servants, and tax collectors, who lived in a client-patron relationship with people of wealth and power. Landless peasants, tanners, sex–trade workers, and beggars generally lived on the periphery outside the walls. The elite avoided direct contact with inferior social groups.[14] Goods and services were acquired through the use of retainers and household slaves, who served as intermediaries. The original audience of the parable would assume that the judge was either a member of the elite or had significant social connections with them. In contrast, the widow, whatever her previous status, had moved towards the bottom of the social hierarchy.

It is critical to give further attention to the social roles associated with the two main characters of the parable. The judge is a "big man" who holds a position of power in the city.[15] Officially, his role is to settle disputes on the basis of the Torah. Unfortunately, the legal system often functioned with a bias toward the most powerful and wealthy sectors of the population. Compliant judges were useful for the schemes of the privileged minority.[16] Legal judgments were a commodity that could be sold or traded for favors—a competition in which the poor had little bargaining power.

This situation of social inequality before the law was not new in Palestine (or most other areas of the world during diverse periods in human history). The prophet Isaiah had taken the side of the poor when he spoke out against judges who acquitted the guilty for a bribe and deprived the weak of their rights (Isa 5:23). Similarly, Amos had criticized the legal administration that took bribes and pushed aside the needy at the gate where cases

13. Rohrbaugh, "Pre–industrial City in Luke–Acts," in Neyrey, ed., *Social World*, 133.

14. Ibid., 136.

15. There is uncertainty about how the judicial system functioned outside of Jerusalem. It may well be that there was not a uniform structure for the administration of justice in each region. However, the meaning of story does not hinge on detailed knowledge of the legal system (Fitzmyer, *Luke X–XXIV*, 1178).

16. Malina, *Social Gospel*, 27.

were heard (Amos 5.10–13). Centuries later, the Talmud spoke of judges who were willing to pervert justice for a dish of meat.[17]

The judge is described as a man who neither fears God nor can be placed in a position of shame by other people in the community. In the language of our time, we would talk about someone who arrogantly abuses his position of power. The fear of God was foundational for Torah obedience and the public administration of justice,[18] as the following text indicates.

> He (Jehoshaphat) appointed judges in the land in all the fortified cities of Judah, city by city, and said to the judges, "Consider what you are doing, for you judge not on behalf of human beings but on the Lord's behalf; he is with you in giving judgment. Now, let the fear of the Lord be upon you; take care what you do, for there is no perversion of justice with the Lord our God, or partiality, or taking of bribes." (2 Chronicles 19.5–7)

The description of the judge who does not fear God and who has no shame about the social impact of his verdicts[19] provides the audience with all the information required about the first character of the parable. This man will render judgments based on a criterion of what works to his personal advantage. He will view people on the margins as a temporary obstacle to the ambitions of his peers and an opportunity to supplement his income through bribes.

The widow lives within a patriarchal society without a husband. Her position is shameful and vulnerable because she evidently has no male protection or representation within the broader community.[20] The audience of the parable is left to conclude that there is no son, no kinsman, and no male in the city who will come to her assistance. The social and cultural position of widows in first-century Palestine was familiar to the audience of the parable. A widow had no inheritance rights, although the husband's estate might include provisions for her maintenance.[21] Widows were required to wear distinctive clothing that identified their social status.[22] A widow who

17. *B.T. Baba Kamma*, 114a.

18. E.g., Lev 19:14, 32; Deut 4:10; 5:29; 6:13; 8:6; 10:12; 13:4; 14:23; 31:12; Ps 110:10.

19. The passive use of the verb *entrepo* implies that the judge does not feel shame about the consequences of his actions in court (Bailey, *Peasant Eyes*, 132).

20. Malina and Neyrey, "Honour and Shame in Luke-Acts," in Neyrey, *Social World*, 63–64.

21. Hanson and Oakman, *Palestine*, 43–47.

22. Gen 38:14; Jdt 8:5; 10:3; 16:7.

wanted to return to her family of origin was forced to negotiate with her own kin for the return of the "bridewealth" that had been paid by her late husband's immediate relatives. As a woman, she was prohibited from making legal representation before a judge. Therefore, deprived of a son and a sympathetic male of the community, she was voiceless before the law. This brief background enables the reader to understand that a widow who felt forced to harass a prominent judge repeatedly had been pushed to lonely desperation. The members of the community may have viewed her conduct as shameful and outlandish.[23] However, there were no respectable options available to her.

The narrative provides no details about the legal issue. The audience might reasonably assume that the dispute involves provisions for the widow's livelihood or her right to continue to live on the property of her late husband. Her repeated and unaccompanied intrusions into the presence of the judge create a disruption in the social code of relationships maintained by the public transcript. On each occasion, the widow presents a simple and unchanging request: "Grant me justice against my opponent." At face value, her words express the desire for a just verdict rather than for unethical gain. Alone, weak, and vulnerable, she faces a judge who is notorious for his perversion of the Torah. The plot prepares the audience for the total failure of justice based on the contrasting social positions of the judge and the widow in light of the former's reputation.[24]

Another man,[25] the adversary who attempts to take advantage of the widow, is an unseen presence in the narrative. Given the confidence of the widow in her claim and the hidden nature of the opponent, his action appears to be unscrupulous. The citizens of the city form a collective fourth character in the social background of the story. Perhaps most members of the community sympathize with the cause of the widow. But they find her behavior to be deviant, and they are aware of their own vulnerabilities before the elite class. The apparent lack of solidarity from men in the city suggests that they are either peers or patrons of the adversary, or are afraid of the consequences of representing the widow in court.

The fifth and final actor is God, who has spoken through the Law and Prophets, expressing his concern for the most vulnerable members of the

---

23. Malina and Neyrey, "Honour and Shame in Luke-Acts," in Neyrey, *Social World*, 63–64.

24. Nolland, *Luke 9:21—18:34*, 871.

25. Note the male gender of the Greek noun *antidikos*.

community—the widow, the orphan and the stranger.[26] It is important to observe that the widow and orphan texts of the Hebrew Scriptures present the needs of people on the margins as a shared community responsibility. This means that God watches and judges the entire city in which the widow has been abandoned to deal alone with her adversary and a disreputable judge.

Most of the narrative is fixed on the judge. He delays dealing with the case of the widow for a prolonged period. Accordingly, she suffers the double injustice of a male opponent who seeks to take advantage of her weak social position and a legal system that does not ensure justice for people on the margins. The delay in action raises suspicions that the judge is either unwilling to confront a powerful opponent or, more likely, is holding out for a larger bribe from the adversary. The soliloquy in 18:4–5 expresses the judge's inner thoughts, which are not evident to the widow, the adversary, or other members of the city.[27] The judge's internal comments reveal that his self-assessment agrees with the initial description of the narrative. He does not fear God and is not disturbed by the shameful nature of his legal decisions. However, "this widow" is causing him trouble in public settings. He even fears that she may escalate her action and give him a black eye.[28] The consequence of a physical assault in a public place by a woman would severely damage his reputation among people who "purchase" his legal decisions. It seems that he cannot curtail an escalation of her behavior, which threatens to make him an object of laughter and derision within the city.[29] His position and power depend on avoiding embarrassing social situations among the elite. Accordingly, the judge decides to grant justice to the widow against her opponent, coldly calculating the cost of her continual annoyance and threatened attack. It is better to decide in her favor even at the cost of disappointing the expectations of a social peer and forfeiting the profit of a bribe.

26. E.g., Exod 22:21–24; Deut 10:17–18; 14:28–29; 24:17–20; 26:12; Isa 10:1–2; Mal 3:5; Ps 146:9; Prov 15:25; Wis 2:1–11.

27. Soliloquies are important in Lukan parables. The self–talk allows the listener to enter into the internal reasoning and motivations of a character. See Luke 12:17, 45; 15:17–19; 16:3–4; 20:13.

28. The Greek verb *hypopiazo* literally means to strike and give a black eye. The figurative meanings are to wear out or to cause shame (Nolland, *Luke 9:21—18:34*, 868).

29. Schottroff, *Parables*, 192. See also Young, *Parables*, 59.

The parable of the widow who demands justice exposes the way "the system" works against people from the margins.[30] Like the parable of the dissenting slave (19:11–27), the story does not create a wild space in which to envision an alternative community of justice, compassion, and love, but rather presents the reality of the world from the perspective of those in the borderlands. I remind the reader of Oscar Romero's comment at the beginning of the chapter: the poor inform us about the way the world works. The widow parable functions in this manner.

In the end, the judge turns out to be a spineless cog perpetuating the social structures of exploitation. The widow's case prevails simply because she has been shameless and insistent.[31] We come to see her as a person of inner strength and tenacity. She exemplifies the great determination of some of the women who work for social transformation and justice in their borderlands in our time.

Application of the Parable (18:6–8)

> And the Lord said, "Listen to what the unjust judge says. And will not God grant justice to his elect ones who cry to him day and night? Will he delay long in helping them? I tell you, he will quickly grant justice to them. And yet, when the Son of Man comes, will he find faith on earth?"

The concluding section connects to the story through the reference to the unjust judge (18:6), the double use of the key word "justice" (18:7–8), and the description of voices raised in desperation (18:7). I propose that there is a deliberate link with the Exodus narrative and that this motif is critical for interpreting the problematic phrase about God acting quickly (18:8a).

This section is introduced with a command to listen carefully to the soliloquy of the unjust judge.[32] It is striking that his character has been described twice in the narrative and now, in the conclusion, we are asked to consider it yet again. As I have suggested, these words represent more than a depiction of an unsavory individual. They are an indictment of the administration of justice and the power exercised by a privileged minor-

30. Herzog, *Parables*, 220–28; Schottroff, *Parables*, 193.

31. Gonzalez, *Luke*, 211.

32. The adjectival genitive *tes adikias* signifies that the judge is rooted in the evil of the current world order that stands in opposition to the values of God's rule. The same expression is found in 16:8.

ity. The entire city's economic and social structure can be characterized as neither fearing God nor feeling shame at the marginalization of people who lack voice and influence. Religion may be present in the city. The fear of God is not so evident.

The application asks three questions. First, will God grant justice to the elect who cry out from the margins? Second, will he delay? Third, will the Son of Man find faith when he comes to earth? The first two questions are concerned about God. The final shifts the focus to the community gathered around Jesus.

WILL GOD NOT ACT ON BEHALF OF THE ELECT WHO CRY OUT TO HIM DAY AND NIGHT?

This question is rhetorical in nature. The negative construction, "will God not act," anticipates an emphatic response.[33] The wording of the question connects both with the story of the widow and the themes of consistent prayer mentioned in 18:1. The introduction, parable, and first question combine to portray a protracted period during which God's action of justice and social transformation seems either delayed or denied. People in the margins continue to call out for relief.

I propose that the portrayal of people crying out to God in desperation creates a deliberate connection with the description of the Hebrew slaves in Exodus 3.

> I have observed the misery of my people who are in Egypt; I have heard their cry on account of their taskmasters. Indeed, I know their sufferings, and I have come down to deliver them from the Egyptians. (3:7–8a)

> The cry of the Israelites has now come to me; I have seen how the Egyptians oppress them. So come, I will send you to Pharaoh to bring my people, the Israelites, out of Egypt. (3:9–10)

This allusion is not accidental. The audience is aware that Passover is approaching, when they will celebrate their ancestors' deliverance from oppression. There is hope that God will act again to liberate his people, who

---

33. As mentioned previously, rhetorical questions are assertions that use the form of a question in order to achieve greater impact than a statement of fact or opinion (Resseguie, *Narrative Criticism*, 61).

are oppressed by the system of Roman domination (including the power of the elite).

I want to make four observations about Exodus 3 in relationship to the widow parable and its application.[34] First, the people whose cries are heard by God are located in the heart of an empire, where Pharaoh exploits their labor and inflicts suffering through his use of military power. Second, God identifies the enslaved women and men who cry out as his people (his elect). He declares solidarity with them and their ancestors, Abraham, Isaac, and Jacob (Exod 2:24–25; 3:6). Third, God is determined to act quickly and decisively on behalf of his people and against Pharaoh's empire. As Brueggemann observes, "The human cry . . . evokes divine resolve."[35] Fourth, God's commitment to intervene requires human agency. God acts by sending Moses, an eighty-year-old shepherd, and his elderly brother, who is a priest.[36]

The term "elect" within Luke's gospel clearly refers to people who live on the margins. They are described as the poor, the captives, the blind, and oppressed (4:18) when Jesus reads from the scroll of Isaiah in the synagogue. In the Lukan beatitudes, the elect are the poor, the hungry, the broken-hearted, and the persecuted (Luke 6:20–23). When John the Baptizer expresses doubt about the Messianic mission of Jesus, his messengers are told to report that the blind, the lame, the lepers, the deaf, the dead, and the poor have been transformed by the coming of God's rule (7:22). Each story of healing and table fellowship further defines the elect to whom Jesus has been sent. Accordingly, the elect are best understood as the humble and marginalized people gathered around Jesus, who cry out to God for salvation and relief from oppression.

Will God Delay Long in Helping Them?

The second rhetorical question is deceptively short and surprisingly difficult to comprehend.[37] One line of translation and interpretation proposes

34. A similar analysis of Exodus 3 is made by Walter Brueggemann in *Journey,* 7–13.

35. Ibid., 11.

36. Moltmann, *Power of the Powerless,* 16.

37. Howard Marshall present nine options for the meaning of the verb *makrothemeo* with the attached preposition and pronoun (*Luke,* 675). The verb is generally defined as "to have patience" or "to wait patiently." The preposition *epi* with the dative case can mean either "on account of" or "toward." The pronoun *autois* logically connects with the elect rather than their oppressors, who have not been mentioned. However, T. W.

that God is patient in hearing the cries of the elect or shows patience towards them by listening to their prayers in spite of their sinful nature.[38] Six decades ago, T. W. Manson dismissed this proposed understanding by observing that "The elect do not want a patient hearing: they want redress. They do not want God to go on patiently listening to their outcry: they want God to take action which will make their crying unnecessary."[39] I choose to follow Joseph Fitzmyer, who translates the phrase, "Will God delay long towards them?" (i.e., in regard to their cries).[40] This second rhetorical question makes the assertion that God will not wait passively while the poor cry out for justice. He will indeed act soon on their behalf.

My line of interpretation is supported by Jesus' solemn pronouncement, which is introduced by the words, "I say to you." This formula invokes the authority of Jesus and signals that something of importance is about to be communicated.[41] The declaration affirms that God is not like the unjust judge, who is unmoved by pleas for justice and relief. He takes the side of the weak and oppressed and acts on their behalf within a social context that deprives them of dignity and threatens their lives.[42]

WILL THE SON OF MAN FIND FAITHFULNESS ON EARTH?

The third question looks both backward and forward. In gazing backward, there is a distant historical reference to Daniel 7:13–14, where the Son of Man is given dominion and kingship so that all people, nations, and languages serve him. The appropriation of the Son of Man title by Jesus raised speculations about the fulfillment of this prophetic word. The backward perspective also includes the short discourse that introduced the widow parable. As we saw previously, Jesus squelched apocalyptic expectations by

---

Manson argues that the original Aramaic saying meant that God postpones his righteous action because he is patient with those who do evil in order to give them time for repentance (Manson, *Sayings*, 397–98).

38. Snodgrass, *Stories with Intent*, 459; Bailey, *Peasant Eyes*, 139.

39. Manson, *Sayings*, 307.

40. Fitzmyer, *Luke X–XXIV*, 1180. See also Hultgren, *Parables*, 256. This is the direction taken by the TNIV and the NRSV in their translations. This translation corresponds with Sirach 35.19, where the same verb has the meaning of delay in executing judgment.

41. See 3:8; 6:27; 7:28; 12:4, 5, 8; 14:24; 17:34; 19:26. The construction is used to introduce pronouncements and statements of urgent action. See Marshall, *Luke*, 667.

42. The phrase *en taxei* describes action that is quick or without delay. Luke uses this expression in a similar way in Acts 12:7; 22:18; and 25:4.

warning his followers of his death and of an extended period of great evil in the world before the eventual revealing of the Son of Man (17:22–37). Accordingly, the third question tempers dreams of a victorious showdown in Jerusalem and introduces the concept of an indefinite time of mission during which despair and doubt might turn members of the movement away from trusting in God's rule.

I prefer to translate the Greek noun *pistis* in 18:6 with the English word "faithfulness" because it seems better suited to the nature of the third question. There is certainty that the Son of Man will come someday in glory, and his concern will be to find women and men who are prayerfully and faithfully engaged in the transforming work of God's kingdom. The third question is not rhetorical in nature, anticipating an emphatic affirmation. Rather, it invites people to enter into a period of deep reflection about how they will pray and act in a world of inequities, oppression, and injustice. Faithfulness will require them to live as dissidents, bringing compassion, justice, and love to the broken and wounded places of the world. These followers of Jesus will be the people through whom God answers cries of despair from the borderlands.

Reflections on the Parable

I want to return our focus to the widow of the parable, along with Lidia and Teresa, whose stories introduced this chapter. One of the discouraging aspects of the parable is that no male figure of the community takes up the widow's cause. She is left to struggle on her own because men in the city fear the social and economic power of her opponent. In El Salvador, Lidia felt deserted by powerful men, such as President Jose Napoleon Duarte and President Ronald Reagan of the USA, who were intent on fighting communism without responding to the root causes of civil violence. Teresa was raped by men who belonged to a paramilitary group, with two Caucasian males standing in the background as passive witnesses. The armed group attempted to crush the union of unarmed female employees, who hoped for better working conditions and equitable wages from the sweatshop that sold products to markets in the Global North.

These three stories represent the testimonies of women from the borderlands, each with its own distinctive account of inequities, disempowerment, and violence. In an earlier book, I wrote that women and girls suffered disproportionately from poverty, human rights violations, and civil violence.[43] Two–thirds of those who are denied primary school education are girls. In many locations, women and girls are subjected to beatings and sexual violence in their homes and communities without effective legal protection and support. In fact, domestic violence is the largest single cause of the unnatural death of women in the world. In some cultures, girls are forced into early marriages when they are still children. Women lack property rights in many countries and find it dangerous to express their political opinions. Organized crime has globalized the human trafficking of women as sex-trade workers. Rape has become a standard weapon of civil conflict around the world. Since the publication of that book in 2011, the oppression of girls and women has become even more aggravated. Taliban militias use violence to keep girls out of school. Boko Haram,[44] operating out of Nigeria and Cameroon, is infamous for the use of female suicide bombers and the kidnapping of school girls. The leaders of the movement announced their intention to treat abducted girls as slaves and war booty. In the Middle East, ISIS uses widespread rape to exert control and spread terror.[45] There are reports from the Ukraine of alarming levels of sexual violence from combatants on both sides of the conflict.[46] In India, dowry expectations have been described as a form of violence against women, resulting in female infanticide, infant killings, family murders, and suicide.[47]

As we are flooded by these statistics of violence and gender discrimination in other countries, it is far too easy to shake our heads in disgust while overlooking the systemic evils in our own nations. I ask readers outside of Canada to note the references I make to my own country while considering policies of exclusion and inequity that prevail within their own borders. Canada ranks eighth place in the UN's Human Development Index ranking, and yet there are widespread gender inequities that discriminate against women.[48] Women are more likely than men to live below the Canadian poverty line and to depend on food banks. Approximately 3,300 Canadian women are in shelters on any given night because of male

43. Nelson et al., *Going Global*, 70–71.

44. The literal translation of *Boko Haram* is "no western education."

45. See Susskind, "What Will it Take." The article relates the story of a fourteen–year-old girl, who was sold to an ISIS combatant and resold fourteen more times to other fighters. Each of her "owners" raped her.

46. See Ferris-Rotman, "Evidence Mounts."

47. See Kale, "Dowry."

48. Most of the following information comes from the research of the Canadian Women's Foundation.

violence—and they are accompanied by about 3,000 children. Alarmingly, another two hundred women are turned away each day because of lack of space in shelters. For single parent mothers, who comprise 21 percent of those living in poverty,[49] Canadian welfare rates barely cover the cost of rent and bus fare in most cities. The largest number of women living in poverty are aboriginal (36 percent), showing that poverty has both gender and racial dimensions. Canadian police estimate that approximately 1,200 Aboriginal women and girls have been murdered or disappeared since 1980, with the average age of the victims at twenty years old.[50] On a national scale, over 50 percent of Canadian women indicate that they have been threatened or been victims of sexual violence. Canadian universities have a reputation for fostering a culture of rape. By grade ten, issues of anxiety, self-esteem, and depression are three times higher for female students than their male counterparts. The wage gap between men and women on the workforce has increased in recent years, and women in Canada are underrepresented at all levels of government.

I am confident that the comparable statistics from other countries of the Global North will provide similar data about the inequities and even dangers of being born a girl. The cumulative impact of these statistics should set off emergency sirens for people drawn to the work of social transformation. Many of us need to confess that we have been inattentive to the cries for justice coming from girls and women in our communities. We have been like the men of the city in the widow parable, because we have failed to raise our voices and to intervene.

I conclude this chapter by returning to the field of international development, which was my vocation for many years. In 2007, a Master's Degree student from Scotland contacted our organization seeking an opportunity to conduct research in Rwanda about child-headed households. The combination of the 1994 Tutsi genocide and the AIDS pandemic had resulted in an estimated 240 thousand children living in households led by a child or adolescent. These existing family units, deprived of parents, lived on the margins of their communities in extreme poverty, vulnerable to predators of various categories (including relatives who wanted their land). Laura Ward Lee's sensitive research methodologies gave voice to the children who lived in these family units.[51] Teenage girls who were heads of households

49. This figure compares to 7 percent of single parent males.
50. See Royal Canadian Mounted Police, "Missing and Murdered Aboriginal Women."
51. The research was published as Ward and Eyber, "Resiliency of Children," 17–33.

identified food and nutrition as a major problem for themselves and their siblings. They told Laura that at times, the only recourse available was informal prostitution in order to earn money to feed their siblings. In a focus group, one girl asked: "What can I do when the children at home are crying because of hunger and a man offers me twenty cents?"[52]

I was unable to control my emotions as I read Laura's report sitting behind a comfortable desk in my office. I had to close the door so that no one would see the tears streaming down my face. I went home that night asking the questions: What kind of a world tolerates that a sixteen-year-old girl must sell her body in order to feed her sisters and brothers? As a global community and as Christian churches, have we become like the men in the city of the widow, who refuse to hear the voice of women from the margins and enter into solidarity with them?

The parable of the widow who demands justice cannot be categorized as a nice devotional text about persistent prayer. The voice of the widow is the determined cry of oppressed and exploited women who still retain hope that God will bring justice and relief. Their words and actions reveal a legacy of betrayals by politicians, government officials, and institutions—sometimes including congregations and denominations. People called to work for transformation in the margins are challenged to understand their roles as agents of God's justice and mercy toward women and girls in their communities, especially those who are living in a borderland.

The story of the widow who demands justice brings my treatment of the parables to an end. I now invite the reader to enter into reflection about the meaning of the parables for the lines that they are writing each day in the stories of their lives.

52. One hundred francs.

CHAPTER 10

Afterword

Good Soil. Good Seed. Good Fruit.

THE JOURNEY THROUGH THIS book has led us into communities located in first-century Palestine as well as into some troubled borderlands of our own time. As we have attended to parables of Jesus from the Gospel of Luke, along with the stories from those living on the margins, we have reckoned with the broken nature of our world. I pray that the pictures of God's rule portrayed in these parables have stimulated you to embrace deeper values in your heart and to commit to actions that are merciful, just, and faithful. For both the parables and the stories from the margins invite us to consider the kind of stories we are writing with our own lives.

As followers of Jesus, we have been entrusted with the task of living fruitfully in a world order threatened by economic disparity, racism, gender violence, rampant consumerism, and environmental destruction. The call to tend the soil of our lives so that it will bear good fruit requires us to do both soul work and to become active participants in bringing healing and transformation to the wounded places of our world. The personal mission of "writing" a good life is far more challenging than the relatively simple project of authoring a book. A good life takes many years, and the lines are written by actions that reveal our core convictions about human life, the created order, and ultimately God.

In the first chapter of this book, I acknowledged my debt to Arthur Frank, who helped me to understand the power of stories. In this closing chapter, I want to pay tribute to Donald Miller, who stimulated my thinking about how the parables of Jesus might encourage us to write good and courageous stories with the narratives of our lives.[1]

Miller proposes that a good life, like a good story, has a central theme. This theme integrates the wide range of experiences that a person accumulates from the date of birth, through childhood, adolescence, the adult years, and into the final season of life. The discernment of a central theme creates a vantage point from which a person can make sense of different places, people, and social environments that have entered into the story (either temporarily or for extended periods). As authors of our stories, we navigate through our past chapters with memories that produce emotions of joy, grief, celebration, regret, solidarity, abandonment, well-being, danger, success, and failure. The central theme enables us to fit the fragments and pieces of our stories into a mosaic that holds the image of who we are and who we are becoming as the future unfolds into the great unknown ahead of us.

According to Miller, compelling stories have conflicts and monumental difficulties that demand courage. Great stories do not require success and public recognition, but they do need bravery, sacrifices, and commitment to truth. At critical moments, the central character will inevitably be shaken by fear or paralyzed by doubt. Often the anxiety is relational in nature, involving apprehensions about rejection, isolation, or misunderstanding. Every good story has two or three "inciting incidents" that emerge from the plot when central characters are forced to make decisions that propel them through doors from which there can be no return. Good stories also have "negative turns," in which a person must deal with personal limitations, flaws, selfish motives, and failure. Conflict, fear, inciting incidents, and negative turns are all related to the primary theme of character development or personal transformation. In a good stories, the central characters deliberately, and sometimes painfully, move toward new understandings of themselves and the world around them. They incorporate new values that distance them from the heritage of the past and propel them into an uncertain future. The intense process of character development creates the space to replace tired or destructive patterns in order to make room for new ways of seeing, analyzing, and interacting in the world.

Miller believes that there is a force in the world that does not want us to live good stories and to contribute something unique with our lives. This negative power becomes evident when we lose hold of our story's

1. Miller, *Million Miles*.

central theme due to pressures or inner compulsions. We enter a period of distraction in which we lose our way, and feel as if the plot has been diverted. During these times, we may discover that God is standing beside us and whispering a better story into our hearts. The quiet words of the Spirit have the potential to restore and redirect our personal narratives into the larger story that God is authoring for our communities, the world, and all creation.

I propose that the central theme of our life story is connected to our personal mission as individuals created in the image of God. Jean Vanier once said that each person has been given a secret name which, when discovered, expresses his or her unique call and contribution to the world.[2] This "call" may be revealed through a momentary, profound experience or alternatively through a long process of reflection and prayer. I think of Gideon Levy, a Jewish journalist, who visited the Palestinian territories and was staggered at the living conditions endured by residents. He knew immediately that he must become their advocate, in spite of the inevitability of public criticism and death threats from his own people. The call came in a moment. Jose Miguez Bonino, a theologian from Argentina, shared that his call came through a longer process. As an adolescent, he had watched his father spend hours at night with lists of dock workers and schedules. As the foreman, he carefully proportioned work so that each man would work enough hours to feed a family. Miguez Bonino was inspired by his father's example of social justice. He sensed a call to forgo a career in law in order to study and teach theology as his contribution to people on the margins. As another example of a longer journey of discovery, I think of Jean Vanier (quoted above) who started his career as a naval commander and later became a university professor. Yet he was drawn to something deeper. Under the guidance of a spiritual advisor, Vanier invited two men with developmental handicaps to live in a house with him in a French village, and so began the international movement known as the L'Arche Communities. Our personal missions will come to us in different ways and circumstances. Our stories will be shaped by how we discern our calls and live them out through our decisions, passions, values, and creativity.

I have organized the remaining section of the book around four topics that are important as we consider the parables and the stories we write with our lives during our brief moment in history.

2. Vanier, *Becoming Human*, 82–83, 102.

Resilience

Our daughter Tara introduced me to the category of people identified as "the done." Though these individuals were once sacrificially involved in community organizations or religious congregations, one day, perhaps after a long period of attrition, they determine that they are done and withdraw from their previous activities and commitments. Their removal is neither a temporary hiatus nor a time of reflection. They are finished.

We probably all know pastoral leaders who have decided that they are "done." The gifted ones move on to other professions, with no intention of returning to parish ministry. Social service agencies and international organizations also have to deal with the departure of formerly productive staff members who become tired of heavy workloads, inadequate budgets, and the unrelenting pressure of human need. They, too, are done. Even more troubling are those clergy, Christian workers and social activists, who lose their passion, yet continue to fill professional roles without engaging their hearts and entering into deep relationships with people. They write proposals, prepare reports, manage budgets, deliver sermons, and protect their careers. But the fires have gone out. Some of these Christian ministers and activists will gradually fall into patterns of depression or addiction.

The parable of the good seed and the good soil addresses the theme of resilience. It reminds us that a fruitful life requires a good heart and steadfast endurance. Most of us who have worked in the borderlands will confess to times of depletion, when our hearts have been compromised by our egos and our motivation to serve has largely disappeared. Sometimes the "funk" lasts a few days. It becomes serious when we sink into an uninspired routine. Ruth Hailey Barton has listed some common characteristics of depletion: irritability, restlessness, emotional numbness, overwork, lack of self-care, the perception of threats, compulsive behaviors, and abandonment of spiritual practices.[3] Many of us have been there. Some of us are wondering if we can ever get out. We want to live good stories of fruitful engagement with the world, but we feel weighed down and unproductive.

The dominant culture promotes busyness and urgency in work, family life, and even recreation. We carry "smart" phones with capacities for conversation, texting, and emails so that we are accessible at any time. We feel pressure to update Facebook with news and photos. We wear devices that track the number of steps we walk each day. We feel guilty if we are

3. Barton, *Soul of Your Leadership*, 104–6.

not doing something. We need to be reminded that Jesus took time away from the crowds to contemplate and to pray. These periods of "time away" did not indicate that he had abandoned his mission. Rather, these periods of withdrawal gave him the solitude to prepare his heart and renew his strength in order to live fully his call.

Readers will be aware that I have been inspired by the example of Oscar Romero. He served as archbishop of El Salvador for only a little more than three years. Ironically, he was chosen because church leaders felt he was a conservative figure that would not upset the institutional and political establishment. The killing of priests and the torture and disappearances of thousands of Salvadorians collectively created what Donald Miller describes as an inciting moment. Romero began to speak forcefully about the violence of El Salvador and its causes. He was criticized by the right for being a communist and by left-wing militants because of his commitment to non-violence. Surely, as people lined up to see him at his office or outside the cathedral each day, and in the face of constant death threats, he must have longed to withdraw into his former career of a seminary teacher.

Romero's resilience was rooted in his spiritual practices. He believed that each human heart contained a secret place where God meets us, where we can perceive the gentle voice of the Spirit, and from which we can cry out for the healing of our wounds and the grace to complete our missions. Several times I visited the small chapel in San Salvador where Romero was shot while celebrating the Eucharist. A framed page from his personal journal hangs on the wall. The extract was taken from his reflections during a spiritual retreat after a new round death threats. He wrote that the date and circumstances of his death would be of little matter. What was important was to give his life each day to God. The inner life of contemplation and prayer gave Romero the resilience to write a good and courageous story with his life under immense pressure and adverse circumstances.

We do not develop a good heart and resiliency by accident, but rather through concrete practices of contemplation and solitude in the presence of God, who searches our hearts and whispers his good story into our lives. The parables of Jesus beckon us to the edges of our imagination, where we can hear those still, quiet whispers of the coming of God's reign into the broken places of the world. The parables are not "easy to understand" stories like most sermon illustrations. The meanings are hidden and require discernment. The stories encourage us to slow down and ponder. We must enter them slowly, imaginatively, playfully, and prayerfully, seeking their meaning for the stories of our lives and our faith communities. As we listen in solitude, we will find strength for our journeys and for the service to which we are called.

Spirit of Restless Discontent

A few years ago, Steve Corbett and Brian Fikkert wrote that Christians in North America should climb out of bed each morning with a deep conviction that something is terribly wrong with the world and with a yearning to strive to act as agents of change. They went on to comment that there was simply not enough yearning and striving amongst North American Christians.[4] Complacency and passivity are the enemies of social change and signs of a shallow spirituality. Unfortunately, many of us, as the prophet Amos says, are at ease in Zion. In our case, Zion represents the culture of the modern world, in which we enjoy the comforts of our homes, sufficient food, entertainment, and annual vacations. The prophet Amos went on to criticize the people around him for their failure to take note of the suffering and ruin of those living on the margins of their social world (Amos 6:1–6). The depiction of eighth-century Israel seems strikingly contemporary.

As Christians, our stories will not be marked by yearning or striving if our worship services and spiritual practices are designed to make us feel comfortable with token acts of charity rather than calling us to become agents of God's transformation in the world. The 2014 World Economic Forum report identified the most pressing global threats to human life as growing income disparity, climate change, high rates of unemployment, hunger, and the loss of biodiversity. Yet in the United States and Canada, these themes seldom penetrate the corporate worship and leadership discussions of most congregations. Apparently, the church has nothing to say about the issues that are destroying the future of our children and grandchildren. By our silence, we are complicit. And so we need the parables of Jesus to remind us that the church has a prophetic calling to be salt and light within a world order that is broken and dark for those living on the margins (Matt 5:13–16).

The parables of Jesus penetrated the public transcript of the Roman Empire and critiqued the social conditions of first-century Galilee and Judea. Certainly, God was not content with the economic inequities that left Lazarus dying outside the gate of a rich man. Nor was God content that

4. Corbett and Fikkert, *When Helping Hurts*, 28.

rich men enjoyed dinner parties while the poor and physically challenged suffered from hunger as in the parable of the Great Banquet. Token efforts, such as occasional food hampers or Thanksgiving dinners at a central hall with kitchen facilities, are not enough. God seeks a deeper transformation that is both personal and structural. The parable of the dissenting slave reveals that God was not satisfied with an economic order that privileged the aspirations of a greedy and unjust ruler. And God was not content with the racialized communities and ethnic divisions that were at the center of the Samaritan parable. Nor did he look favorably on a city in which men abandoned the righteous cause of a marginalized woman. We are left to conclude that Jesus, the story teller, had a restless discontent with the structures and dominant discourse of his time. Therefore his parables can nourish our restless discontent so that we can regain our prophetic voice and become agents of God's transformation.

This attitude of restless discontent continues to inspire prophetic voices and actions in our own time. I have been moved by the quiet but determined work of Marcia Owen in Durham, North Carolina. Marcia Owen refused to accept passively the proliferation of guns and violence as a constitutional right and a cultural heritage of America.[5] She was troubled by the statistic that children in the United States are sixteen times more likely to be killed by a gun than the combined number of their age cohort in twenty-five other developed countries. Appalled that parents in some parts of Durham put their children to bed in bathtubs in order to protect them from drive-by shootings, she began to hold a prayer meeting at the site of each murder by gunshot in Durham. Her words, actions, and community-based advocacy led to a broad movement for social change and the building of relationships across the borderlands of her city. I would never have imagined that people gathering for prayer at crime scenes could be such a powerful expression of radical discontent.

The message of the parables can help us to rediscover that God's message to our communities extends beyond themes of individual morality. God wants to speak into the ways in which we have structured the economic and social patterns that shape our shared lives. The parables invite us to evaluate our communities on the basis of how people on the margins receive care and support. The stories remind us that an element of restless discontent should be part of our personal stories.

5. The story of Marcia Owen and the Religious Coalition for a Nonviolent Durham is told in Wells and Owen, *Living without Enemies*.

Rich Images of Transformation

Though restless discontent is a character trait of prophets (and should be incorporated into our stories), the ability to critique excesses and injustices can easily become part of what Richard Rohr calls an "ugly morality."[6] Unfortunately, we all know people of faith who become defined by a hostile attitude to those who hold different opinions and a negative approach to virtually every contested issue. These moral zealots often speak at length about what is wrong, yet fail to extend a positive vision of the future built on compassion, justice, and faith.

I was in grade nine when Martin Luther King Jr. gave his "I have a dream speech." I found his words to be mesmerizing. I longed to leave my home, school, and the family farm in rural western Canada to join in the struggle for racial equality. Over the years, I have shown a video recording of that speech to development workers in Africa and India and also to theology students in Canada. I am always amazed by the way they listen attentively, their eyes fixed on Dr. King and the crowds. His evocative speech turns around several powerful images that provoke the listeners' imagination of a different world order. "We refuse to believe that the bank of justice is bankrupt." "Let us not seek to satisfy our thirst for freedom by drinking from the cup of bitterness and hatred." "I have a dream that one day on the red hills of Georgia, the sons of former slaves and the sons of former slave owners will be able to sit down together at the table of brotherhood." "I have a dream that my four little children will one day live in a nation where they will not be judged by the color of their skin but by the content of their character." "I have a dream that one day every valley shall be exalted, and every hill and mountain shall be made low, the rough places will be made plain, and the crooked places will be made straight; and the glory of the Lord shall be revealed and all flesh shall see it together." Even reading these words today can make chills go up and down our spines.

Simon Sinek observes that Martin Luther King Jr. did not inspire us with a ten-point program for change or a hundred-day action plan with measurable indicators.[7] Rather, he spoke to our hearts, using images that inspired a creative and shared effort to build something better in the social lives of communities divided by race and ethnicity. In the same way, the parables contain images that reach into our hearts and inspire us to imagine

6. Rohr, *Eager to Love*, 63.
7. Sinek, *Start with Why*, 4–5.

renewed communities that reflect God's values and compassion for people in the borderlands. These images encourage us live as dissidents who are determined to write good stories with our lives. The stories of Jesus do not allow us to wallow in the mud simply complaining about what is wrong with the world.

Richard Rohr, the Franciscan priest to whom I referred above, proposes that the world of the imagination has the power to change us and to steer history more than the physical and quantifiable world around us. He quotes Einstein, who said that imagination was more important than intelligence. Rohr adds that God's best work is often done by rearranging our assumptions and giving us rich dreams of the future, which transform us and make us participants in his work of transformation.[8] Rohr's description is strikingly similar to Chris Hedges' expression, "sublime madness," as well as Sally McFague's notion of wild spaces, which I have cited at different places in this book. The parables speak to our imaginations about alternative ways of structuring our individual lives in community with other people. When we make contemplative space to reflect on the stories of Jesus within the secret places of our hearts, the Spirit hovers over us, whispering in our ears the good and fruitful story of God, who is inviting us to participate in the work of healing and transforming the world. In this way, the parables told by Jesus draw us into the larger story of God. We may be led to repentance as we review past chapters of our lives. We may feel overwhelmed by God's faithfulness and inspired by new images of a good story for ourselves and our communities. The parables, because they are stories, draw on our capacity to imagine a world that can be called the new creation of a loving God.

An Alternative to the Public Transcripts of our Times

In conclusion, I want to return to James C. Scott's social theory of public transcripts of domination and hidden transcripts of resistance. Readers will recall that Scott proposes that the content of a public transcript is composed of what the dominant economic and political powers want the rest of us to believe, along with the social norms that regulate our lives in compliance with their agenda. Such public transcripts are communicated through media, cultural expressions, political speeches, advertising, and symbolic acts. Hidden transcripts of resistance are the like the cracks in the walls

8. Rohr, *Eager to Love*, 247–65.

through which we can see from a different perspective and nourish our commitments to alternate patterns of living.

Regine and I visited the border area of China and North Korea in 2010. Across the Tuman River, the supreme leader Kim Jong II allowed people to starve while providing state resources for one of the world's largest standing armies, making massive investments in nuclear arms, and staging public executions in stadiums. His son, Kim Jong-un, maintains the detention camps of his father and has ordered guards to shoot desperate North Koreans that attempt to escape into China. Given this context, it seemed surprising when approximately one hundred thousand North Koreans turned out in November 2014 in Pyongyang to protest a United Nation's human rights report that condemned North Korea. This massive show of support was undoubtedly organized by the government, and ordinary citizens dutifully fulfilled their roles under duress. It was an obvious manifestation of a public transcript of domination.

The situation is markedly different in developed countries, such as the United States, Canada, Australia, and the states of the European community. We like to believe that our nations are models of democracy and protectors of individual freedoms. We find comfort in thinking that regular elections will allow citizens to determine the future social and economic policies that will guide our countries. We want to believe that our elected officials will work in a collaborative way for the well-being of our communities and the world as a whole. Issues of justice can be left to our courts (provided one can afford lawyers). We still hold to various forms of the Horatio Alger myth that any child can rise from rags to riches. We are confident that we have the right to intervene in the affairs of other counties, whether that means demanding new trade laws or sending in our armed forces to neutralize threats to our security. We are often dismissive or defensive of critiques that challenge our assumptions of superiority. This public transcript is embraced and maintained by people who present a tight and articulate message of patriotism, tradition, and faith.

Joerg Rieger describes our political and economic world as a soft form of empire when compared to Rome in the first century or the kingdom of Kim Jong-un in North Korea.[9] Yet the neo-liberal empire's agenda of economic and cultural globalization claims more and more of the earth's peoples. Control is no longer a matter of political rule or military occupation. Rather, the power of the empire is exercised through finances, tech-

9. Rieger, *Christ & Empire*, 313–16.

nology, resource extraction, and regulation of information. Rieger observes that the public transcript of this new empire reaches further around the world and deeper into the collective unconsciousness of people than any form of rule in history. He suggests a starting point of political discernment for those who are concerned that something is wrong. People should ask who or what entities ultimately benefit from the current world order.

One of the myths of the public transcript is that the reporters and journalists (print and electronic) form the fourth estate, which ensures that citizens have access to impartial information so that they can make informed choices and ensure that their elected representatives fulfill their oaths of office. Today, five corporations own over 90 percent of the media outlets in the United States. Canada has the highest concentration of ownership and control of vertically integrated media (TV stations, cable and satellite, radio, print, internet) among the G-8 countries. The situation in Great Britain is similar, as media ownership becomes concentrated into fewer corporations. Investigative reporting has been eroded by entertainment journalism, which is creating what Carl Bernstein describes as a talk–show nation and an idiot culture. We are exposed to about three thousand advertisement messages and images a day from companies that want us to believe that their products will give us personal fulfillment, along with white teeth, shapely bodies, faces without wrinkles, clean laundry, freedom from pain, and healthy pets. Self-worth is evidently more of a commodity to be packaged and purchased than a long-term project of building a meaningful life. Perhaps this explains why consumer debt has risen at an alarming rate in the developed countries of the global north.

Higher levels of family debt, the decline of meaningful community participation, and the dumbing down of democracy are related factors in the social life of our countries. Thoughtful citizens increasingly see through the rhetoric of political parties and paid advertisements of corporations. Cynicism is prevalent. Civil violence emerging from the margins is a frightening prospect. Many Christians, observing these trends, have been further shaken by the decline in church attendance over the past decades. They wonder about the future of their congregations and tinker with different styles of music and technology to attract people. The real problem for the future of our churches may be that most Christians have blended indistinguishably into the culture around them. Over a decade ago, Robert Webber urged that effective witness needed to demonstrate compassion, justice, and faith both in the personal lives of congregants and also in their shared engagement with people in their communities.[10] Conservative and liberal Christians have distinguished themselves by articulating what they are against. Yet our contemporary culture needs a positive transcript of resistance that expresses, through word and deed, God's creative transformation in the borderlands.

Gary Nelson provides a helpful analysis that divides problems and challenges into three broad categories.[11] Simple problems are straightforward. They can be resolved by following instructions that are clear and easily understood. One might think of a congregation that wants to reduce power consumption by moving from standard to LED light bulbs. A chart will assist in making purchases to ensure an equivalent amount of illumination. A complicated problem involves a number of considerations that need to be taken into account in order to arrive at a satisfactory solution. In this case, an appropriate example would be the selection and installation of a new air conditioning or heating system for a church. Energy requirements, the capacity of air ducts, potential renovations to the facility, purchase price, the cost of labor, financing, and warranties are some of the factors that would need to be considered. Complex problems are even more difficult. They are rooted in fluid circumstances, different personalities of people, and unpredictable issues. Raising children is a complex problem because no two children are alike, new challenges emerge at different stages in life, parents face their own personal issues, teachers and friends play roles, and no one can accurately predict the influences and events that will impact on a child's life. In a similar manner, developing, implementing, and managing a congregational mission strategy is a complex problem.

Gary and I have proposed that a congregational mission strategy has the potential to make a bold statement into the prevailing public transcripts of our time. Church leaders could consider developing their own mission strategy around four key activities while still attending to the institutional nature of the local church.[12] We believe that governance structures, financial accountability, human resource management, and facility maintenance are important institutional needs. The problems that arise in in attending to the church as an institution generally can be described as simple

10. Webber, *Ancient-Future Evangelism*, 40.

11. Nelson and Dickens, *Disorienting Times*, 75–92.

12. Workshop on "Living the Tension: Evangelism and Social Justice as Holy Discontent,"Assembly of Canadian Baptists of Ontario and Quebec, Toronto, 12 June 2015.

or complicated. Looking after institutional needs is not a substitute for a mission strategy that involves church members in evangelism, justice, and acts of compassion beyond the congregational community. We encourage congregations to give attention to four areas in developing a mission strategy. First, there is a need for a deeper understanding of local and global needs. Individuals and groups are challenged to understand both the symptoms and the causes of the brokenness and wounds in their communities and the world. This means going deeper than the explanations offered by the public transcript. Second, congregations are encouraged to articulate God's message of salvation in response to these needs. The following questions can be used to foster fruitful discussion: How will God manifest his presence to transform lives and give hope? What does our understanding of the scriptures and the rich history of the church teach us about God's work in similar situations? What is the good news to be proclaimed inside and outside of the church? Third, congregational leaders will need to determine prophetic actions that can be like mustard seeds of the new creation. We cannot resolve all the problems around us. But we can bear witness to the kingdom in word and deed in ways that bring God's transformation and healing to wounded people. Individuals and congregations will benefit from discovering the fruitful practices of others who are engaged in similar ministries. Fourth, pastors and leaders will need to ask themselves about building a community of faith that nurtures those who engage in mission and, at the same time, embraces those women and men who have been pushed to the margins in one way or another. There are not many places in the world where individuals can experience acceptance, affirmation, the love of God, and the care of his people. Pastors and other leaders can pose questions about the kind of community that is being developed by the congregation as they gather for worship, study, fellowship, and service.

Mission is God's way of bringing healing to a wounded world. Mission is always contextual. Mission is always complex. There is no detailed set of instructions to be followed whether one is in Charlotte, North Carolina, Regina, Saskatchewan or Managua, Nicaragua. The parables of Jesus can help individuals and congregations to discern their shared call to mission and participate in God's transformation of the world.

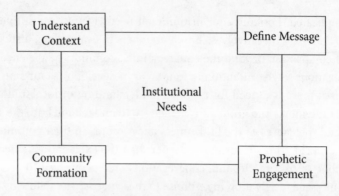

FIGURE 1: Mission is complex involving context, message, engagement, and community formation.

Through the use of stories, Jesus cast a vision of an alternative empire—the kingdom of God. He invited diverse people to participate in this kingdom by joining together as a renewed community that shaped its life around the double–love command. The practices of this community included shared meals at a common table, affection for children, respect for women, generosity with resources, concern for those with mental and physical health problems, and an inclusiveness that embraced people from the borderlands of villages and cities. We know these stories inspired his early followers, for they took the trouble to pass them on orally to one another and eventually to write them down. They have become part of the proclamation and teaching of the church through the centuries. I pray that the parables may continue to speak to our hearts as we yearn and strive to write good stories with our lives for the salvation and healing of a broken and wounded world.

In our era, the road to holiness necessarily passes through the world of action. —Dag Hammarskjold.

Bibliography

Abuelasish, Izzeldin. *I Shall Not Hate: A Gaza Doctor's Journey*. Toronto: Random, 2010.

Adiga, Aravind. *The White Tiger*. New Delhi: HarperCollins, 2008.

Alonso Schokel, Luis. *La Biblia de Nuestro Pueblo: Biblia del Peregrino America Latina*. Bilbao, Spain: Ediciones Mensajero, 2006.

Arnal, William E. *Jesus and the Village Scribes: Galilean Conflicts and the Setting of Q*. Minneapolis: Augsburg, 2001.

Arndt, William F., and F. Wilbur Gingrich. *A Greek-English Lexicon of the New Testament and Other Early Christian Literature*. Chicago: University of Chicago Press, 1957.

Bailey, Kenneth E. *Jesus through Middle Eastern Eyes: Cultural Studies in the Gospels*. Downers Grove, IL: InterVarsity Academic. 2008.

———. *Poet and Peasant and Through Peasant Eyes: A Literary-Cultural Approach to the Parables of Luke; Combined Edition*. Grand Rapids: Eerdmans, 1983.

Barrett, C. K. ed. *The New Testament Background: Writings from Ancient Greece and the Roman Empire That Illuminate Christian Origins (Revised Edition)*. San Francisco: HarperCollins, 1989.

Barton, Ruth Hailey. *Strengthening the Soul of Your Leadership*. Downers Grove, IL: InterVarsity, 2008.

Bauer, Walter, W. F. Arndt, and F. W. Gingrich, *A Greek-English Lexicon of the New Testament and Other Early Christian Literature, 2nd ed.* Chicago: University of Chicago Press, 1979.

Bauman, Zygmunt. *Collateral Damage: Social Nequalities in a Global Age*. Cambridge: Polity, 2011.

Berry, Wendell, *The Unsettling of America: Culture and Agriculture*. San Francisco: Sierra, 1997.

Blass, Friedrich, Albert Debrunner, and Robert W. Funk. *A Greek Grammar of the New Testament and Other Early Christian Literature*. Chicago: University of Chicago Press, 1961.

Bolton, Giles. *Poor Story: An Insider Uncovers how Globalisation and Good Intentions have Failed the World's Poor*. London: Ebury, 2007.

Borg, Marcus J. *Jesus: Uncovering the Life, Teaching and Relevance of a Religious Revolutionary*. San Francisco: Harper, 2006.

Boucher, Madeline I. *The Parables*. Dublin: Veritas, 1981.

Braun, Willi. *Feasting and Social Rhetoric in Luke 14*. Cambridge: Cambridge University Press, 1995.

Brown, Colin, ed. *The New International Dictionary of New Testament Theology*. Exeter: Paternoster, 1975–1978.

BIBLIOGRAPHY

Browning, W. R. F. "Mystery." In *A Dictionary of the Bible*. Online: http://www.highbeam. com/doc/1O94-mystery.html.

Brueggemann, Walter. *Journey to the Common Good*. Louisville: Westminster John Knox, 2010.

Callender, Jr., Dexter E. "Servants of God(s) and Servants of Kings in Israel and the Ancient Near East." in Allen Callahan, Richard A. Horsley and Abraham Smith, eds. *Semeia*, 83–84. Atlanta: SBL, 1998.

Cardenal, Ernesto. *The Gospel in Solentiname*, Vol. 1– 3. Maryknoll: Orbis, 1975–79.

Chambers, Robert. *Ideas for Development*. London: ITDG, 2005.

——. *Whose Reality Counts? Putting the First Last*. London: ITDG, 1997.

Charlesworth, James H. ed. *The Old Testament Pseudepigrapha, Volume 1: Apocalyptic Literature and Testament*. Garden City, NJ: Doubleday, 1983.

——. *The Old Testament Pseudepigrapha, Volume 2: Expansions of the "Old Testament" and Legends, Wisdom and Philosophical Literature, Prayers, Psalms and Odes, Fragments of Lost Judaeo-Hellenestic Work*. Garden City: Doubleday, 1985.

Chilton, Bruce. *Pure Kingdom: Jesus' Vision of God*. Grand Rapids: Eerdmans, 1996.

Coggins, R. J. *Samaritans and Jews: The Origins of Samaritanism Reconsidered*. Atlanta: John Knox, 1975.

Collier, Paul. *The Bottom Billion: Why the Poorest Countries are Failing and What Can Be Done About It*. Oxford: Oxford University Press, 2007.

Corbett, Steve, and Brian Fikkert. *When Helping Hurts: How to Alleviate Poverty Without Hurting the Poor . . . and Yourself*. Chicago: Moody, 2009.

Crossan, John Dominic. *God and Empire: Jesus against Rome, Then and Now*. San Francisco: HarperCollins, 2007.

Dallaire, Romeo. *Shake Hands With The Devil: The Failure of Humanity in Rwanda*. Toronto: Random House Canada, 2004.

Dana, H. E., and Julius R. Mantey. *A Manual Grammar of the Greek New Testament*. Toronto: MacMillan, 1955.

Danker, Frederick W. *Jesus and the New Age: According to St. Luke*. St. Louis: Clayton, 1972.

Das, Rupen. *Compassion and the Mission of God: Revealing the Invisible Kingdom*. Carlisle, UK: Langham Global Library, 2015.

Davis, Ellen F. *Scripture, Culture, and Agriculture: An Agrarian Reading of the Bible*. Cambridge: Cambridge University Press, 2009.

Davis, Joseph E., ed. *Stories of Change*. Albany, NY: State University of New York Press, 2002.

Dennis, Marie, Renny Goldden and Scott Wright. *Oscar Romero: Reflections on his Life and Writings*. Maryknoll: Orbis, 2000.

Donahue, John R. *The Gospel in Parable*. Minneapolis: Fortress, 1990.

Duling, Dennis. *The New Testament: Proclamation and Parenesis, Myth and History*. 3rd Edition. New York, Harcourt Brace, 1994.

Ferris-Rotman, Amie. "Evidence Mounts in Ukraine that Both Sides are Committing Sexualized Violence." *Website of Women Under Siege*. December 29, 2014. Online: http://www.womenundersiegeproject.org/blog/entry/evidence-mounts-in-ukraine-that-both-sides-are-committing-sexualized-violence

Fitzmyer, Joseph A. *The Gospel According to Luke I–IX*. New York: Doubleday, 1981.

——. *The Gospel According to Luke X–XXIV*. New York: Doubleday, 1985.

Frank, Arthur W. *Letting Stories Breathe: A Socio-Narratology.* Chicago: The University of Chicago Press, 2010.

Freyne, Sean. *Galilee and Gospel: Collected Essays.* Leiden: Brill Academic, 2002.

———. *Jesus, A Jewish Galilean: A New Reading of the Jesus-Story.* London: T. & T. Clark, 2004.

Garcia Martinez, Florentino. *The Dead Sea Scrolls Translated: The Qumran Texts in English.* Grand Rapids: Eerdmans, 1996.

Giroux, Henry A. *The Giroux Reader.* Boulder: Paradigm, 2006.

Glancy, Jennifer A. *Slavery in Early Christianity.* Minneapolis: Fortress, 2006.

Gonzalez, Justo L. *Luke.* Louisville: Westminster John Knox, 2010.

Goodman, Martin. "The First Jewish Revolt: Social Conflict and the Problems of Debt." *Journal of Jewish Studies* 33 (1982) 417-427.

———. *Rome and Jerusalem: The Clash of Ancient Civilizations.* New York: Vintage, 2007.

Gourevitch, Philip. *We Wish to Inform You that Tomorrow We Will Be Killed with Our Families: Stories From Rwanda.* New York: Picador, 1998.

Green, Joel B., ed. *Dictionary of Jesus and the Gospels, 2nd edition.* Downers Grove: InterVarsity Academic, 2013.

Gutierrez, Gustavo. *We Drink from our Own Wells.* Maryknoll: Orbis, 1988.

Hanks, Thomas D. *God So Loved the Third World: The Bible, the Reformation and Liberation Theologies.* Maryknoll: Orbis, 1983.

Hanson, K. C. "The Galilean Fishing Economy and the Jesus Tradition." *Biblical Theology Bulletin* 27 (1997) 99–111.

Hanson, K. C., and Douglas E. Oakman. *Palestine in the Time of Jesus: Social Structures and Social Conflicts, 2nd Edition.* Minneapolis: Fortress, 2008.

Hardoon, Deborah. *Wealth: Having It All and Wanting More.* Oxfam Issue Briefing, Oxford: Oxfam International, 2015.

Hatzfeld, Jean. *The Antelope's Strategy: Living in Rwanda After the Genocide.* New York: Farrar, Straus and Giroux, 2009.

Hauerwas, Stanley. *The Hauerwas Reader.* Durham: Duke University Press, 2001.

Hedges, Chris. *The World As It Is: Dispatches on the Myth of Human Progress.* New York: Nation, 2009.

———. *Wages of Rebellion: The Moral Imperative of Revolt.* Toronto: Alfred A. Knopf Canada, 2015.

Hendrickx, Herman. *The Gospel for the Third World, Volume Three B: Travel Narrative. Luke 13.22-17.10.* Collegeville, Minnesota: Liturgical, 2000.

———. *The Third Gospel for the Third World. Volume Two: Ministry in Galilee (Luke 3.1-6.49).* Collegeville, Minnesota: Liturgical, 1997.

Herzog II, William R. *Parables as Subversive Speech: Jesus as Pedagogue of the Oppressed.* Louisville: Westminster John Knox, 1994.

———. *Prophet and Teacher: An Introduction to the Historical Jesus.* Louisville: Westminster John Knox, 2005.

Horsley, Richard A. *Covenant Economics: A Biblical Vision of Justice for All.* Louisville: Westminster John Knox, 2009.

———. *Jesus and Empire: The Kingdom of God and the New World Disorder.* Minneapolis: Fortress, 2003.

———. *Jesus in Context: Power, People, & Performance.* Minneapolis: Fortress, 2008.

———. "The Slave Systems of Classical Antiquity and Their Reluctant Recognition by Modern Scholars." In *Semeia,* Atlanta: SBL, 1998.

Horsley, Richard A., ed. *Hidden Transcripts and the Arts of Resistance: Applying the Work of James C. Scott to Jesus and Paul*. Atlanta: Society of Biblical Literature, 2004.

———. *In the Shadow of Empire: Reclaiming the Bible as a History of Faithful Resistance.* Louisville: Westminster John Knox, 2008.

Horsley, Richard A., and John S. Hanson. *Bandits, Prophets and Messiahs: Popular Movements in the Time of Jesus*. Harrisburg, PA: Trinity, 1999.

Horsley, Richard A., and Neil Asher Silberman. *The Message and the Kingdom: How Jesus and Paul Ignited a Revolution and Transformed the Ancient World*. New York: Grosset, 1997.

Howell, Crawford, and Samuel Krauss. "Pseudo Phocylides." *Jewish Encyclopedia*. Online: http://www.jewishencyclopedia.com/pseudo-phocylides.

Hultgren, Arland J. *The Parables of Jesus: A Commentary*. Grand Rapids: Eerdmans, 2002.

Ignatieff, Michael. *Blood and Belonging: Journeys into the New Nationalism*. Toronto: FSG Adult, 1995.

———. *The Warrior's Honour: Ethnic War and the Modern Conscience*. Toronto: Viking, 1998.

Institute for Economics and Peace. *Global Peace Index Report*. New York: IEP, 2015.

Jeffers, James S. *The Greco-Roman World of the New Testament Era: Exploring the Background of Early Christianity*. Downers Grove, IL: InterVarsity Academic, 1999.

Jeremias, Joachim. *Jerusalem in the Time of Jesus*. Philadelphia: Fortress, 1969.

———. *The Parables of Jesus: Revised Edition*. London: SCM, 1975.

Jersak, Brad. "Interview with Dave Diewert." *Clarion Journal of Spirituality and Justice*. June 9, 2006. Online: http//clarionjournal.typepad.com/clarion_journal_of_spirit/2006/06/safe_injection_.html.

Johnson, Luke Timothy. *The Gospel of Luke*. Collegeville, MN: Liturgical, 1991.

Kale, Vidyut. "Dowry: The Number One Killer of Women in India." *Intellectual Anarchy*. November 2011. Online: https://aamjanata.com/dowry-the-number-one-killer-of-women-in-india/.

Kapur, Akash. "The Secret of His Success." Review of *The White Tiger,* by Aravind Adiga. *New York Times*. November 7, 2008. Online: www.nytimes.com/2008/11/09/books/review/Kapur/http.

Kartveit, Magmar. *The Origin of the Samaritans*. Leiden: Brill, 2009.

Katongole, Emmanuel. *A Future for Africa: Critical Essays in Christian Social Imagination*. Chicago: University of Scranton Press, 2005.

Katongole, Emmanuel with Jonathan Wilson-Hartgrove. *Mirror to the Church: Resurrecting Faith after Genocide in Rwanda*. Grand Rapids: Zondervan, 2009.

King, Thomas. *The Inconvenient Indian: A Curious Account of Native People in North America*. Toronto: Doubleday, 2012.

———. *The Truth About Stories*. Toronto: House of Anansi, 2003.

Lehtipuu, Outi. *The Afterlife Imagery in Luke's Story of the Rich Man and Lazarus*. Leiden: Brill, 2007.

Lindhout, Amanda, and Sara Corbett. *A House in the Sky*. New York: Scribner, 2014.

Livermore, David A. *Cultural Intelligence: Improving your CQ to Engage our Multicultural World*. Grand Rapids: Baker Academic, 2009.

Longenecker, Richard N., ed. *The Challenge of Jesus' Parables*. Grand Rapids: Eerdmans, 2003.

Maier, Paul L. *Josephus: The Essential Works*. Grand Rapids: Kregel, 1994.

Malina, Bruce J. *The Social Gospel of Jesus: The Kingdom of God in Mediterranean Perspective*. Minneapolis: Fortress, 2001.

———. "Wealth and Poverty in the New Testament and Its World." *Interpretation* 61.4 (1987) 354–67.

Malina, Bruce J. and Richard L. Rohrbaugh. *Social-Science Commentary on the Synoptic Gospels*. Minneapolis: Fortress, 1992.

Manson, T. W. *The Sayings of Jesus*. London: SCM, 1949.

Marshall, I. Howard. *The Gospel of Luke: A Commentary on the Greek Text*. Grand Rapids: Eerdmans, 1978.

McClendon, James Wm. Jr. *Biography as Theology: How Life Stories can Remake Today's Theology*. Philadelphia: Trinity, 1990

MacDonald, Nancy. "Welcome to Winnipeg." *MacLeans* (2015) 16–24.

McFague, Sallie. *Life Abundant: Rethinking Theology and Economy for a Planet in Peril*. Minneapolis: Fortress, 2001.

McKenzie, John L. *A Theology of the Old Testament*. New York: Doubleday, 1974.

McKibbon, Bill. *Deep Economy: The Wealth of Communities and the Durable Future*. New York: Times, 2007.

Meier, John P. *A Marginal Jew: Volume 2: Mentor, Message, and Miracles*. New York: Doubleday, 1993.

———. *A Marginal Jew: Rethinking the Historical Jesus. Volume 3: Companions and Competitors*. New York: Doubleday, 2001.

———. *A Marginal Jew: Rethinking the Historical Jesus. Volume 4: Law and Love*. New Haven, CT: Yale University Press, 2009.

Meredith, Martin. *The State of Africa: A History of Fifty Years of Independence*. London: Free Press, 2005.

Merton, Thomas. *No Man is an Island*. Boston: Shambhala, 2005.

Metzger, Bruce M. and Michael D. Coogan, eds. *The Oxford Companion to the Bible*. Oxford: Oxford University Press, 1993.

Micklethwait, John and Adam Wooldridge. *The Fourth Revolution: The Global Revolution to Reinvent the State*. New York: Penguin, 2014.

Miller, Donald, *A Million Miles in a Thousand Years: What I Learned While Editing My Life*. Nashville: Thomas Nelson, 2009.

Moltmann, Jurgen. *The Power of the Powerless: The Word of Liberation for Today*. San Francisco: Harper and Row, 1983.

Moxnes, Halvor. *Putting Jesus in His Place: A Radical Vision of Household and Kingdom*. Louisville: Westminster John Knox, 2003

———. *The Economy of the Kingdom: Social Conflict and Economic Relations in Luke's Gospel*. Eugene, OR: Wipf and Stock, 2004.

Nave Jr., Guy D. *The Role and Function of Repentance in Luke-Acts*. Atlanta: Society of Biblical Literature, 2002.

Nelson, Gary V., and Peter M. Dickens. *Leading in Disorienting Times: Navigating Church and Organizational Change*. Columbia: TCP, 2015.

Nelson, Gary V., Gordon W. King, and Terry G. Smith. *Going Global: A Congregation's Introduction to Mission Beyond Our Borders*. St. Louis: Chalice, 2011.

Neufeld, Dietmar and Richard DeMaris, eds. *Understanding the Social World of the New Testament*. London: Routledge, 2010.

Neyrey, Jerome H., ed. *The Social World of Luke-Acts*, Peabody, MA: Hendrickson, 1991.

Nolland, John. *Word Biblical Commentary Vol. 35a, Luke 1:1–9:20*. Dallas: Word, 1989.

————. *Word Biblical Commentary 35B Luke 9.21—18.34*. Dallas: Word, 1993.

Northup, Solomon. *Twelve Years a Slave*. New York: Atria, 2013.

Oakman, Douglas E. *Jesus and the Peasants*. Eugene, OR: Cascade, 2008.

Padilla, Rene, *¿Que es la Mision Integral?* Buenos Aires, Ediciones Kairos, 2006.

Palmer, Parker J. *Let Your Life Speak: Listening for the Voice of Vocation*. San Francisco: John Wiley and Sons, 2000.

Pegg, Shawn, and Diana Stapleton. *Hunger Count 2014*. Mississauga: Food Banks, 2014.

Pronzato, Alessando. *Las Parabolas de Jesus: Tomo 1*. Salamanca: Ediciones Sigueme, 2003.

————. *Las Parabolas de Jesus en el Evangelio de Lucas: Tomo 2*. Salamanca: Ediciones Sigueme, 2003.

Reguly, Eric. "Crime and Punishment for Banks (Or Not)." *The Globe and Mail Report on Business*. October 2014. Online: http://www.theglobeandmail.com/report-on-business/rob-magazine/crime-and-punishment-for-banks-not/article20768992/

Resseguie, James L. *Narrative Criticism of the New Testament: An Introduction*. Grand Rapid: Baker Academic, 2005.

Rieger, Joerg. *Christ & Empire: From Paul to Postcolonial Times*. Minneapolis: Fortress, 2007.

Rittner, Carol, John Roth, and Wendy Whitworth, eds. *Genocide in Rwanda: Complicity of the Churches?* St. Paul: Paragon, 2004.

Roberts, Paul Craig. "The Difficulty of Being an Informed American." Online: http//www.informationclearinghouse.info/January 8, 2009.

Rohr, Richard. *Eager to Love: The Alternative Way of Francis of Assisi*. Cincinnati: Franciscan Media, 2014.

Romero, Oscar. *Dia y Dia con Monsenor Romero: Meditaciones para Todo el Ano*. San Salvador: Publicaciones Pastorales, 2000.

————. *The Violence of Love*. Maryknoll: Orbis, 2004.

Roth, S. John. *The Blind, The Lame, and the Poor: Character Types in Luke-Acts*. Sheffield: Sheffield University Press, 1997.

Royal Canadian Mounted Police. "Missing and Murdered Aboriginal Women: A National Operational Overview, 2014." Online: http://www.rcmp-grc.gc.ca/pubs/mmaw-faapd-eng.pdf.

Ruiz de Galarreta, Jose Enrique. *Para Leer el Reino en Parabolas*. Navarra, Spain: Verbo Divino, 2007.

Russell, Sharman Apt. *Hunger: An Unnatural History*. New York: Basic, 2005.

Sainath, P. *Everybody Loves a Good Drought: Stories from India's Poorest Districts*. New Delhi: Penguin, 1996.

Sakenfeld, Katherine Doob, ed. *The New Interpreter's Dictionary of the Bible*. Nashville: Abingdon. 2009.

Schottroff, Luise. *The Parables of Jesus*. Minneapolis: Fortress, 2006.

Scott, Bernard Brandon, *Re-Imagine the World: An Introduction to the Parables of Jesus*. Santa Rosa: Polebridge, 2001.

Scott, James C. *Domination and the Arts of Resistance: Hidden Transcripts*. New Haven: Yale University Press, 1990.

Sen, Amartya, *Development As Freedom*. New York: Anchor, 1999.

————. *Poverty and Famines: An Essay on Entitlement and Deprivation*. Oxford: Clarendon, 1981.

Sen, Amartya, and Jean Druze. *Hunger and Public Action*. Oxford: Clarendon, 1989.

Sinek, Simon. *Start with Why: How Great Leaders Inspire Everyone to Take Action*. New York: Portfolio, 2011.

Smallwood, E. Mary. *The Jews Under Roman Rule: From Pompey to Diocletian.* Leiden: E. J. Brill, 1976.

Smil, Vaclav. "China's Great Famine: 40 Years Later." *British Medical Journal* 319 (1999) 1619–21.

Snodgrass, Klyne. *Stories with Intent: A Comprehensive Guide to the Parables of Jesus.* Grand Rapids: Eerdmans, 2009.

Sobrino, Jon. *The Principle of Mercy.* Maryknoll: Orbis, 1992.

———. *Where is God? Earthquake, Terrorism, Barbarity and Hope.* Maryknoll: Orbis, 2004.

Sotolongo, Pedro Luis. *Ernesto Che Guevara: Ethics and Aesthetics of an Existence.* Habana: Editorial Jose Marti, 2002.

Stegemann, Wolfgang, Bruce J. Malina, and Gerd Theissen, eds. *The Social Setting of Jesus and the Gospels,* Minneapolis: Fortress, 2002.

Steves, Rick. *Portugal.* Berkeley, CA: Avalon, 2013.

Steward, John. *From Genocide to Generosity: Hatreds heal on the Rwandan Hills.* Carlisle: Langham, 2015.

Stiglitz, Joseph E. *Freefall: America, Free Markets, and the Sinking of the World Economy.* New York: W. W. Norton, 2010.

Susskind, Yifat. "What Will It Take to Stop ISIS Using Rape as a Weapon of War?" *The Guardian.* February 17, 2015. Online: http://www.theguardian.com/global-development/2015/feb/17/disarm-isis-rape-weapon-war.

Talbert, Charles H. *Reading Luke: A Literary and Theological Commentary on the Third Gospel.* Rev. ed. Macon: Smyth and Helwys, 2002.

Thurow, Roger, and Scott Kilman. *Enough: Why the World's Poorest Starve in an Age of Plenty.* New York: Public Affairs, 2009.

Vanier, Jean. *Becoming Human.* Toronto: House of Anansi, 1998.

Volf, Miroslav. *Exclusion and Embrace: A Theological Exploration of Identity, Otherness, and Reconciliation.* Nashville: Abingdon, 1996.

Ward, Laura May, and Carola Eyber, "Resiliency of Children in Child-Headed Households in Rwanda." *Intervention* 7.1 (2009) 17–33.

Webber, Robert E. *Ancient–Future Evangelism: Making Your Church a Faith–Forming Community.* Grand Rapids: Baker, 2003.

Weinfield, Nancy S., et. al. *Hunger in America 2014. National Report Prepared for Feeding America.* Chicago: Feeding America, 2014.

Wells, Samuel, and Marcia Durham. *Living without Enemies: Being Present in the Midst of Violence.* Downers Grove, IL: InterVarsity, 2011.

West, Cornel, with David Ritz. *Brother West: Living and Loving Out Loud.* New York: Smiley, 2009.

Westley, Frances, Brenda Zimmerman, and Michael Quinn Patton. *Getting to Maybe: How the World is Changed.* Toronto: Vintage Canada, 2007.

William Whiston, trans. *Josephus: The Complete Works.* Nashville: Thomas Nelson, 1998.

Wright, N. T. *Jesus and the Victory of God.* Minneapolis: Fortress, 1996.

Wright, Scott, et al. *El Salvador: A Spring Whose Waters Never Run Dry.* Washington: Ecumenical Program on Central America and the Caribbean, 1990.

York, John O. *The Last Shall Be First: The Rhetoric of Reversal in Luke.* Sheffield: JSOT Press, 1991.

Young, Brad H. *The Parables: Jewish Tradition and Christian Interpretation.* Peabody, MA: Hendrickson, 1998.